CLEAN ENERGY TRANSITION AND DIGITAL TRANSFORMATION

Building
Better Less Different

CLEAN ENERGY TRANSITION AND DIGITAL TRANSFORMATION

Fundamentals
Case Studies
Strategies

Felix Heisel, Dirk E. Hebel
with Andreas Wagner, Moritz Dörstelmann

BIRKHÄUSER
BASEL

Better

Less

Different

Better + Less + Different

PREFACE

A surprising amount is happening already – and still it is not enough if we are to seriously tackle the enormous transformations needed in the building sector. On the one hand, the realization that the world's material resources are finite and that their continued unsustainable extraction for use in the construction industry is causing immense damage to the planet is now not only common knowledge but has also reached the level of national and international politics and is finding its way into corresponding legislation. On the other, for a variety of reasons, the resulting implications and regulatory mechanisms have yet to be incorporated into everyday construction practice. While sustainable behaviour and management must become the guiding principle of social action, the ways and means by which we will achieve this are far from clear. As a holistic praxis, sustainability must combine technical and material as well as social, economic, ecological and also ethical strategies, which have multiple complex interactions and all too often also conflicting goals and priorities. In the design, organisation, planning and construction of the built environment we encounter the complexities of sustainable action including all its various experiences, problems and potential solutions. And while we look ahead to a – hopefully – better future, we must also address the enormous existing stock built long before the new guidelines were negotiated and that now needs to be adapted and converted according to this new understanding.

This series of publications aims to help guide us along this path and examines the central topics of the process and its interactions and dependencies from both a scientific and practical perspective. Each volume of *Building Better – Less – Different* details two fundamental areas of sustainability, whose respective dynamics and interactions are particularly relevant but also revealing and instructive. After introductory overviews, each book presents established methods and current developments along with analyses of potential conflict points and relevant international case studies. The sustainability strategies of efficiency ("better"), sufficiency ("less") and consistency ("different") form the framework for each book. Together, the volumes provide a systematic and up-to-date compendium of sustainable building.

This first volume, *Circular Construction and Circular Economy*, published in 2022, presents concepts, methods and examples of circularity in construction and the economy, focusing particularly on the question of resources: where will raw materials for future construction activity come from, given the increasing bottlenecks in supplies and depleting reserves? What role will the bio-economy play? Which methods and processes do we need to trial, implement and politically establish for us to achieve the goals of a circular economy? How can urban mining and circular construction be realized using techniques such as mono-material constructions and design for disassembly, and be facilitated by tools such as materials passports and databases? The circular economy is not solely about closing materials loops but also encompasses a wide range of strategies from local community projects to new ownership and service models and steering mechanisms such as carbon fees and dividends.

This second volume in the series extends the discourse on sustainability to encompass the topics of *Clean Energy Transition and Digital Transformation*: How can we meet the energy needs of our built environment for heating, cooling and electricity – better, less or differently? Which energy sources are feasibly scalable to such an extent? And what role do technical and digital solutions play in this transformation? Can digital processes bring about a revolution in our design and production mechanisms that allow us to profoundly rethink the energy and resource question? For example, do robotic prefabrication, machine learning or parametric design offer new ways of making unconventional or non-standardized materials from biological processes or urban mining suitable for use at a larger scale? And what role does the user and society play in this new world? Can digitalization take over certain necessary tasks, through suitable means of human-machine interaction, and thus counter the shortage of skilled workers?

We must learn to understand the dynamics and interdependencies of these and other related topics to avoid the pitfalls of blinkered silo thinking. This book is therefore more than a linear sequence of articles, case studies and commentaries; it is also a field of relationships defined by the strategies "better", "less" and "different" as well as "clean energy transition" and "digital transformation". A corresponding visual table of contents (see p. 9) aims to encourage a variety of ways of accessing the topics within. Further references at the end of each article help readers extend their perspective and establish links between the different subject areas in this book, and in the other books of the series. It is important that each area and aspect can learn from one another: to incorporate and apply economic and constructional models and ideas from the fields of energy and resources to the construction industry, and vice versa.

Accordingly, the various introductions, articles, case studies and commentaries in this book highlight – and (re)introduce – the inherent relationships within this field to further vital discourse on implementing and establishing sustainable models. The third decade of the 21st century will be crucial to whether we succeed in finding ways to live and act consistently, i.e., in harmony with the environment and its natural cycles and processes. Only then will we be able to dispense with the human-conceived distinction between the built and natural environment, so that we may exist together in dignity on this planet without exploiting one or the other.

Felix Heisel, Dirk E. Hebel, Andreas Wagner and Moritz Dörstelmann, July 2023

SUSTAINABILITY

Strategies for Action

Introduction by Felix Heisel and Dirk E. Hebel

A HUMAN-MADE EPOCH

The term Anthropocene was coined to denote the geochronological period in which we currently live and describes an age in which humans and human activity have become the defining factor for the planet Earth. The impact that our activities have on the planet's geological, biological and atmospheric ecosystems is now traceable. Even though not officially recognized yet, the Anthropocene will be the first epoch to be defined not solely geologically. The term derives from the Greek *anthropos* for human and *zen* for time, and was widely established in 2000 by the Dutch chemist and atmospheric scientist Paul Crutzen and the US biologist Eugene Filmore Stoermer in their article "The 'Anthropocene'". In their contribution to the discourse on a new epoch, which they see as succeeding the current age of the Holocene,[1] they describe humanity's interventions in the natural environment as being recognizable and demonstrable from the 19th century onwards, and cite a list of significant, visible and measurable influences along with corresponding phenomena such as climate change, species extinction or the emergence of new diseases. In their article, they propose that the epoch started in the second half of the 18th century, as it is from this period that atmospheric concentrations of greenhouse gases – caused by the onset of fossil industrialization – are first detectable in ice core drillings taken in Antarctica.

In 2008, the Stratigraphy Subcommission of the Geological Society of London, the oldest national geological society in the world, began considering whether the designation proposed by the two scientists was justified. However, it was not until 2016 that the International Commission on Stratigraphy first discussed the possible official introduction of the geochronological term Anthropocene, based on recommendations made by the "Anthropocene" Working Group convened at the 35th International Geological Congress in Cape Town. After evaluating the evidence presented – in particular the increased presence of greenhouse gases in the atmosphere, the extent of human intervention in the natural landscape over and above natural changes resulting from erosion and sedimentation, ocean acidification resulting from CO_2 input, perturbations of the nitrogen and carbon cycles, habitat loss and the progressive extinction of species – the commission concluded that there were sufficient grounds for naming a new epoch. On 21 May 2019, the working group published the minutes of their vote,[2] in which most members agreed on the recommendation to formally adopt the Anthropocene epoch but that it should begin much later than Crutzen and Stoermer's proposal – at around 1950. The reason given is that an epoch requires a distinct boundary in both time and place, a so-called golden spike, that is evident and verifiable in geological deposits. For this, they proposed the nuclear fallout resulting from the first US nuclear weapons tests in 1945 in the state of New Mexico. In 2023, Crawford Lake in Canada was identified as a suitable site for the golden spike as its sediment layers exhibit multiple traces of human activity, including carbon dioxide, nitrogen and plutonium-239.

Although, at the time of writing, the Anthropocene epoch has yet to be officially declared, the magnitude of the discussion shows just how crucial it is that we adopt a holistic approach to sustainable action: while the climate of planet Earth has been shaped over some 800,000 years by planetary constellations, in the last 70 years, it is us humans who have had a greater impact.

GLOBAL WARMING

Far and away the most intensively discussed human-made impact on our natural ecosystems is that of the warming of our planet. The Paris Framework Convention on Climate Change in 2015 declared that global warming must not exceed 2 °C, and ideally be limited to no more than 1.5 °C above pre-industrial levels. A corresponding agreement was adopted in December of that year at the 21st Conference of the Parties to the United Nations Framework Convention on Climate Change (COP21) in Paris. To come into effect approval from at least 55 states responsible for at least 55% of global greenhouse gas emissions was needed. These two conditions were met on 5 October 2016, allowing the agreement to formally enter into force on 4 November 2016. Since August 2021, 191 of the 197 Parties to the Framework Convention on Climate Change have formally agreed to its

1 Paul J. Crutzen and Eugene F. Stoermer, "The 'Anthropocene'", in *IGBP Global Change Newsletter*, no 41, Stockholm: IGBP, May 2000, pp. 17–18, https://www.igbp.net/download/18.316f18321323470177580001401/1376383088452/NL41.pdf (accessed 21 August 2022).

2 Subcommission on Quarternary Stratigraphy, Results of binding vote by the Anthropocene Working Group, http://quaternary.stratigraphy.org/working-groups/anthropocene/ (accessed 21 August 2022).

1

The Green Deal focus areas as published by the EU in 2019, with the shift to a comprehensive circular economy as top goal.

Based on: European Green Deal, European Commission, 2019.

adoption. To comply, countries must submit details of the measures taken to limit global warming, a process that began in 2020.[3]

Updated national plans must be submitted every five years along with a review of the steps taken so far and any adjustments needed. These measures are at present still voluntary, as the rules lack any form of sanctions for non-compliance. The Convention does, however, require individual nation states to draw up roadmaps on how to progressively strengthen measures to reach successively stricter greenhouse gas reduction targets. There is now broad consensus that a radical reduction of carbon dioxide (CO_2), methane (CH_4), nitrous oxide (N_2O) and all fluorinated greenhouse gas emissions is imperative to combat global warming.

It was therefore perceived as extremely disappointing that the most recent, 27th World Climate Change Conference (COP27), which began on 6 November 2022 in Sharm El Sheikh, Egypt, failed to live up to this spirit. In his address to the assembled heads of states and governments, the United Nations Secretary General, António Guterres, emphatically outlined the options facing the global community: to join forces in a climate solidarity pact or embark on a "collective suicide". Unfortunately, despite a call by some 80 countries to collectively "phase down" fossil fuels, such a resolution failed due to massive opposition from Saudi Arabia and Russia. Also lacking in the concluding cover decision is a declaration of intent to reach peak greenhouse gas emissions before 2025, which makes the target of limiting mean global warming to 1.5 °C barely feasable.[4] One historic breakthrough was, however, achieved: the establishment of a Loss and Damage (L&D) fund. After decades of demands from vulnerable states, the Fund is an important statement of solidarity in climate issues. Nevertheless, there are still many open questions regarding its implementation.

THE EUROPEAN GREEN DEAL

The European Union aims to become the first continent to reduce net greenhouse gas emissions to zero by 2050. To this end it has put together its own package of measures as part of the so-called European Green Deal. It foresees a total of ten fields of action, including the introduction of a circular economy, a zero-pollution strategy, the transformation of agriculture, sustainable transport concepts, sustainable financing strategies for these measures and the production of clean, reliable and affordable energy. To mandate this climate action, the EU issued the European Climate Change Act, which stipulates that net greenhouse gas emissions from the entire economy in the EU should be reduced by at least 55 % compared to levels in 1990 by as early as 2030. Regulation (EU) 2021/1119 entered into force on 29 July 2021 after several rounds of negotiations and stricter adjustments of targets.[5] To implement the European Climate Law, an action plan of directives and regulations was drawn up: the so-called "Fit for 55" package of measures, whose title refers to the target of a 55 % reduction in greenhouse gas emissions by 2030.

THE EU'S "FIT FOR 55" PACKAGE

A cornerstone of the "Fit for 55" package is the introduction of emissions trading, which will initially apply only to energy companies and energy-intensive industrial sectors as well as parts of the aviation sector. From 2024 it will also apply to the shipping sector, and from 2027 also to individual mobility and heavy goods transport and the heating sector – including heating for buildings – as well as smaller and less energy-intensive industrial sectors. Emissions trading puts a price on greenhouse gases. To establish a market, the EU issues so-called emissions allowances that greenhouse gas producers can purchase and trade with. By capping the number of emissions allowances, the EU can drive up their market price, thereby creating incentives for individual sectors to reduce their greenhouse gas emissions. The package explicitly includes a mechanism for successively raising the price of the allowances. Part of the revenue generated by the emissions trading systems in the energy, industry, aviation and shipping sectors will flow into an innovation fund to promote investment in climate-friendly technologies, and into a social fund to support low-income sections of society in working towards climate change. In addition, the package includes a Carbon Border Adjustment Mechanism to levy tariffs on goods imported from countries outside the

3 Plan, implement, review: How the Paris Agreement works, 2021, World Ressources Institute, Washington DC, https://www.wri.org/paris-rulebook (accessed 28 July 2023).

4 Outcomes of the 27th World Climate Change Conference, 2022, German Environment Agency, Dessau-Roßlau, https://www.umweltbundesamt.de/themen/ergebnisse-der-27-weltklimakonferenz (accessed 28 July 2023); https://www.wri.org/insights/cop27-key-outcomes-un-climate-talks-sharm-el-sheikh.

5 Regulation (EU) 2021/1119 of the European Parliament and of the Council of 30 June 2021, establishing the framework for achieving climate neutrality and amending Regulations (EC) No 401/2009 and (EU) 2018/1999 ('European Climate Law'): https://op.europa.eu/en/publication-detail/-/publication/365a2e8e-e04f-11eb-895a-01aa75ed71a1/language-en/format-PDF/source-284562315.

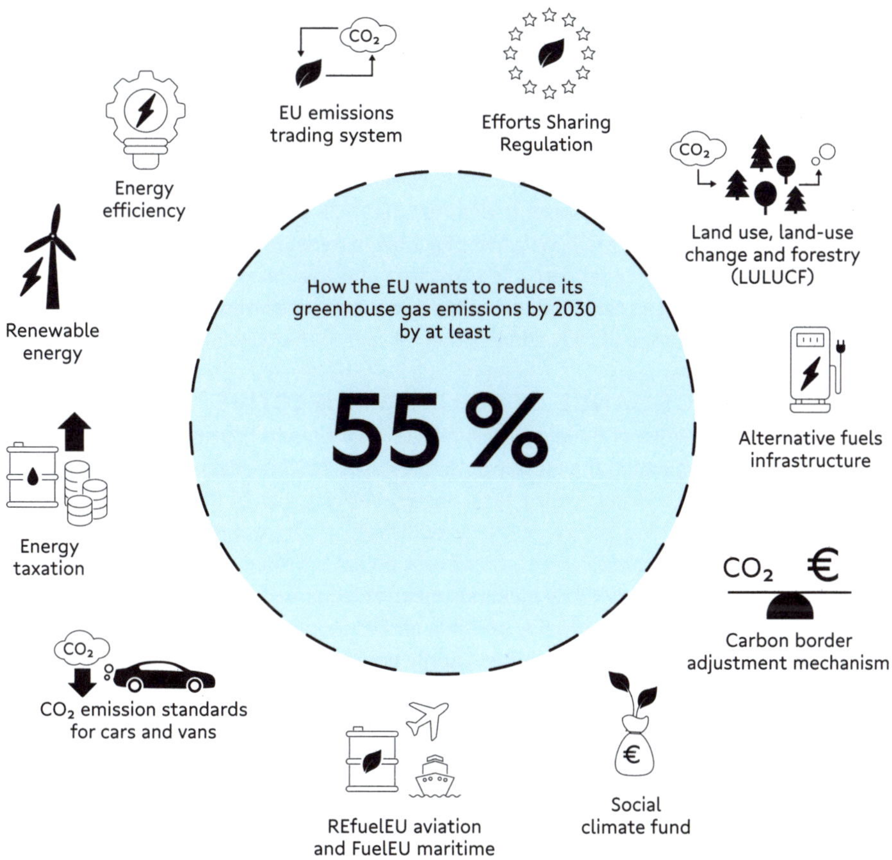

2

The "Fit for 55" package consists of a series of measures on how the EU and its 27 member countries intend to achieve a 55 % reduction in their greenhouse gas emissions compared to the year 2005.

Based on: Fit for 55 – the EU's plan for a green transition: renewable-carbon.eu (accessed 13 August 2023).

EU not subject to emissions allowances, with the intention that European producers are not put at a disadvantage. It also aims to prevent businesses relocating production to non-EU countries with less stringent climate policies.

The package also includes measures to promote renewable energy production and energy efficiency strategies in the building sector. The European Commission sees construction as one of the sectors with the greatest need for action. According to the "Level(s)" paper issued by the European Commission, buildings over their entire life cycle account for "half of all energy use, 40% of all greenhouse gas emissions, half of all raw material extraction and one third of all water use" on the European continent.[6] To take clear, unequivocal and verifiable action in response to this, the European Commission revised the Energy Performance of Buildings Directive, first issued in 2010, to specifically address these issues in the building sector.

THE ENERGY PERFORMANCE OF BUILDINGS DIRECTIVE

The Energy Performance of Buildings Directive (EPBD) aims to improve the energy performance of buildings within the European Union. In the 2023 revision, the European Parliament voted for stricter rules on the total energy performance of buildings. It brings forward target dates requiring all new buildings built from 2028 (rather than 2030 as in the original version) to be emission-free, and all new public buildings already from 2026 (previously 2027). Additionally, all new buildings must be equipped with solar technologies from 2028 at the latest where technically possible and economically feasible. For residential buildings requiring major renovations, this will apply beginning in 2032. From 2030, residential buildings must achieve an Energy Performance Class (EPC) of at least E, and from 2033 class D on a scale of A to G, where A means zero emissions and G corresponds to the 15% worst-performing buildings in a country (or a higher percentage if the country-specific scale for class E should be below the EU minimum standard). Non-residential and public buildings will be required to achieve these EPCs from 2027 and 2030 respectively. The EPBD therefore ultimately affects almost all buildings within the European Union – albeit not all at once – regardless of size and use, and applies equally to new buildings and existing buildings when refurbished or modernized, or on the renewal of a lease.

BUILDING CODES FOR CLIMATE PROTECTION IN THE USA

In countries outside the European Union without such a coordinated and comprehensive package of measures, model regulations such as the International Building Code (IBC), the International Energy Conservation Code (IECC) or the International Green Construction Code (IgCC) are often used as a basis for the ongoing development of building legislation.[7] Following the model of the 10th Amendment to the US Constitution, which delegates all powers not governed or prohibited by the US Constitution to the states, many state-level constitutions delegate legislative powers, including those relating to the built environment (building permits, building codes, planning and zoning), in turn to city or town councils. Consequently, most states have agreed on some form of IBC (albeit sometimes quite outdated) that serves as the basis for building regulations and sets minimum standards for public health, safety and general welfare. Specifications exceeding these minimum standards – especially with regard to environmental protection – require a majority consensus at the respective political levels. As a result, there are numerous ordinances across the USA that vary considerably in form and stringency. A positive example is the California Green Building Standards Code (CGBSC), also known as CALGreen, which the State of California began developing back in 2007. The legislative package, the product of Assembly Bill 32, or California Global Warming Solutions Act, has the explicit goal of reducing the state's greenhouse gas emissions to 1990 levels by 2020 – which was actually achieved for the first time on 11 July 2018.[8] The CGBSC includes regulations and design principles for efficiently using, conserving and recovering energy, water and materials, and to protect the environment and well-being, and applies to new and remodelled residential, industrial and public buildings.

Another example is that of the City of New York: based on the finding that two thirds of greenhouse gas emissions in the metropolitan area result from the building sector, and the

6 European Union (ed.), LEVEL(S), Luxembourg, 2019, https://ec.europa.eu/environment/eussd/pdf/LEVEL(S)%20CONFERENCE%20REPORT.pdf, p. 5 [Version from 10 April 2021].

7 International Code Council, ICC, https://www.iccsafe.org/about/overview/international-code-adoptions/ (accessed 28 July 2023).

8 California Building Standards Commission, Sacramento, https://www.dgs.ca.gov/BSC/About/History-of-the-California-Green-Building-Standards-Code-CALGreen (accessed 28 July 2023).

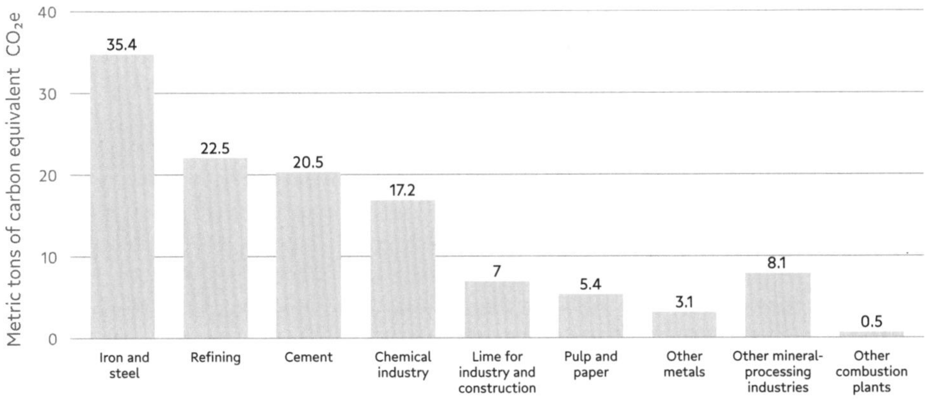

3

Greenhouse gas emissions by industrial sector in Germany in 2021.

Based on: Statista 2023, original source: German Federal Environment Agency; German Emissions Trading Authority.

goal of achieving carbon neutrality by 2050, the City Council passed Local Law 97 (LL97) in 2019 as part of the Climate Mobilization Act. LL97 introduces new targets for energy performance and limiting greenhouse gas emissions from building operations for all new buildings and all existing buildings with a gross floor area of over 25,000 square feet (2.323 m²) in the city from 2024 onwards, making upgrades mandatory, although some exceptions apply. The city estimates that without such improvements some 20–25% of the building stock in 2024 will exceed these emission limits, and that in 2030 – when stricter limits come into force – this could apply to as much as 75–80% of all buildings. A catalogue of penalties for non-compliance, starting at USD 268 per metric ton of CO_2 emissions over the limit (and USD 500,000 for misreporting), was introduced to motivate building owners to undertake the necessary upgrading measures.[9]

The small City of Ithaca in New York State goes a step further. Also in 2019, the city council adopted the Ithaca Green New Deal, which aims to achieve community-wide carbon neutrality by 2030. The measures targeted at the building sector include new building legislation that sets efficiency targets for building envelopes and building operations at 80% above New York State levels – and establishes a programme to completely decarbonize all existing buildings in the city. As part of a public-private partnership established in 2022, the programme includes electrifying all buildings, heating and other appliances, decoupling from fossil fuels, providing for electricity needs using 100% renewable sources, installing heat pumps in all buildings – also entailing mandatory upgrades – and a retrofitting programme to reduce electricity loads and improve the insulation of buildings across the city. By leveraging creative financial models, many of these measures will be implemented at little or no upfront costs to the building owners, thereby contributing to reducing both existing and future social and economic inequalities.[10]

FROM AN ENERGY PROBLEM TO AN EMISSIONS PROBLEM

Given this book's focus on clean energy transition and digital transformation, it may seem unusual to devote such attention to aspects of climate protection in the discourse on sustainability. From the first oil crisis in the 1970s until well into the first decade of the 21st century, little attention has been given to how our energy supply systems impact the climate. Public discourse was instead more concerned with ensuring a consistent supply of affordable energy. The paradox is that we have never had, nor will have, an energy availability problem on Earth! As discussed in detail in the introduction to the first volume of *Building Better – Less – Different*,[11] the energy input, and also energy output through radiation, is the only open system on our planet. Energy arriving as solar irradiance on this planet costs nothing; it is essentially a free service of the galaxy we live in. The planet itself provides associated additional sources of energy in the form of wind, water or geothermal. The problem we have is on the one hand, that such energies are distributed unevenly and people have unequal access to them – and, on the other, and related to this, a massive emissions problem resulting from our dependency on access to and continued use of fossil fuels.

9 NYC Buildings, Greenhouse Gas Emissions Reporting, https://www.nyc.gov/site/buildings/codes/greenhouse-gas-emission-reporting.page (accessed 28 July 2023).

10 City of Ithaca, Green New Deal, https://www.cityofithaca.org/642/Green-New-Deal (accessed 28 July 2023).

11 Dirk E. Hebel and Felix Heisel, "Sustainability – The Importance of a Holistic Approach", in Felix Heisel, Dirk E. Hebel with Ken Webster, *Building Better – Less – Different: Circular Construction and Circular Economy*, Birkhäuser, 2022, pp. 10–21.

The oil crises of the 1970s should have served as warnings. The first oil crisis began in October 1973 when the member states of the Organization of the Petroleum Exporting Countries (OPEC) stopped oil exports to the USA, Europe and Japan in response to the Yom Kippur War in the Sinai and the Golan Heights, causing oil prices to multiply within a short space of time. The USA and its allies responded with economic sanctions against the OPEC countries. The impact on the world economy was significant, especially for those industrialized countries heavily dependent on oil imports, which saw a rise in inflation and a decline in economic growth. The second oil crisis in 1979 was again triggered by the OPEC countries reducing oil production following supply disruptions resulting from the revolution in Iran, causing a corresponding rise in oil prices. What the western world has chosen to perceive as crises is a product of longstanding dependencies on oil and reveals the extent to which our modern societies have manoeuvred themselves into a dead end from which it has become difficult to escape. Instead of developing technologies to better exploit renewable sources of energy such as solar, wind or the carbon cycle, we have focused mainly on extracting fossil fuels – with the associated negative consequences.

More recent events have once again made us painfully aware of the consequences of our dependency on fossil fuels. Russia's attacks on Ukraine since 2014 and 2022 and the resulting economic sanctions against the aggressor have revealed Europe's dependency not only on oil but also on natural gas. Fifty years after the first oil crisis, the situation is similarly dramatic with comparable economic consequences. Had we used those 50 years to achieve greater independence from fossil fuels, we would have had half a century more to combat climate change, and the situation now may not have been as pressing as it is. Instead, time is running short, and we are now attempting to turn the tide within a timespan of just 25 years. We have since also realized that producing heat and cooling from regenerative sources is just as challenging as producing electricity from renewable energies, as the EU Energy Performance of Buildings Directive shows. In short: without proper answers to the issue of energy provision, it will not be possible to decarbonize the sectors of transport, mobility, industry, and also building.

DECARBONIZATION THROUGH DIGITALIZATION

Closely linked to the question of new ways of providing energy is that of new technologies and specifically digitalization, for which the past 50 years have been a decisive period. Existing power supply systems are based on a small number of large power plants that serve as central nodes in a large-scale power distribution grid. With the shift towards power generation from wind and solar energy, which unlike power plants do not produce a constant supply of energy but fluctuate on a daily or even hourly basis, comes a paradigm shift in the design of production and supply systems. At a local level, this can mean systems that oscillate continually between the provision and use of energy, and these require a corresponding adaptive system that can intelligently control energy flows with the help of digitalization. Such systems then also make it possible to integrate electrochemical energy accumulators or hydrogen storage systems along with a swarm of small to medium-sized energy generating plants. In the electricity sector, these can range from smaller or larger solar panel installations on roofs or open land to individual wind turbines or entire wind parks with many turbines. Digital control systems for routing electricity flows in real time can also incorporate forecasting for both power generation (i.e., weather data) as well as power consumption (empirical data), turning them into intelligently predictive and adaptive systems.

The capabilities of digital systems do not stop there. Vehicle transport will continue to play an important role in future: vehicle batteries of all kinds can help stabilize energy flows when parked and connected to the power grid – studies show that private cars are parked for an average of 23 hours per day – by absorbing and releasing energy at short notice in a controlled and targeted manner in response to digital, networked real-time data. This so-called sector coupling that digital networks enable also highlights the importance of promoting a switch to electromobility as a key building block in the path to a decarbonized future, and not just as a matter of principle.

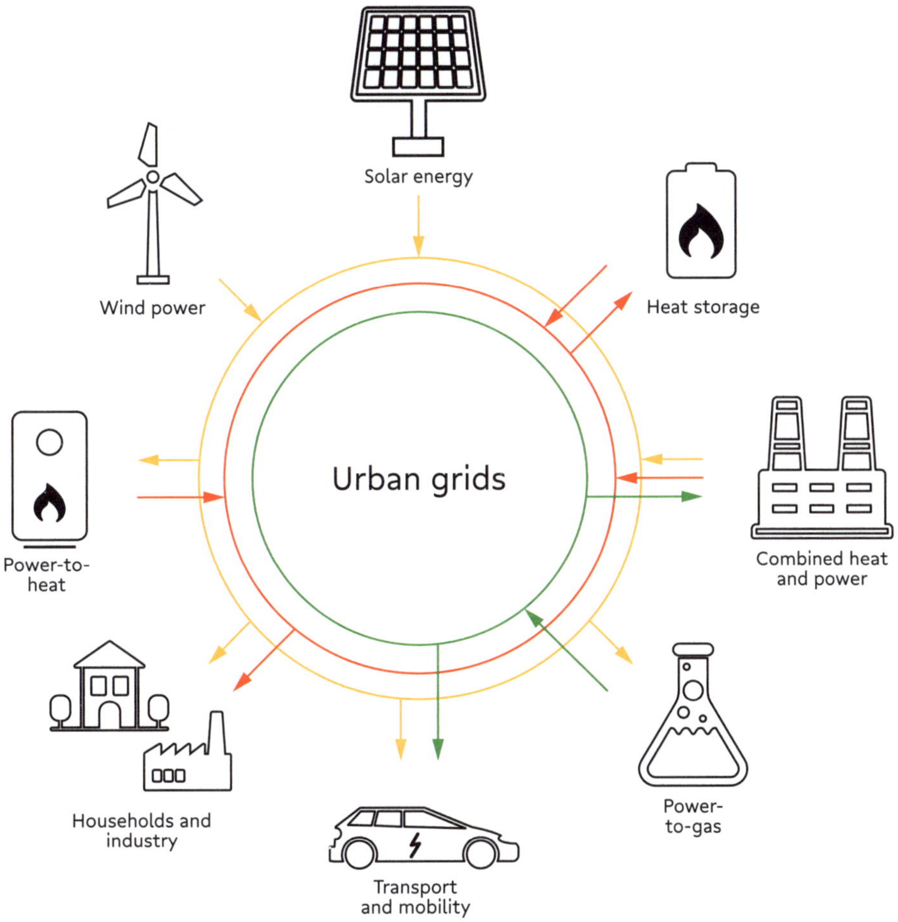

4

Sector coupling in urban grids.

Electricity

District heating

Gas

Based on: Fraunhofer SCAI.

The same applies to coupling with the heating sector. There are already millions of autonomous heating systems which currently burn fossil fuels and produce emissions. Replacing these with heat pumps not only replaces the energy source, but also enables them to be incorporated into digitally controlled networks, creating an opportunity to use their potential more efficiently.

Digitalization is thus helping to create emerging networks in which the areas of energy, transport and buildings are closely linked. This publication describes several small- and large-scale variants. Neighbourhoods and local communities in particular stand to benefit from the immense advantages of this new approach. The digital serves here as a connecting nervous system exchanging information between devices and infrastructure in real time. In future, networks will distribute not just energy but also information, communicating how, when and where energy is being generated, supplied and consumed. Networks will then no longer be one-way systems and we become simultaneously consumers and producers of energy. Similar to the introduction of a circular economy, the clean energy transition is creating new needs and business models for products ranging from smart electricity meters to inverters to vehicles that contribute to providing comfort at home. Here we see the interlinking of building and mobile systems.

THE DIGITAL TRANSFORMATION OF ARCHITECTURAL PRODUCTION

Computational design and production have transformed the way living and working environments are provided. Digital tools first began to be used for architectural design in the early 1980s. Initially, they focused on improving efficiency ("better"), i.e., in optimizing known methods. The first software packages simulated drawing tools, digital 3D models simplified perspective drawings, and the first 3D printing tools and digital cutters improved

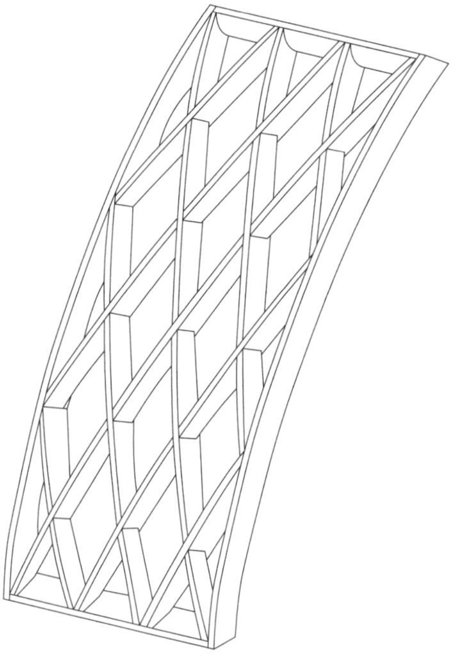

5

The Zollinger Gridshell comprises many small individual elements that together form a load-bearing structure.

Based on: Friedrich Zollinger.

model building. Sometimes software from other branches was employed. Frank Gehry, for example, employed the aircraft design tool CATIA by Dassault Systems to digitize hand-built models using a digitizing wand to transpose points from a physical model, measured in relation to a defined point of origin, into three-dimensional digital objects. The software then derived the corresponding two-dimensional drawings for communicating the design to construction companies.

The first digital production chains were likewise informed by a drive for greater efficiency. Computer-controlled milling machines transformed digital data into complex geometries at considerable speed, making, for example, traditional carpentry joints in wood construction economically attractive again. In the same way that CAD programs replaced architectural draughting, milling machines replaced more time-consuming craftship. As more and more synergies have emerged, the architectural plan itself has become increasingly obsolete: digital planning and models can now flow directly into production processes. This same development also creates opportunities for strategies of sufficiency ("less") by, for example, linking computational design to engineering in order to place material only where it is structurally and constructively required. At present, concrete slabs are still cast according to the one-size-fits-all principle at a single thickness that corresponds to that needed for the point that sustains the greatest load: we deploy material at a thickness not needed throughout. As Philippe Block demonstrates compellingly in the first volume of *Building Better – Less – Different*,[12] progressive digital planning and production is bringing about a paradigm shift. Through the intelligent interplay of computational design and production, we can, on the one hand, improve the effectiveness, i.e. performance, of the material used and on the other reduce the overall amount of material used.

Another example of this is a concept for functionally graded concrete developed by Werner Sobek, which also achieves significant material savings: "In structural components made of functionally graded concrete, the material properties such as strength, density, stiffness or thermal conductivity are specifically adapted to the stress profile prevailing in the interior structure of the component. By varying the mortar and concrete composition using lightweight aggregates or pore-forming agents, material is used only where actually needed. As a result, the components' total mass is drastically reduced, while retaining stability and functionality."[13]

In the building sector, we can identify a further example of sector coupling, this time in the areas of design and manufacturing – a coupling which is established by the nervous system of digital information exchange, just as previously explained with regard to the area of energy. This leads to a third strategy of sustainable building, namely consistency ("different"). By coupling computational design and production, we can increasingly utilize building materials and elements previously considered too weak or not performant enough. Consequently, we are experiencing a renaissance of traditional building methods and biological building materials. Computational production makes it possible, for example, to economically fabricate a Zollinger roof, a lattice shell made of many small interlocking rods that is self-supporting and requires neither columns nor a supporting structure. Developed by Friedrich Zollinger at the beginning of the 20th century, the construction method, while comparatively labour-intensive, was designed to make sparing use of the available materials. In times of need, such as after both World Wars, when long wooden beams were hard to come by, such structures could be built with 40 % less material than conventional roof structures. In the modern day, computational production methods make it possible to utilize, for example, substandard or non-standardized wood that would otherwise be deemed unsuitable for use in construction. Similarly, we are seeing a resurgence in the use of biological materials such as willow rods, hemp fibres or mushroom mycelium in building structures. The digital transformation of the design process enables such materials to be used intelligently, economically and efficiently, leveraging their performance to address new tasks in building structures while maintaining their ability to be returned to pure natural cycles without contaminating or even compromising them.

12 Philippe Block, "Strength Through Geometry and Material Effectiveness", in Felix Heisel, Dirk E. Hebel with Ken Webster, *Building Better – Less – Different: Circular Construction and Circular Economy*, Birkhäuser, 2022, pp. 72–77.

13 https://gradientenbeton.eu/. Daniel Schmeer, Mark Wörner, Harald Garrecht, Oliver Sawodny and Werner Sobek, "Optimal structures made of functional graded concrete – design, dimensioning and automated production", in Silke Scheerer and Manfred Curbach (eds.), Final Report SPP 1542, Concrete Light, Technische Universität Dresden, 2022, https://doi.org/10.25368/2022.331.

14 https://www.epo.org/about-us/annual-reports-statistics/statistics/2022_de.html.

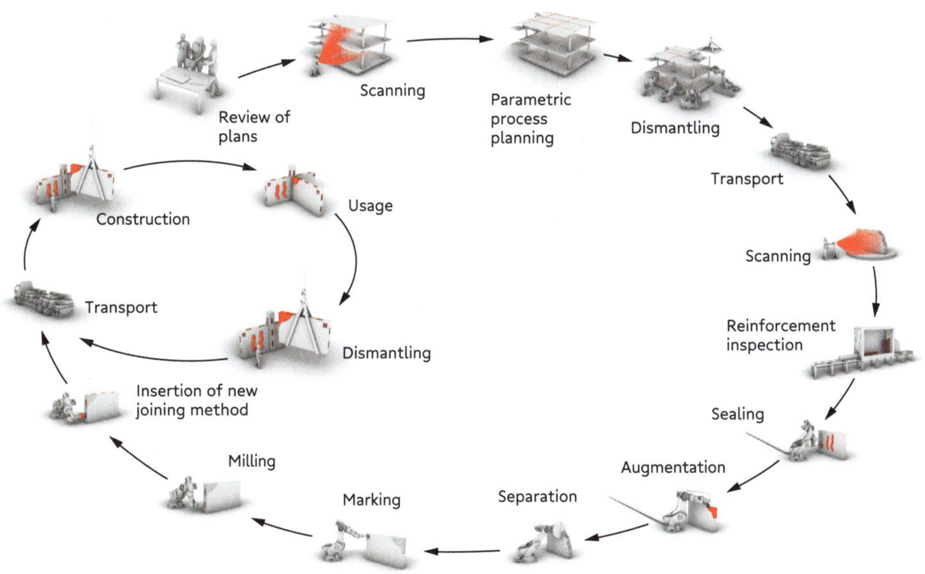

This volume provides an overview of the possibilities and potentials present in the building industry from the viewpoint of building better, less and different, and attempts to reveal where these overlap, connect and generate synergies, also in relation to the previous volume on *Circular Construction and Circular Economy*. Just how topical and significant the fields of clean energy transition and digital transformation are for sustainable construction can be seen in the 2022 statistics published by the European Patent Office where "digital and clean energy technologies have driven up patent applications in the EU to a record level".[14] Alongside clean energy technology and other methods of generating, distributing and storing electricity, including battery technology, digital communications remains the frontrunner in annual filings. With this volume, our intention is to relate this surge in innovation to the issues and strategies for sustainable action in architectural design, construction, operation and at the end-of-use of buildings.

6

Digital tools provide a means of making the reuse of entire building components cost-effective.

Based on: Vincent Witt, *KITBauTech - eine neu Bauforschungsinfrastruktur für das KIT*, Master's thesis, KIT Faculty of Architecture, Karlsruhe, 2023.

THE CLEAN ENERGY TRANSITION IN THE CONTEXT OF SUSTAINABILITY

Introduction by
Andreas Wagner

The topic of energy has informed the design of buildings since the 1970s – although the underlying motivation has shifted considerably over the years. Sadly, then as now, it was war that prompted worldwide energy security fears: the oil crisis resulting from the Yom Kippur War – in response to which the Organization of the Petroleum Exporting Countries (OPEC) drastically cut its oil supplies to Western industrialized countries – made it clear how dependent countries without own oil production were on foreign petroleum.[1] Looking back, the ad hoc reaction of the West German government – to introduce car-free Sundays – seems almost tragicomic. But this first taste of the need to address the topic of energy marked the beginning of a successively more substantial agenda for conserving energy (along with various measures designed to secure the country's energy supply), among them the Energy Savings Act (Gesetz zur Einsparung von Energie in Gebäuden).[2] At that time, the building stock in Germany was predominantly a mix of either pre-turn-of-the-century or post-war buildings, many industrially fabricated but all, by current standards, poor in terms of energy efficiency. Interestingly, buildings from around and after the turn of the century were often of a better standard than their later counterparts.

FROM ENERGY-EFFICIENT BUILDING ENVELOPES TO INTEGRAL BUILDING AND ENERGY CONCEPTS

The introduction of the Energy Savings Act in 1976 confronted architects and planners with the need to tackle the topic of energy use in buildings. Germany's early action and long-time pioneering role in developing energy conservation measures for buildings serves as a good example of similar steps taken subsequently in other countries.

The first legislation to be derived from the Act was the Thermal Insulation Ordinance (Wärmeschutzverordnung, WSchVo) in 1977, which initially only set out explicit specifications for the heat transfer coefficient of building elements and for reducing heat loss through leaks in the building envelope.[3] In 1995 it was amended in response to pressure from architects to include a calculation procedure that eventually took into account the contribution of solar gains for heating. Research into passive solar strategies began in the early 1970s and numerous notable prototypes were constructed, mostly in the USA and to a lesser degree in southern Europe, predominantly with single glazing and adobe for energy storage. In Germany too, protagonists such as Rolf Disch from Freiburg and Thomas Herzog from Munich propagated the principles of solar architecture in a series of model buildings, and the revised ordinance corroborated their approach, although the actual energy gain was not always as promising as hoped: ultimately it came down to the fact that the American and southern European models only functioned due to the significantly higher availability of solar energy in those regions.

Over time, improvements in the thermal insulation properties of glazing (heat protection glass) and the advent of translucent thermal insulation made it possible to significantly reduce heating demand with the help of solar energy, also in Central European climates. Milestones from this era of progressive development in the 1990s include the energy self-sufficient solar house in Freiburg[4] and the first passive house in Darmstadt[5] – which, despite their quite different approaches, were both the product of systematic research into solar-based energy concepts combined with highly efficient building envelopes. At the time, design concerns still took a back seat to the extremely ambitious energy objectives, but this would change, as many excellent subsequent examples have shown.

In their conceptual approach, both these buildings anticipated a significant legislative change that was to come: in 2002, the Energy Saving Ordinance (Energieeinsparverordnung, EnEV)[6] was introduced that marked a shift from optimizing the building envelope to considering it alongside the technical systems used in the building in the form of an overall energy balance. In addition, it introduced a new assessment parameter: the primary energy demand for heating, ventilation, cooling/air conditioning, hot water supply and lighting. By focusing on targets for the total energy demand of a building, it gave architects and planners greater scope to develop alternative integral building and energy concepts, while minimum thermal transfer specifications for the building envelope still applied. At the same time, the primary

1 See, for example, History, Energy Crisis (1970s), https://www.history.com/topics/1970s/energy-crisis.

2 See, for example, Energy Savings Act, https://www.bbsr-geg.bund.de/GEGPortal/DE/Archiv/EnEG/EnEG1976/1976_node.html. (accessed 24/03/2023).

3 See, for example, Thermal Insulation Ordinance from 1977 to 2002, https://www.energie-experten.org/energie-sparen/energieberatung/gebaeudeenergiegesetz/waermeschutzverordnung (accessed 24 March 2023).

4 Architects: Planerwerkstatt Hölken & Berghoff, Freiburg, 1992. See, for example, W. Stahl, K. Voss, A. Goetzberger, "The self-sufficient solar house in Freiburg", *Solar Energy*, Volume 52, Issue 1, 1994, pp. 111–125, https://doi.org/10.1016/0038-092X(94)90085-G.

5 Architects: Prof. Bott/Ridder/Westermeyer, Darmstadt-Kranichstein, 1991. See, for example, https://passipedia.de/beispiele/wohngebaeude/mehrfamilienhaeuser/das_erste_passivhaus_in_darmstadt-kranichstein_deutschland.

6 See, for example, Das neue Gebäudeenergiegesetz (GEG) im Überblick; https://www.energie-experten.org/energie-sparen/energieberatung/gebaeudeenergiegesetz (accessed 24 March 2023).

energy demand ensured that consideration must still be given to energy resource usage, in turn elevating the advantages of renewable energy sources over finite fossil and nuclear energy sources.

A whole range of exciting approaches to building design have since emerged, including various concepts for passive cooling utilizing night-time ventilation and the stack effect to discharge a building's thermal mass, geothermal heat exchangers to cool supply air or thermo-active building systems that employ subsurface geothermal or groundwater sources. In such integral concepts, the building design and construction become part of the energy concept, necessitating a new, more cooperative understanding of design. Similar developments can be seen in new approaches to incorporating solar modules into the building envelope where technical and design demands need to be reconciled with one another. Ongoing innovations by the PV industry show impressively how PV modules have developed from the standard sizes of the past to samples which can now be fabricated in numerous shapes and sizes, no longer limited to planar geometry and with different surface patterns, colours and three-dimensional forms to address a wide range of design requirements.

NEW GOALS: FROM CONSERVING RESOURCES TO CLIMATE PROTECTION

In the early 2000s, the various national initiatives across Europe aiming to improve the energy efficiency of buildings were unified in a European framework in the form of the Energy Performance of Buildings Directive (EPBD).[7] With this came a fundamental shift in focus in response to the aims of the UN Kyoto Protocol[8] that served as a basis for the Directive, in which the signatory states made a binding commitment to reduce greenhouse gas emissions. The main goal was – and still is – to limit anthropogenic global warming to a minimum: the current target is to remain under 1.5 °C. Through the focus on limiting climate change by reducing greenhouse gas emissions – specifically combustion-related CO_2 emissions – the directives and regulatory frameworks for buildings have given rise to a new set of terms such as climate-neutral, zero-carbon or net-zero-emissions buildings.[9]

Given that the building sector is one of the largest consumers of energy in Europe, accounting for about 40 % of total energy consumption and 36 % of CO_2 emissions in the EU, and that analyses have shown that some 75 % of the existing building stock is energy inefficient and thus responsible for the lion's share of building-related emissions,[10] there is an urgent need for action in this sector if we are to meet climate targets. At the same time, we need to convert the energy supply of buildings to emission-free technologies, which entails huge changes to current systems, especially where heat supply is concerned. Alongside heat pumps, (cold) heat grids have a major role to play in future. To meet the accompanying significant increase in electricity demand, for example for running heat pumps, it will be necessary to further expand wind farms, both on open land and offshore, as well as to activate much more roof and other surfaces in cities and urban conurbations for photovoltaic systems, which will undoubtedly have an impact on the future urban townscape.

Another aspect that will change the face of the urban realm, along with the buildings that shape it, is the problem of overheating as rising temperatures cause hot spells in summer to become more prolonged and intense. Here both technological as well as climate-adaptive design measures can help improve health and comfort in inner-city environments. To mitigate the potentially rapid rise in energy demand in this field, such approaches should be coupled with predominantly passive, or solar-assisted active cooling systems.

With respect to the objectives, goals and methods for limiting climate change, they do not seem all that different to those for conserving energy resources, with the exception perhaps that emissions are used for the assessment. What is certainly different, however, is that the timeframe we have to meet the current goal of no-more-than-1.5 °C global warming by reducing emissions to net-zero is much shorter: 2050 is only a little more than 25 years away!

7 Energy performance of buildings directive, https://energy.ec.europa.eu/topics/energy-efficiency/energy-efficient-buildings/energy-performance-buildings-directive_en (accessed 6 August 2023).

8 Kyoto Protocol, https://unfccc.int/kyoto_protocol (accessed 6 August 2023).

9 Nearly Zero-Energy Buildings, https://energy.ec.europa.eu/topics/energy-efficiency/energy-efficient-buildings/nearly-zero-energy-buildings_en (accessed 6 August 2023).

10 See, for example, European Commission, *Making our Homes and Buildings Fit for a Greener Future*, 15 December 2021, https://energy.ec.europa.eu/system/files/2019-01/buildings_performance_factsheet_0.pdf (accessed 13 August 2023).

BROADENING HORIZONS: THE EUROPEAN GREEN DEAL

With the European Green Deal in 2019,[11] the EU set new, very ambitious targets for reaching net-zero emissions. Of particular relevance for the building sector are targets for implementing an effective circular economy and for energy-efficient and resource-conserving construction and renovation. Part of this will be a comprehensive life cycle analysis for buildings to record and assess resource use and environmental impacts. The most recent amendment of the EPBD,[12] for example, sets out corresponding requirements for verifying greenhouse gas emissions over a building's entire life cycle. For the integrated building and energy concepts mentioned earlier, this will influence both building material choices as well as concepts for technical services. By way of example, the RoofKIT project (see p. 142), winner of the Solar Decathlon Europe 21/22, showed that when predominantly natural, recycled/recyclable and reused/reusable building materials are used, the proportion of greenhouse gas emissions produced by the building services is far greater than for the building construction itself – and this is in a project where careful attention has been paid to simplifying building services through the use of decentralized (i.e., ductless) facade ventilators, short services paths thanks to a central technical core and exclusively passive cooling.

The holistic perspective has given rise to new debates, for example on the target values for future energy standards and their consequences for the use of materials in the building envelope and the associated emissions. Or in the context of digitalization, on whether more technology in the form of intelligent systems (e.g., sensors and building automation) can close the so-called performance gap of buildings, or whether perhaps allowing more user control (e.g., natural ventilation) in conjunction with simple laws of physics might ultimately be more resilient. A radical example is the 2226 building concept (see p. 70), which has no heating system at all and uses internal heat sources along with good thermal insulation and an intelligent (albeit sensor- and automation-based) ventilation concept to maintain sufficient levels of thermal comfort.

ENERGY AND SUSTAINABILITY – THE CONTRIBUTIONS IN THIS BOOK

Although the concept of sustainability in its many different dimensions is now widely acknowledged and increasingly determines our political agendas and social behaviour, sustainable building focused for a long time almost exclusively on energy. Thankfully, this is no longer the case, and issues such as the environment, resources, and health as well as social developments and values are increasingly shaping the process of designing, constructing and using buildings. Indeed, even our perspective on energy in the context of sustainability strategies for building has expanded significantly, as we have shown here.

Climate change, even more than conserving resources, is now the primary challenge we face for our future on Earth. For the energy-hungry and emissions-producing construction sector, this means we must act swiftly and effectively to meet these climate goals. The articles in this second volume of *Building Better – Less – Different* aim to show how this can be achieved and the range of possibilities available to us. They ask, for example: How can we better shape the so-called heat transition? How do we develop new energy concepts at a neighbourhood level with the help of digital planning tools? How can we use improved technological approaches for climate-neutral heating? Is it also possible to reduce the environmental impact of buildings over their entire life cycle with less technical means and simpler overall concepts? Should we assess buildings differently in future so that we can properly evaluate their climate-relevant greenhouse potential? Should we give users more opportunities in their use of buildings? Do we need completely different energy supply strategies? And how do we address the impact of rising temperatures without incurring a sharp rise in energy consumption for cooling?

11 European Green Deal, https://commission.europa.eu/strategy-and-policy/priorities-2019-2024/european-green-deal_en (accessed 6 August 2023).

12 Energy performance of buildings directive, https://energy.ec.europa.eu/topics/energy-efficiency/energy-efficient-buildings/energy-performance-buildings-directive_en (accessed 6 August 2023).

DIGITAL TRANSFOR-MATION

A Techno-optimistic Outlook

Introduction by
Moritz Dörstelmann

Digital tools are an indispensable part of our daily lives and industrial applications. Whether we take a photo with a smartphone, or a machine efficiently produces injection-moulded parts, both are enabled by the productive use of machine learning. In the construction sector, digital design and fabrication methods are now widely used to efficiently realize construction projects. While these are still mostly incremental improvements of existing processes, there are numerous diverse and innovative start-ups just waiting to bring digital business models and construction technologies to established construction and design practice. The technical foundations for a profound digital transformation of the construction industry to create resilient, low-emission buildings are already in place. Similarly, the political mechanisms discussed in the preceding introductions, the recognizable social will and, not least, the expected rise in energy and material costs, combined with the availability of new technological possibilities, create a promising climate for a fundamental paradigm shift towards digitally enabled low-emission construction methods. Together, these have the potential to make a considerable contribution to tackling the climate crisis, one of the most significant challenges we are facing as society today.

Social transformation and technological innovation have always gone hand in hand in humanity's efforts to respond to fundamental challenges. From the early days of digital proto-technologies to the current digital permeation of almost every aspect of our lives, new digital tools have helped us to simplify tedious processes and make them more efficient and productive. The most profound impact on our society, however, has rather come from fundamentally new ideas and concepts that have transferred, adapted and combined available technologies to new fields of application and naturally incorporated them into their implementation.

The transition towards circular and low-emission building methods involves and affects large parts of our society and besides architectural and construction technological developments requires a differentiated view within each respective socio-economic context. Many parts of the world have a huge building stock that, on the one hand, contains numerous potentially reusable components and building materials, and on the other uses available space very inefficiently. A digital transformation must therefore be accompanied by a corresponding societal shift that is open to a more flexible use of existing resources, be they building components or living space, and that questions established expectations of durability and permanence through a new understanding of ongoing change in the use of space and materials. Closely linked with this is the societal notion of sufficiency, with great potential in architectural design to develop new types of living concepts and working environments.

Digital technologies can support and enable such change. To do so, they must be applied in parallel at multiple levels: in the context of the existing building stock to make better use of existing resources; in the development of low-emission construction methods to significantly reduce the burden on the atmosphere in the short and medium term; and in the development of circular construction methods as medium and long term evolution of the existing building stock towards a material repository that will significantly reduce the ecological cost of future buildings.

Here too, digital technologies can help unlock the potential of the urban mine. Modern scanning and imaging technology can be used to capture extensive data sets on heterogeneous building components and materials. With the help of artificial intelligence, these can be evaluated, categorized and qualified for future use, making it possible to track the life cycle of building components and stocks of materials. By linking data and material flows, digital tools can establish local material cycles and, in combination with the use of decentralized low-energy processing methods, have the potential to significantly reduce emissions in the construction industry.

At the same time, the established paradigm of absolutely quantifiable and qualifiable building materials can also be questioned with computational methods and challenge our current understanding of safety by exploring alternative concepts of statistical probability, robustness and redundancy to ensure structural integrity.

Adaptive digital design and cyber-physical fabrication concepts enable us to respond to the inhomogeneity and non-standardized material behaviour we often encounter in reclaimed or grown building materials. This opens new material side streams and a diversification of resources which can be sustainably used in the construction industry. Alongside tapping into new material cycles, and in the context of skilled labour shortage, the digital reinterpretation of historical and artisanal building methods can bring about a renaissance in the use of local natural materials and enable their technically and economically scalable application.

In the age of Big Data, architectural designs and district and urban planning can draw on an increasingly diverse and detailed information basis. The problem then turns to how one can manage the multitude of interacting design parameters so that they can contribute to the design process. Integrative computational design methods provide such ways of navigating huge solution spaces. Not only do they offer ways of incorporating differently weighted ecological and economic factors into the generation of a design through the use of multi-criteria optimization, but they also impact on the original sphere of architectural and spatial design. This does not render architects obsolete through design automation, but rather allows them to harness novel A.I.-based tools to explore their designs.

Such profound changes bear opportunities and risks for all players in the construction sector. They open up opportunities for new business models and the emergence of new disciplines in the Architecture, Engineering and Construction (AEC) sector, while at the same time necessitating greater transdisciplinary collaboration and coordination. As a discipline that has always operated at the intersection of the humanities and engineering, it falls within the cultural remit of the profession to actively shape such changes and drive digital transformation: to balance the timeless poles of *firmitas*, *utilitas* and *venustas* through the simultaneous exploration of a novel architectural design repertoire and sustainable construction technologies.

This second volume of *Building Better – Less – Different* focuses on two intertwined themes: Clean Energy Transition and Digital Transformation. We ask how the digital reinterpretation of historical building techniques can bring about a renaissance of natural building materials using scalable digital building technologies. And how digital deconstruction and reuse strategies can transform the existing building stock into a resource for future building. We explore the potential of customized digital production as a means of reducing resource usage. We look at ways in which innovative building technologies can make inroads into a predominantly conservative sector. And we want to explore the future role of architects as an interdisciplinary mediator and digital master builder who can reunite design and fabrication through digital craft.

This book explores these questions in a series of articles that show how the circularity of current architectural practice can be greatly enhanced by digital design and fabrication technologies and that demonstrate how we can design *better* today. In addition, we examine how new digital circular construction concepts could develop in the near future, and illustrate, using examples, how these could evolve into material and process-driven explorations that lead to *less* carbon emissions and less waste-intensive construction. Finally, we look further into the future to see how fundamentally *different* concepts for the design and material composition of our built environment could potentially challenge the current paradigms within our discipline.

Better

BETTER

Efficiency as the Basis for a Successful Clean Energy Transition

Introduction to Clean Energy Transition by Andreas Wagner

Even though figures on the availability of conventional energy resources and reserves are continually being revised – due to better exploration methods but also the changing accessibility of geographical regions – it is already clear that these energy resources will fall far short of meeting the world's ever-growing demand for energy. At present the per capita energy demand of developing and emerging economies is much less than that of industrialized nations, but as global imbalances gradually recede (as they must), this margin will decrease, causing a significant rise in energy demand. In addition, the global population continues to grow.

To this we must add the impact of converting fossil fuels on the climate, whether through combustion in power plants to produce electricity or to generate heat. More than half the greenhouse gas emissions that are ultimately responsible for global warming can be attributed to energy conversion. This alone means that continuing to bank on fossil fuel reserves for future energy provision scenarios is a counterproductive scenario – even disregarding the fact that their extraction will cause further environmental pollution (as seen, for example, in the current recovery of oil through tar sands extraction in Canada) and will increasingly be nonviable economically compared with harvesting renewable energy sources.

It is already becoming clear that the target of limiting global warming to 1.5 °C will not be met. If we are not to massively endanger the conditions for life on Earth, there is urgent need for action. If we consider solar energy alone, the solution seems simple: annual solar irradiance – the energy supplied by the sun measured at the Earth – is 10,000 times greater than our total annual energy demand. While the theoretical potential is enormous, seen against the background of technical and economic circumstances as well as regional variances in availability, it quickly becomes clear that to transition to power from renewable energy sources such as the sun, two key aspects need to be addressed with respect to both supply and demand.

In industrialized nations, the building sector is responsible for about 40 % of total primary energy consumption, and that does not include the energy consumed to produce building materials. The construction sector is therefore the single largest and most important field of action in which we can mitigate the progress of climate change. And we must act quickly: the time we have to achieve the objective of transforming the energy system is relatively short – current scenarios for limiting global warming to a (perhaps still) manageable level require that the building sector must achieve net-zero emissions by 2045.

One key pillar for effecting a transition to renewable energy sources in the building sector is to improve the energy efficiency of buildings. Without reducing the heating capacity of buildings, and thus their energy demand, the available alternative technical means of energy supply will not adequately cover their needs.

Given that in Europe alone some 75 % of the existing building stock is estimated to be inadequate in energy efficiency terms, this is a Herculean task – especially considering the diverse types of buildings from various eras and with different construction methods. Approaches therefore need to be specific and appropriate. Universal energy performance targets that are overambitiously set for a non-negligible number of individual buildings are not feasible and would founder on the various legal, structural and economic restrictions and constraints. Similarly, retrofitting measures must respect the architectural character and cultural identity of buildings and cities. At the same time, these hurdles must not be taken as a blanket excuse for inaction: the rate at which energy efficiency upgrades are taking place already lies far behind what is needed to achieve the declared targets. There are many very good examples of retrofitting measures for improving energy efficiency that are appropriate to the construction method and architecturally compatible. For a large proportion of buildings, such (energy-related) refurbishments will bring significant design improvements. What is needed are refurbishment roadmaps that are tailored to the individual project. They must be technically robust with regard to sustainable solutions for preserving the building fabric and sensible with respect to their energy-related targets. Then they create conditions that are conducive to alternative forms of energy supply.

What form could this target take? Because most of the energy consumed in the building sector is used for the provision of heat, this needs to be converted into combustion-free methods to eliminate emissions at the place of use. In theory, hydrogen represents a conceivable alternative energy source, either converted in suitable boilers or in fuel cells. However, the poor conversion rate of renewable electricity into hydrogen, and the huge demand for hydrogen especially in industrial sectors, makes it unlikely that this solution will see broad adoption in buildings in the short and medium term. The favoured option at present is therefore the provision of heat by electrically driven heat pumps (both individual or communal installations) that, on the one hand, leverage renewable environmental sources for heat and on the other are powered by electricity from renewable sources.

The EU's Energy Performance of Buildings Directive (EPBD) sets out the goal of zero-energy or zero-emission buildings – understood as an annual balance rather than a building's complete self-sufficiency. The question here is where the renewable electricity for operating the heat pumps and the building's various other needs will be sourced. From the broader perspective of grid load, the most desirable option is that a building covers as much of its own energy demand as possible so that grid interactions and load are minimized – i.e., the building is grid-efficient. In practice, this means utilizing as much of the building's – and possibly the plot's – external surfaces as possible to generate electricity.

For smaller, especially freestanding buildings of up to three or four storeys, the roof area is usually sufficient to cover the electricity demand using PV. This is less easily achieved in urban environments with many multi-storey buildings where facades are often shaded by surrounding buildings. Accordingly alternative areas for generating electricity will be needed to meet the demand. Aside from the fact that there are also accompanying system-related challenges, such as the feed-in of solar power at different grid voltage levels, it becomes clear that we must once again act to improve efficiency – in this case the efficient use of available surface areas, which is defined essentially by the relationship between reducing energy demand and the best possible conversion of all energy forms. The same principle also applies to leveraging other environmental sources for heat generation via heat pumps – for example through geothermal energy or hybrid PVT photovoltaic thermal collectors – regardless of whether at an individual level or supplied via a heat grid. Without such efficiency optimizations, the demand for land on which to install renewable energy systems may soon rise immeasurably.

Improving the resilience of buildings is another topic discussed in this chapter, which can be achieved through energy-efficiency oriented retrofitting measures but also by transforming the energy system. This means making buildings more robust against system failures so that living conditions can be maintained for a certain time and to a certain degree in the case of energy supply outages or fluctuations. This is especially important in countries without stable energy supplies. A further advantage of decentralizing the energy system through a multiplicity of small photovoltaic systems on individual buildings is that it reduces the risk of systemic failure and supply shortages due to the higher degree of redundancy resulting from the many installations.

THE SCALE AND IMPACT OF THE CLEAN HEATING TRANSITION

Reconciling Thermal Insulation, Renewable Energies and Social Justice

Commentary by Martin Pehnt

From 2014 until 2021, energy use in buildings has not decreased. Larger house and apartment sizes, decades of cheap energy and a lack of political will have meant that the pace of transition to clean heating has been slow, despite the increasingly apparent consequences of climate change and the fact that space and water heating in buildings accounts for a third of all energy consumed in Germany.[1]

The events of 2022 have given renewed urgency to the need to transition to decarbonized heating. The outbreak of the war in Ukraine has made the untenability of the present situation painfully apparent. The high price of energy has thrown the vulnerability of a wasteful building stock into sharp relief. Unlike the electricity sector, in which the share of renewable energy sources is increasingly rising, the share of renewable energy used in the building sector is much lower. Much of the existing building stock needs renovation, and many buildings are still very inefficient. In short, there is a considerable backlog to catch up on if we are to achieve the long-term goal of net-zero carbon emissions in the building stock by 2045, not to mention the more immediate target of halving greenhouse gas emissions in the decade from 2020 to 2030. That means that skilled labour, materials and equipment will be in short supply over the next seven years and beyond.

This timeframe is one of the main challenges of the clean heating transition. As refurbishments are typically undertaken at extended intervals, opportunities missed now will not recur again soon. Those who recently installed a gas heating system – which despite the gas crisis amounted to some 600,000 of the roughly one million heating systems installed in Germany in 2022[2] – may find they will have to decommission it prematurely or switch to expensive green gas sources. Similarly, those putting up scaffolding to renovate their building exterior would be well advised to do more than just a "paint job", and to apply insulation.

It is unfortunate that in Germany the issue of transitioning to decarbonized heating got caught up in other, often polemic debates in past legislative periods. The standpoints of competing concepts on how best to achieve a turnaround became increasingly entrenched. A central point of contention was the question of "energy efficiency *or* renewable energy". It is quicker and easier to increase the proportion of renewable energy, they argued, and thus not necessary to improve the efficiency of the building stock. As a result, insulating buildings was portrayed as being only for the over-zealous.

And yet even the switch to renewable energy sources has fallen behind. In fact, many of the associated aims, such as making more sparing use of renewable energies, avoiding peak loads, leveraging the thermal storage capacity of buildings, or utilizing low-temperature heating systems that work with highly efficient heat pumps or heat grids benefit significantly from good thermal insulation. The combination of a district-wide heat-pump-based energy supply, suitable thermal insulation and an integrated building operation system can reduce the load on the electricity grid by a factor of six.[3]

The debate has since begun to shift from "energy efficiency *or* renewable energy" towards "energy efficiency *enables* renewable energy". The focus here is not solely on insulation but on finding intelligent, low-cost solutions to creating efficient building envelopes that work architecturally and are also circular in their construction. For this we can draw on a wide range of concepts and materials. In the context of the existing building stock, this means maximizing the potential of modernization and refurbishment activities.

An important instrument to this end is the elaboration of a "renovation roadmap" that has the long-term goal of achieving net-zero carbon emissions. In discussion with an experienced energy consultant, an individual building renovation strategy is developed that considers the future plans and wishes of the owners along with any necessary modernization and upkeep measures and looks at how these can be cost effectively aligned with climate protection goals. The renovation roadmap also serves to avoid wrong decisions being made: for example, make sure the roof overhang of a new roof extends out far enough to accommodate later insulation of the external walls; plan replacement windows so that they can be shifted out into the insulation layer to reduce thermal bridging; ensure building materials are climate-friendly; pre-install conduits ready for the later installation of a solar panel

1 AG Energiebilanzen e. V. (AGEB), *Anwendungsbilanzen zur Energiebilanz Deutschland. Endenergieverbrauch nach Energieträgern und Anwendungszwecken*, as of December 2022, https://ag-energiebilanzen.de/wp-content/uploads/2023/01/AGEB_21p2_V3_20221222.pdf (accessed 12 March 2023).

2 Bundesverband der Deutschen Heizungsindustrie (BDH), Jahresbilanz 2022: Heizungsmarkt boomt, Pressemitteilung 2023, https://www.bdh-industrie.de/presse/pressemeldungen/artikel/jahresbilanz-2022-heizungsmarkt-boomt (accessed 12 March 2023).

3 FIW, ifeu, *Wärmeschutz und Wärmepumpe – warum beides zusammengehört.* Study commissioned by VDPM, Munich, Berlin, Heidelberg, 2023, https://www.ifeu.de/fileadmin/uploads/pdf/2023_FIW_ifeu_Wärmeschutz_und_Wärmepumpe.pdf.

system; identify where geothermal probes for a heat pump system can be drilled; examine how heating systems can operate at lower supply temperatures, and so on. State funding is already available for developing an individual building renovation roadmap.

Another area of contentious debate that has since abated in Germany is that of the value of district heating versus individual central heating. While some assert the right to have a central heating boiler in their own home and object to being forced to join a heating supply network, others see the only reasonable solution in large-scale district heating. Since then, the pressing need to advance the decarbonization of heating supply has given way to a broader acceptance that multiple climate-friendly solutions can exist alongside one another.

Heat grids are essential for distributing energy from geothermal sources, large solar energy farms, river heat or recovered waste heat. In densely built-up urban areas especially, existing as well as new heat networks represent a vital pillar in the supply of heat to households and other consumers. New players are needed that can operate such networks professionally and cost effectively. Municipalities must play a key role here through local heat planning and the development of heat supply networks. Early adopter bonuses but also the declaration of suitable areas for implementing heat grids in which gas supply infrastructure will be dismantled on the long run, can help accelerate their implementation. Here too, significant state subsidies are available to assist in the transformation of heat supply infrastructure in Germany.

Nevertheless, most buildings will still be heated individually. As such, new, easy-to-implement approaches to incorporating heat pumps and attaching solar systems are needed. Standardized solutions that can be produced at scale and thus lower the cost of adoption will play a key role, especially when made available as pre-configured heating systems. Local heat sources that can supply groups of buildings and their heat pumps, for example as cold district heating networks, improve efficiency and reduce the number of external units for heat pumps. As with building insulation, the aim should be to promote the adoption of cost-effective variants through the means of scaling, competition and simplification.

Alongside the technical and commercial aspects, policymakers will also need to address a particular challenge: the socially just design of the transition to clean heating. This applies not just to the appropriate distribution of costs between building owners and tenants but also to ways of financing modernization measures for socially disadvantaged and low-income households. While the proportion of social housing in Germany continues to decline, the burden of energy costs and rent prices is increasing each year. The current system of subsidies and instruments has to be restructured in future. The proportion of the cost of refurbishments that building owners can pass on to their tenants will need to be reformed, the support provided to households must better reflect the income levels and more support will be needed to fund climate-friendly social housing.

Only with swift action in identifying and using the right instruments in each case will it be possible to shape the transition to decarbonized heating in a climate-friendly and socially just way.

Further Reading

▶ Gas crisis, "Sustainability – Strategies for Action", p. 10
▶ Renovation wave, "The Clean Energy Transition in the Context of Sustainability", p. 20
▶ Heat pump, "Heat Pumps – A Solution for the Transition from Fossil Fuels to Sustainable Heating Sources?", p. 32

HEAT PUMPS – A SOLUTION FOR THE TRANSITION FROM FOSSIL FUELS TO SUSTAINABLE HEATING SOURCES?

Article by Sebastian Herkel and Peter Schossig

Defossilizing the operation of buildings will make a key contribution to their sustainability. After years of focusing efforts on reducing energy consumption to minimize CO_2 emissions, attention has now shifted to the complementary strategy of targeting low-carbon ways of providing energy services. Not only is this often more cost-effective than energy efficiency improvements, it can also be implemented more quickly due to shorter renewal cycles. The switch to renewable energy sources means in essence a switch to electrification, as its primary sources – the sun and wind – are most easily converted into electricity.[1] Electricity, and other downstream synthetic material energy carriers such as hydrogen, then serve as the energy carrier. Heating grids, too, will play an increasingly important role, so that, along with wind power and photovoltaics, geothermal energy by means of large-scale heat pumps and solar thermal energy can be tapped as energy sources. When examining the available options in terms of their economic viability, feasibility and temporal availability, it becomes clear that heat pumps and heat grids have a vital role to play in achieving net-zero greenhouse gas emissions in buildings.

THE CURRENT SITUATION

Around half of all heating energy in the housing sector in Germany is consumed by the so-called Worst-Performing Buildings – that is buildings in efficiency classes G and H with an annual heat demand of 200 kWh/m² or more. Larger apartment buildings are responsible to a slightly lesser degree than detached or semi-detached buildings, due to their greater compactness and typically more frequent renovation cycles.

In 2021, 76 % of all buildings in Germany were still heated using systems powered by fossil fuels. 14 % were supplied by district heating,[2] while the share of electric heating systems was 5 %. A significant proportion of these heating systems – some 30 % – are more than 20 years old and thus due for replacement soon. By the end of 2022, approx. 7 % of the 21.3 million heating systems in German residential buildings were heat pump systems, with a strong upward trend. In 2022 some 230,000 heat pump systems were newly installed, and the German Heat Pump Association predicts that the number of new installations per year will rise to around 900,000 by 2030.[3]

In detached and semi-detached houses, heat pumps have been state of the art in both new and existing buildings for several years. Performance monitoring over a period of more than ten years has shown that systems have continually improved and become easier to install. Recordings taken of 41 systems in 2018 and 2019 show varying average annual performance factors depending on the source: around 3.1 for air-source systems and 4.1 for geothermal systems. Closer examination also reveals the relevance of the heat transfer systems and their dimensioning: in existing buildings, systems with underfloor heating perform very well, but buildings with generously dimensioned radiators that can operate with relatively low supply temperatures also achieve good results.[4]

Less empirical knowledge is currently available on the use of heat pumps in unrenovated or partially renovated apartment buildings, but current findings suggest that such systems can achieve good levels of energy efficiency. An analysis of three different apartment buildings showed that the use of heat pumps achieved annual performance factors of between 2.8 and 3.2.[5]

CHALLENGES AND SOLUTIONS

While the feasibility and also scalability of heat pump technology has been proven many times over, some challenges remain – especially when it comes to converting the heating supply systems of multi-storey apartment buildings.[6] Compared with detached and semi-detached buildings, apartment buildings have different requirements and conditions. Due to the greater number of residents, hot water supply represents a higher share of the total heat demand, and higher temperatures are necessary to ensure water quality. Most apartment buildings are also in urban environments where space is more limited and noise emissions are more problematic, making it more difficult to leverage environmental heat sources. Heat pumps also typically require more installation space than conventional

1 G. Luderer, C. Kost et al., "Deutschland auf dem Weg zur Klimaneutralität 2045 – Szenarien und Pfade im Modellvergleich", ein Ariadne Report, 2021, https://ariadneprojekt.de/media/2022/02/Ariadne_Szenarienreport_Oktober2021_corr0222.pdf.

2 BDEW, *Entwicklung des Wärmeverbrauchs in Deutschland. Basisdaten und Einflussfaktoren*, 6th edition (2022), 16 March 2022, https://www.bdew.de/media/documents/20220511_W%C3%A4rmeverbrauchsanalyse_Foliensatz_2022_final.pdf.

3 Bundesverband Wärmepumpe e.V. (ed.), *Branchenstudie 2023: Marktentwicklung – Prognose – Handlungsempfehlungen*, Berlin, 2023, https://www.waermepumpe.de/fileadmin/user_upload/waermepumpe/05_Presse/01_Pressemitteilungen/BWP_Branchenstudie_2023_DRUCK.pdf.

4 D. Günther et al, *Wärmepumpen in Bestandsgebäuden. Ergebnisse aus dem Forschungsprojekt "WPsmart im Bestand"*, Fraunhofer ISE, 2020, https://www.ise.fraunhofer.de/content/dam/ise/de/downloads/pdf/Forschungsprojekte/BMWi-03ET1272A-WPsmart_im_Bestand-Schlussbericht.pdf.

5 C. Bongs, J. Wapler, J. Metz, M. Miara and M. Lämmle, "Wärmeversorgung im Geschosswohnungsbau mit Wärmepumpen", nbau Nachhaltig Bauen, https://www.nbau.org/2023/02/26/waermeversorgung-im-geschosswohnungsbau-mit-waermepumpen.

6 Ibid.

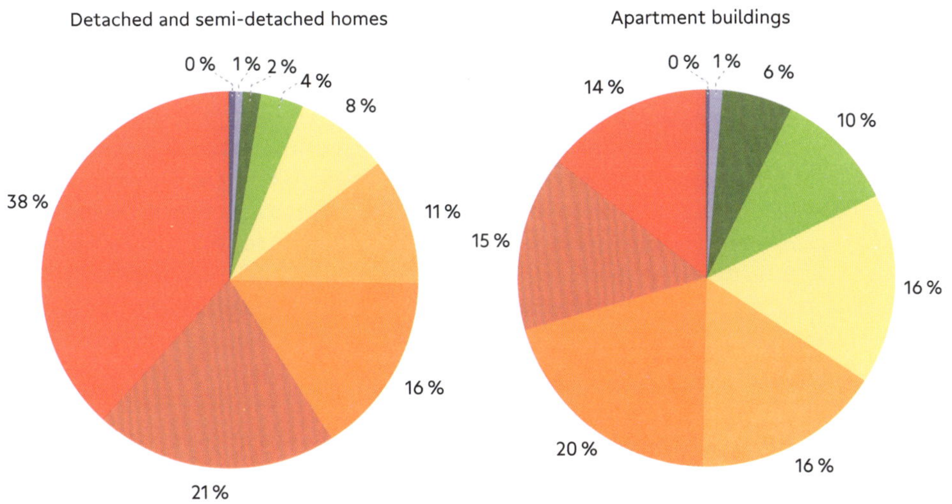

1

Distribution of energy standards in the building stock for different types of buildings, weighted by energy consumption.

Based on data from dena, ifeu, Prognos, Öko-Institut, Navigant, adelphi (2019), *Vorbereitende Untersuchungen zur Erarbeitung einer langfristigen Renovierungsstrategie nach Art 2a der EU-Gebäuderichtlinie RL 2018/844 (EPBD)*, https://www.bmwi.de/Redaktion/DE/Publikationen/Studien/vorbereitendeuntersuchungen-zur-langfristigen-renovierungsstrategie.pdf.

- A+ 0–30 kWh/m²a
- A 30–50 kWh/m²a
- B 50–75 kWh/m²a
- C 75–100 kWh/m²a
- D 100–130 kWh/m²a
- E 130–160 kWh/m²a
- F 160–200 kWh/m²a
- G 200–250 kWh/m²a
- H > 250 kWh/m²a

boilers. Other current challenges affect all building types, for example the availability of suitably skilled personnel for planning and installing such systems, as well as the provision of sufficiently high electrical connection power, a problem exacerbated by the demand for additional power for personal e-mobility. These challenges can be answered in part by technological developments but will also entail changes to processes.

Energy source	**Heat pumps**	**Transfer system**	**Planning / Installation / Power connection**
Challenges			
— Tapping the energy source — Air-source heat pumps: noise emissions problematic for some locations — Ground source heat pumps: Available surfaces for drilling	— Switch to more climate-friendly refrigerants (e.g., propane) — More efficient provision of higher temperatures — Units with greater (thermal) power	— Reduction of system temperatures — Continued use of existing hydraulics — User acceptance for low heat supply temperatures	— Lack of qualified personnel for planning and installation — Qualifying heating installers in new systems — Weak power supply networks
Possible solutions			
— Utilizing the building envelope to exploit energy sources — Photovoltaic thermal hybrid solar collectors — Multivalent energy source systems — Bivalent systems	— Ongoing development of propane-based heat pumps and safety concepts — Cascading of heat pumps with different (thermal) power levels	— Selective replacement of radiators and hydraulic adjustment — Decentralized freshwater stations — Central freshwater stations with ultrafiltration	— Standardization of processes — Digitalization of planning and installation processes — Immigration and training — Local demand management, expansion of networks

2

Challenges and possible solutions for heat pumps in existing buildings, especially in multi-storey apartment buildings.

Based on: C. Bongs, J. Wapler, J. Metz, M. Miara and M. Lämmle, "Wärmeversorgung im Geschosswohnungsbau mit Wärmepumpen", nbau Nachhaltig Bauen, https://www.nbau.org/2023/02/26/waermeversorgung-im-geschosswohnungsbau-mit-waermepumpen.

INNOVATION AND SUSTAINABILITY

The solutions outlined here show that alongside the will to effect a transition in the provision of heat and the training of necessary skilled personnel to implement it, further innovations are also necessary for a socially just transition to renewable heating energy provision. Many of the solutions discussed are systemic in nature and relate to the integration of heat pump systems into existing buildings and their heat distribution networks. Some concern the heat pumps themselves. For example, the refrigerants used in the cooling circuits of heat pumps vary significantly in their impact on the climate (Global Warming Potential, GWP). Up to now, synthetic refrigerants have been used on a large scale, but have a significant global warming potential and can also form compounds that contaminate the environment (per- and polyfluoroalkyl substances, PFAs). As regulations such as the EU Refrigerant Directive (F-Gas Regulation) become increasingly strict in the coming years, these will give way to natural refrigerants such as R290 (propane), which are thermodynamically very well suited for the higher supply temperatures typically required in existing buildings, but partly require additional safety measures.

Alongside the shift from fossil fuels towards renewable electricity needed to achieve climate protection targets, it will also be necessary to consider the overall heating supply system from a broader perspective than just the operation phase of buildings. As heat pumps and low-carbon electricity bring about significant reductions in emissions, other sustainability criteria become more significant, such as the embedded grey energy in the heating unit. In future, it will be essential to consider the entire life cycle of heat generation also in terms of the circular economy.

CONCLUSION AND OUTLOOK

There is no doubt that transforming our heating supply systems requires effort from all sides – building owners, their tenants, as well as the heating and construction industries. It will entail changes and inevitably some conflicts – but there is nevertheless a good chance of its successful implementation: the technical prerequisites for relatively cost-effective and fast defossilization are given, the heat pump industry is working hard and investing heavily to facilitate a swift market ramp-up, and skilled trades are building capacity through corresponding training to support the transformation. At a political level, too, a shift is underway in industry from burning fossil fuels to using local renewable energy sources which presents great opportunities.

Further Reading

▶ Scalability, "Cooling as a Service (CAAS)", *Circular Construction and Circular Economy*, p. 130

▶ Efficiency class, "Sustainability – Strategies for Action", p. 10

▶ Thermal resilience, "Evaluating and Improving the Thermal Resilience of Residential Buildings", p. 36

EVALUATING AND IMPROVING THE THERMAL RESILIENCE OF RESIDENTIAL BUILDINGS

A Retrofit Strategy Using CityBES for Fresno, CA

Case Study by Tianzhen Hong, Max Wei and Kaiyu Sun

Buildings in cities consume 30–70 % of the cities' total primary energy. Retrofitting the existing building stock to improve energy efficiency and reduce energy use, energy costs and carbon emissions is a key strategy for cities to achieve their climate goals. Planning and evaluating retrofit strategies for buildings requires a deep understanding of the physical characteristics, operating patterns and energy use of the building stock. This is a challenge for city managers as data and tools are limited and disparate.

Various computational tools have been developed and used to model the performance of buildings and identify energy conservation measures (ECMs) to support stakeholders and decision makers. These tools vary by scales, data requirements, user experience, modelling approaches and use cases. The recently emerged urban building energy modeling (UBEM)[1] aims to create a digital model that combines building information modeling (BIM) and building energy modelling for buildings at the district or city/region scale. UBEM tools use a city's increasingly available open datasets on building footprint, land use, tax assessor records and permits to create energy models for each individual building in the study area. These models may be fine-tuned or calibrated with various types of building energy usage data if available. Compared with top-down or data-driven analysis tools, UBEM tools can capture details of individual buildings and evaluate them, using physics-based simulation engines to provide more accurate and specific mitigation or adaptation measures for each building.

City Buildings, Energy, and Sustainability (CityBES) is a UBEM tool that won an R&D 100 Award in 2022. CityBES[2] is an open web-based data and computing tool for district- to urban-scale building modelling to assess energy use, carbon emissions and thermal resilience of buildings in their existing conditions and improvements with up to 110 energy conservation measures.[3, 4, 5] CityBES uses an international open data standard, City Geography Markup Language (CityGML), to represent and exchange 3D city models. It employs EnergyPlus to simulate building energy and thermal performance. EnergyPlus[6] is a physics-based building performance simulation program developed by the U.S. Department of Energy.

CityBES provides a suite of features for urban planners, city energy managers, building owners, utilities, energy consultants and researchers. Fig. 1 shows the three layers of the software architecture of CityBES: the data layer, the algorithms and software layer and the use cases layer. The data layer includes weather data, the 3D city model (CityGML or GeoJSON) created with multiple data sources such as geographic information system (GIS), land use and assessor records, and also a database of energy efficiency measures and utility rates as well as building energy codes and standards. The software layer includes EnergyPlus as a simulation engine and the software development kit CBES SDK, which is built upon OpenStudio. The use cases layer provides examples of applications, among them energy benchmarking, energy retrofit analysis, district heating and cooling system modelling, renewable energy analysis, building performance visualization and heat resilience modelling as well as urban scale mapping of microclimate and heat vulnerability at census tract level.

APPLICATION OF cityBES – CASE STUDY OF TWO NEIGHBOURHOODS IN FRESNO, CA

As the world gets warmer from climate change, the frequency, intensity and duration of heat waves are increasing worldwide. This affects mostly underserved, low income or disadvantaged communities, which are least able to adapt to increasing heat since these people typically reside in older, less well-insulated dwellings, may lack the income to purchase, install or upgrade cooling resilience measures and may not be able to afford higher electricity bills in the summer to keep their homes comfortable. Therefore, the focus of this study is on disadvantaged communities (DAC) to better understand the impact of passive cooling measures to improve thermal resilience in residential buildings during heat waves. DACs are defined in the State of California as the areas which suffer the most from a combination of economic, health and environmental burdens,[7] i.e., areas with high unemployment, low incomes, poor underlying health and high exposure to pollution. Areas such as Fresno are especially vulnerable since the poor baseline

1 T. Hong, Y. Chen, X. Luo, N. Luo and S. H. Lee, "Ten questions on urban building energy modeling", *Building and Environment*, 168, 2020, Article 106508. https://doi.org/10.1016/j.buildenv.2019.106508.

2 T. Hong, Y. Chen, S. H. Lee and M. A. Piette, "CityBES: A Web-based Platform to Support City-Scale Building Energy Efficiency", *Urban Computing*, 14, 2016.

3 K. Sun, W. Zhang, Z. Zeng, R. Levinson, M. Wei and T. Hong, "Passive cooling designs to improve heat resilience of homes in underserved and vulnerable communities", *Energy and Buildings*, 252, 2021, https://doi.org/10.1016/j.enbuild.2021.111383.

4 K. Sun, P. Kusumah, W. Zhang, M. Wei and T. Hong, "Exploring Decarbonization and Clean Energy Pathways for Disadvantaged Communities in California", International COBEE Conference, Montreal, Canada, 2022.

5 L. Teso, L. Carnieletto, K. Sun, W. Zhang, A. Gasparella, P. Romagnoni, A. Zarrella and T. Hong, "Large scale energy analysis and renovation strategies for social housing in the historic city of Venice", *Sustainable Energy Technologies and Assessments*, 52A, https://doi.org/10.1016/j.seta.2022.102041.

6 Building energy simulation software, US Department of Energy, "EnergyPlus", 2023, https://EnergyPlus.net.

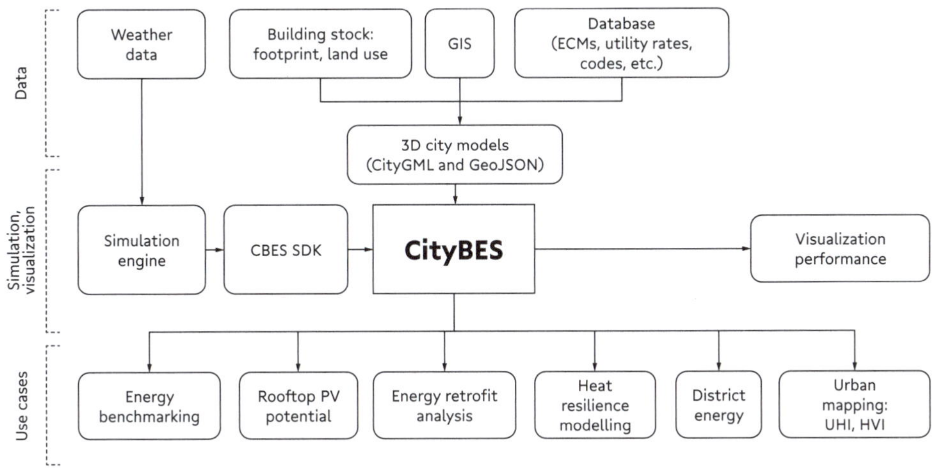

1

CityBES data, workflow and major use cases.

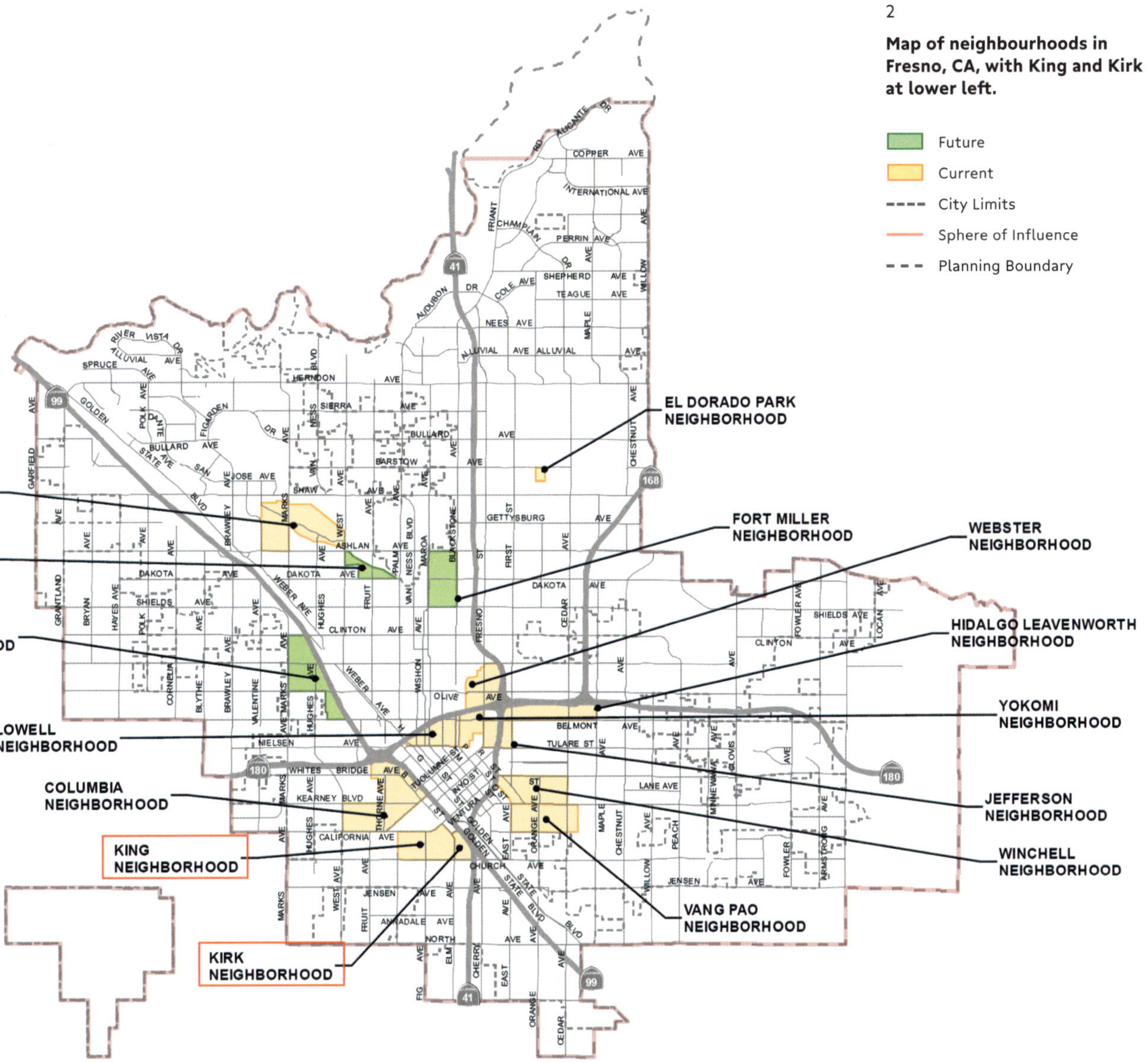

2

Map of neighbourhoods in Fresno, CA, with King and Kirk at lower left.

Future
Current
City Limits
Sphere of Influence
Planning Boundary

air quality is worsened during summer heat,[8] and the hot, dry conditions – Fresno experienced a record 69 days over 37.8 °C in 2021 – lead to high amounts of agricultural and road dust, which further exacerbates summer air quality.

There is an urgent need to characterize passive and low-energy active cooling measures that can provide greater resilience to occupants during extreme heat waves in these communities. Such data and characterization can inform heat reduction programmes, building retrofit programmes and more resilient building energy codes.

DISTRICT CHARACTERIZATION AND MODELLING

The King and Kirk neighbourhoods in Fresno (Fig. 2), identified as DAC using the CalEnviroScreen tool,[9] were selected as the case districts for this study. Extensive community outreach was utilized to inform the technical modelling described here. Building characteristics were collected from several sources for creating the dataset to be used in CityBES,[10] which included building footprints, use type, height, number of stories and year built. The building footprints were extracted from the Microsoft building footprint database[11] with the boundaries of the neighbourhoods. The year built, use type and number of stories of these buildings are mainly from query results using Atom API, a real estate service.

There are 814 residential buildings in the King neighbourhood and 280 residential buildings in Kirk. All buildings are either one storey or two stories, and most of them are single-family homes built before the 1970s. Prototype models were developed to represent existing buildings, calibrated against energy usage based on the CBECC-RES tool certified for use for California residential building code compliance and the International Energy Conservation Code (IECC) prototype models. For the district-scale modelling, the prototype models were scaled to the actual floor area of each building in the building stock, with the aspect ratio retained. Building properties were also modified to reflect our best estimates of in-place equipment. Buildings constructed in different years are assumed to comply with Title 24, California's building energy efficiency standards, of the corresponding vintages, including envelope properties, internal loads, HVAC efficiencies, etc. We also considered possible retrofits implemented in older buildings, such as buildings constructed prior to the introduction of Title 24.

DEFINITION OF ENERGY CONSERVATION MEASURES

Eleven most representative types of passive measures were selected for modelling and the assessment of their performance in improving the heat resilience of the buildings. Passive measures are defined as technologies that function fully without using electric power. The definition and key assumptions related to each passive energy conservation measure (ECM) are summarized in Fig. 3.

We focus on the grid-off scenario to show the performance of various ECMs during a worst-case scenario of a heat wave with power outage. The results presented here comprise the baseline performance and variability of resilience across different single-family homes, and the performance of ECMs across all residential buildings in one district. We used standard effective temperature unmet degree-hours (SETUDH) as a resilience metric, which considers indoor air temperature, relative humidity, mean radiant temperature, air velocity, occupants' metabolic rate and clothing insulation. The upper limit of "Livable Temperatures" is set to 30 °C, based on the USGBC LEED passive survivability criteria.[12]

7 California Public Utilities Commission (CPUC), *Disadvantaged Communities*, 2021, https://www.cpuc.ca.gov/industries-and-topics/electrical-energy/infrastructure/disadvantaged-communities (accessed 15 January 2023).

8 NWS (National Weather Service) (n.d.), *Clearing the Air on Weather and Air Quality*, https://www.weather.gov/wrn/summer-article-clearing-the-air (accessed 15 January 2023).

9 California Office of Environmental Health Hazard Assessment, 2022, *CalEnviroScreen 4.0*, https://oehha.ca.gov/calenviroscreen/report/calenviroscreen-40 (accessed 15 January 2023).

10 Y. Chen, T. Hong, X. Luo and B. Hooper, "Development of City Buildings Dataset for Urban Building Energy Modeling", *Energy and Buildings*, 183, 2018, https://doi.org/10.1016/j.enbuild.2018.11.008.

11 Microsoft, *Building Footprints – Bing Maps*, 2019, https://www.microsoft.com/en-us/maps/building-footprints (accessed 15 February 2021).

12 A. Wilson, "Passive Survivability", Building Green, 14, 12, 2005, https://www.buildinggreen.com/op-ed/passive-survivability.

Measure	Measure description	Baseline assumption	ECM assumption
Roof insulation	Reroof and add roof insulation	Roof does not have insulation layer	Add R-24.83 insulation layer to roof
Ceiling insulation	Add insulation to top-floor ceiling	Applicable for buildings built before 1992, whose ceiling has R-16.67 insulation	Improve the insulation layer to R-38
Cool roof	Increase roof solar reflectance by applying a reflective asphalt shingle product	Exterior layer material properties: solar reflectance 0.20 thermal emittance 0.75	Exterior layer material properties: solar reflectance 0.40 thermal emittance 0.90
Cool wall	Increase wall solar reflectance by painting	Exterior layer material properties: solar reflectance 0.30 thermal emittance 0.90	Exterior layer material properties: solar reflectance 0.60 thermal emittance 0.90
Interior blinds	Install and use window blinds	No window shades	Add interior blinds to windows
Exterior overhang	Add exterior overhang shades	No exterior overhang shades	Add overhang shades with depth of 0.76 m (2.5 ft) and offset of 0.55 m (1.8 ft) from window upper edge
Exterior storm window	Add exterior storm window layer	No storm window	Add an exterior storm window layer, assumed to be 3-mm E-glass
Interior storm window	Add interior storm window layer	No storm window	Add an interior storm window layer, assumed to be 3-mm E-glass
Window film	Add solar-control window film	No window film	Apply window film to the interior surface of the existing window (characteristics refer to LLumar Solar Control Film)
Natural ventilation	Enable natural ventilation for rooms with windows	No natural ventilation	Enable natural ventilation for each window, controlled by indoor and outdoor temperature difference
Radiant barrier	Add radiant barrier	No radiant barrier	Reduce the material's thermal emittance on the bottom of the roof to 0.10

3

Summary of baseline and passive measure assumptions.

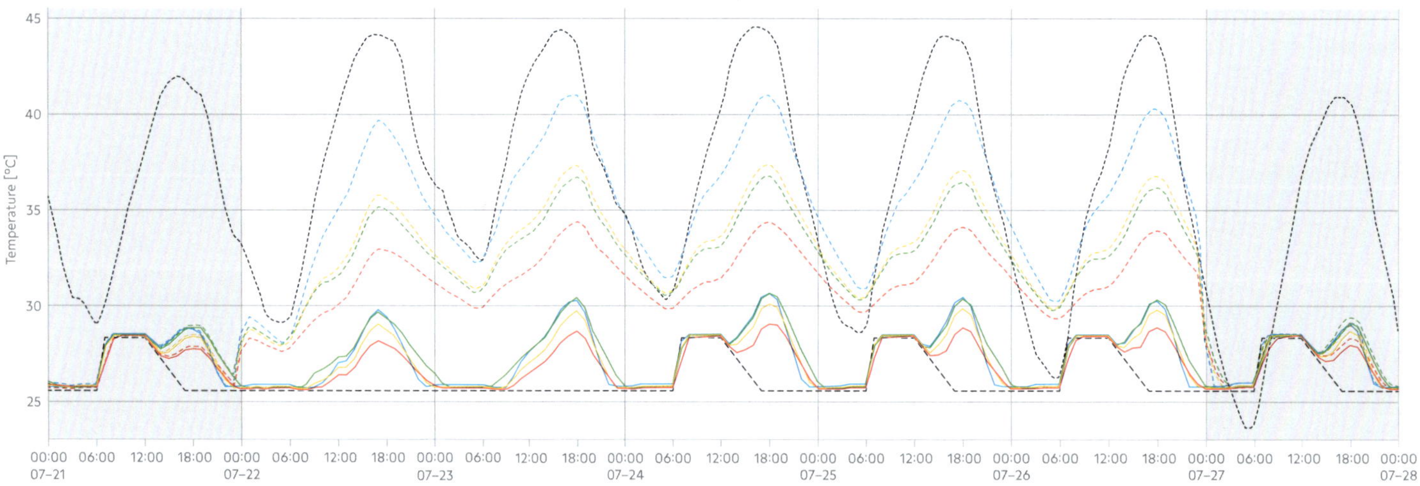
Temperature [°C]
45
40
35
30
25
00:00 07-21
06:00
12:00
18:00
00:00 07-22
00:00 07-23
00:00 07-24
00:00 07-25
00:00 07-26
00:00 07-27
00:00 07-28

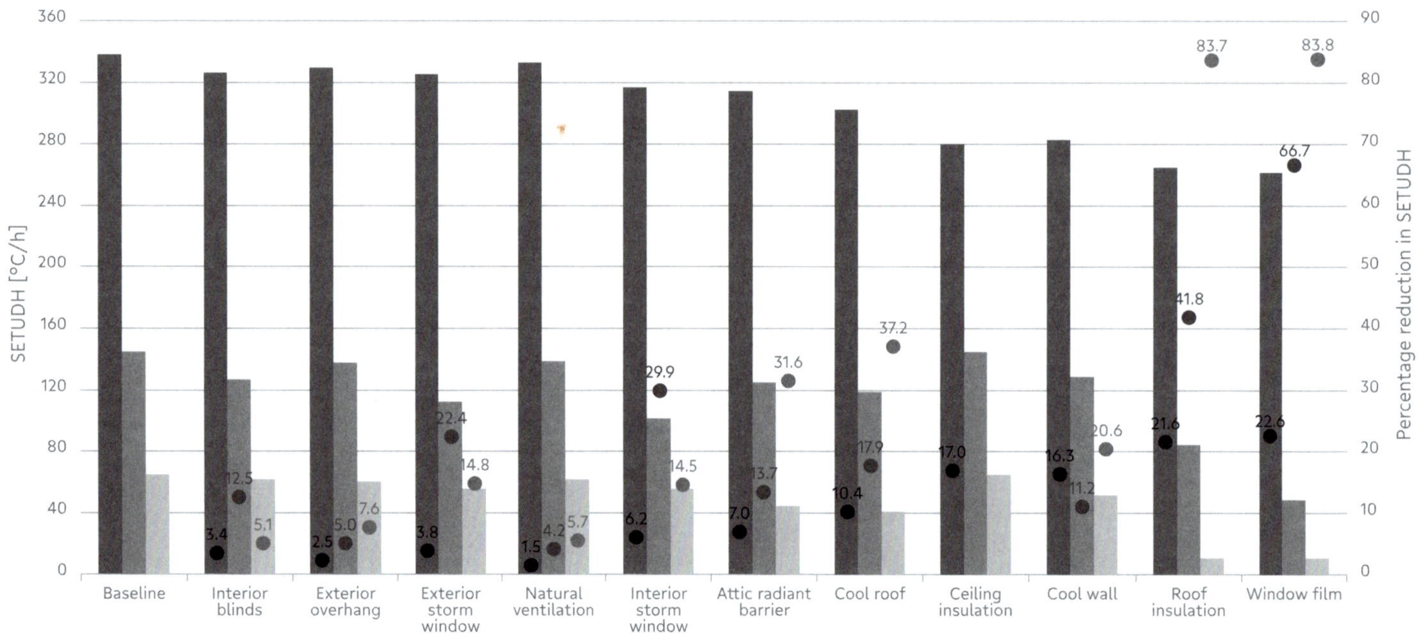
SETUDH [°C/h]
Percentage reduction in SETUDH
Baseline
Interior blinds
Exterior overhang
Exterior storm window
Natural ventilation
Interior storm window
Attic radiant barrier
Cool roof
Ceiling insulation
Cool wall
Roof insulation
Window film
3.4
12.5
5.1
2.5
5.0
7.6
3.8
22.4
14.8
1.5
4.2
5.7
6.2
29.9
14.5
7.0
13.7
31.6
10.4
17.9
37.2
17.0
16.3
11.2
20.6
21.6
41.8
83.7
22.6
66.7
83.8

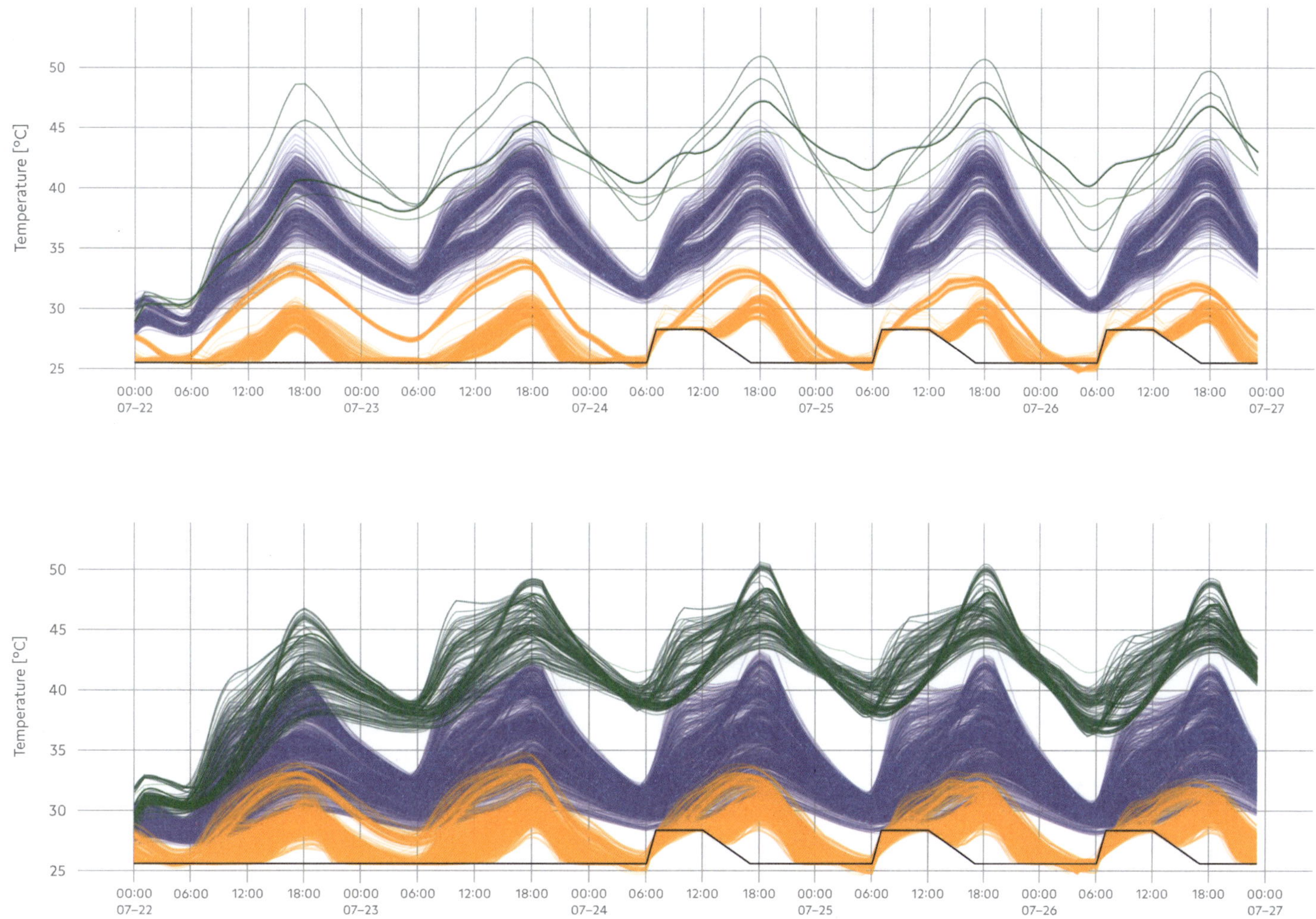

4 ↖

Living zone air temperature for single-family homes as a function of vintage and grid electricity availability. The heat wave days are the five non-grayed days, indicating the worst-case historical heat wave conditions in July 2006.

- 1976 – grid on, no retrofit
- 1976 – grid off, no retrofit
- 2004 – grid on
- 2004 – grid off
- 2015 – grid on
- 2015 – grid off
- 1976 – grid on, retrofitted
- 1976 – grid off, retrofitted
- Outdoor
- Setpoint

5 ←

Standard effective temperature unmet degree hours (SETUDH) for the baseline case and for each ECM during the heatwave for single-family homes of different vintages in the grid-off scenario. Absolute values are represented by columns, percentage reductions are shown by dots.

- 1976 value
- 2004 value
- 2015 value
- 1976 % reduction
- 2004 % reduction
- 2015 % reduction

6 ↑

Indoor air temperature profiles for homes in the King district.

Temperature profile
Top: **single-family homes**
Bottom: **multi-family homes**

- All-floors – grid on
- Lower-floor – grid off
- Top-floor – grid off
- Cooling setpoint

SINGLE-FAMILY HOMES

The indoor air temperatures of single-family homes for three vintages (1976, 2004, 2015) are shown in Fig. 4 for the worst-case historical five-day heat wave in July 2006, with and without grid power. Even with grid power available, indoor temperatures in the afternoon cannot achieve the cooling set-point of 25.5 °C, because the sizing of the air conditioning units is not sufficient to cover the extreme heat days (which represent 0.4 % of the hottest days) and because the AC units' capacity is assumed to degrade over the years.

When grid power is unavailable, the indoor air temperature of a non-retrofitted home built in 1976 exceeds 40 °C for some hours during the middle three days of the heat wave. Newer buildings have cooler air temperatures due to better envelope construction. The indoor air temperature for the 2015 homes, for example, can be 4 °C cooler than those of 1976 homes when grid power is unavailable – but is still 5–9 °C higher than the cooling setpoint of 25.5 °C!

The reduction in SETUDH compared to the baseline for the three single-family home vintages is shown in Fig. 5 for the grid-power-available and grid-power-unavailable scenarios. Absolute values of the metric are represented by columns, while percentage reductions for each measure compared to the baseline are shown by dots.

Adding window film and adding roof insulation are generally the most effective ECMs for all vintages in terms of reducing SETUDH. Adding window film reduces the heat gain from windows and lowers the Solar Heat Gain Coefficient (SHGC). Adding roof insulation dramatically lowers the attic air temperature, which reduces the heat transfer from the attic to the living zone. Taking the representative home built in 1976 as an example, these two measures can reduce SETUDH by 21.6 % and 22.5 %, respectively, with grid power available. Without roof insulation, the air temperature in the attic can reach almost 70 °C; this can be decreased by more than 20 °C by adding roof insulation.

DISTRICT-SCALE RESILIENCE ANALYSIS

Fig. 6 shows the indoor temperature profiles of all residential buildings in the King district. For single-family homes, each curve represents the temperature of one floor, while for multi-family homes, each curve represents the temperature of one unit (apartment). The profiles for the two types of homes are plotted in separate panels to avoid overlapping. The three clusters of curves correspond to all-floor grid on, lower-floor grid off, and top-floor grid off. The temperature in the grid-off scenario is significantly higher than that in the grid-on scenario. When the grid is off, top-floor zones perform much worse than lower-floor ones, due to the extra heat gain through the roof and the absence of free cooling via the cool ground.

RESILIENCE MEASURE PERFORMANCE UNDER POWER OUTAGES

The distribution of SETUDH for all homes in the King District is shown in Fig. 7, for the baseline and after applying each of the ECMs during the heatwave with power outage. The window film has the best performance overall, while natural ventilation has the best performance in top-floor zones. Ceiling insulation, wall insulation and cool walls emerge as the measures with the next-best reductions in SETUDH.

CONCLUSION

Several measures provide substantial reductions in the SETUDH resilience metric for both single and multi-family homes: window films, roof and ceiling insulation and cool walls. Natural ventilation is especially helpful in the top floors for single-family and multi-family homes. However, it can be problematic when outdoor air is polluted or for some residents who have home security and safety concerns. Indoor air temperatures can reach dangerous levels when there is a heat wave coincident with power outage, suggesting that the situation for many homes in Fresno that lack air conditioning but with grid power available would be very similar. It is recommended that California's building standards should be upgraded to promote extreme-heat solutions based on

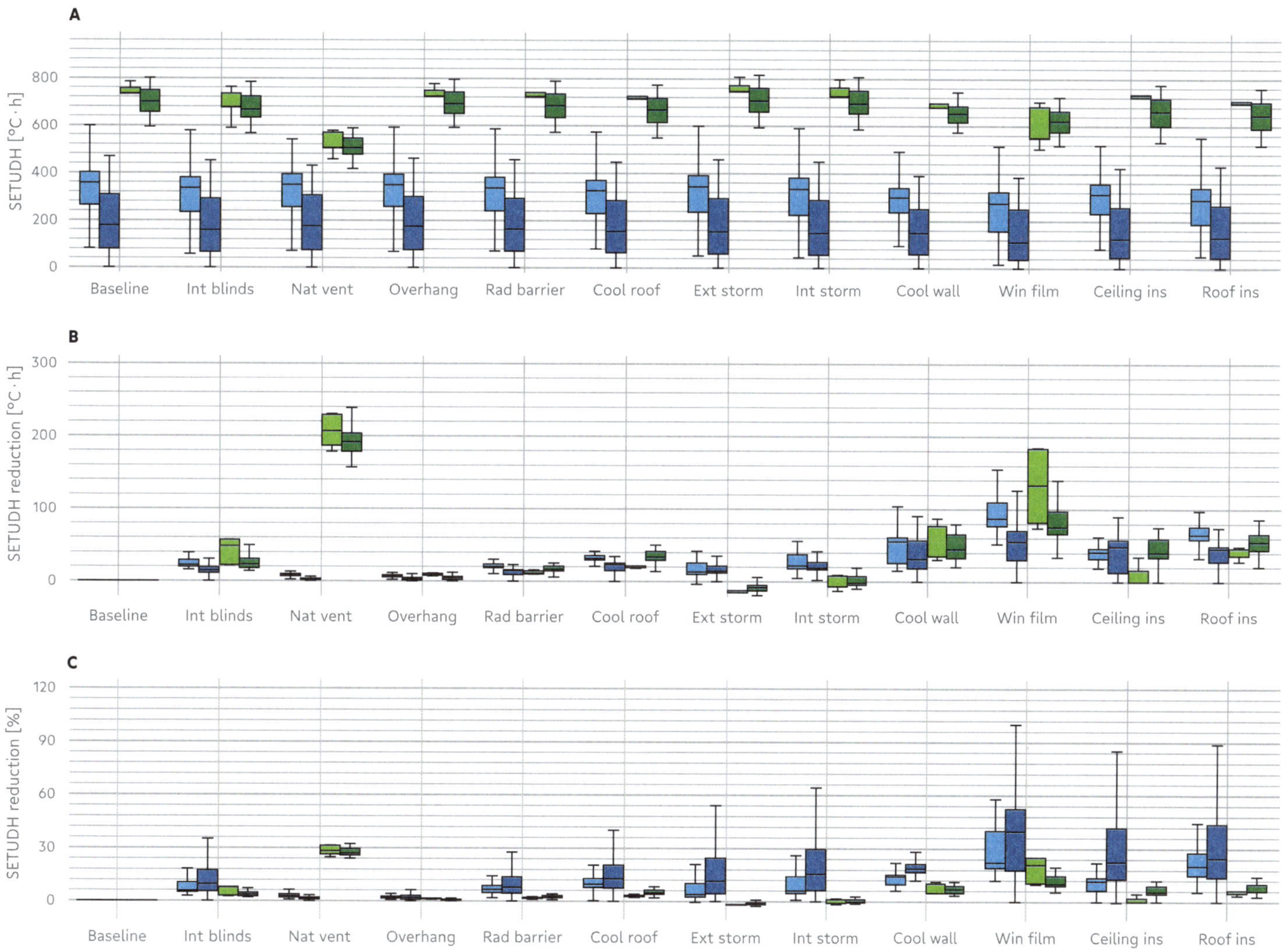

7

The distribution of standard effective temperature unmet degree hours (SETUDH) in the King neighbourhood in the baseline case and for different ECMs during the heat wave with no grid power available.

A
Passive 5-day

B
Passive 5-day absolute reduction

C
Passive 5-day relative reduction

- Single-family – lower floor
- Multi-family – lower floor
- Single-family – top floor
- Multi-family – top floor

human outcomes and to minimize excess mortalities and morbidities. All homes should have a minimum cooling standard or equivalently a maximum indoor temperature allowed to ensure a healthy and safe indoor environment for all. Expanding existing home weatherization audits focused on energy efficiency to include climate resilience assessment and recommended resilience strategies and/or measures would help to identify homes most in need of heat resilience upgrades.

Urban building modelling tools like CityBES can represent the building stock in a digital model integrating a city's open datasets, create detailed energy models for each individual building, then simulate their energy and thermal performance. Tools like CityBES are powerful simulation platforms to investigate different resilience and energy efficiency measures for buildings on a large scale; besides being planning tools for stakeholders they can serve as instruments on a political level (communities, state governments) for decision making with regard to regulations, mitigation plans, funding programmes etc. This case study shows how important it is to address social and political topics in addition to the technical aspects while planning energy efficiency and resilience measures for the built environment.

Further, CityBES is a very good example of how digitalization opens the door to underserved areas of the real world and how it can help to improve thermal conditions of the built environment by making evidence of aspects which could not be considered with "analogue" processes. Creating such computational models of urban buildings at scale requires the availability and integration of diverse data sources which unavoidably involve uncertainties of inputs to the models and the simulation results. Reliable building stock data is key to such model creation. Actual measured energy use data at different levels of detail (e.g., annual electricity and gas usage, monthly utility bills, and time-series of hourly or sub-hourly smart meter data) are valuable and essential to finetune and calibrate the models, ensuring the simulation results are reliable. Tapping into the advances in AI, machine learning, cloud computing and big data is a major research topic in the field. Also, feedback from users and stakeholders on the adoption of such modelling tools is crucial to improve their usability and support the global transition of building decarbonization and climate resilience.

Further Reading

▶ Decarbonization, "Sustainability – Strategies for Action", p. 10
▶ Thermal insulation, "The Scale and Impact of the Clean Heating Transition", p. 30
▶ Existing buildings, "Building Capacity and Knowledge in the Local Economy", *Circular Construction and Circular Economy*, p. 38

BETTER

Digital Strategies for Reusing Building Materials

Introduction to Digital Transformation by Moritz Dörstelmann and Vincent Witt

Building construction and the operation of buildings are major contributors to the climate crisis: almost 40 % of global CO_2 emissions[1] are attributed to the building sector, as is around 55 % of annual waste generation.[2] Architecture and the construction industry must address climate change, but how? Which digital strategies can help make building climate-friendly? Climate change is not the only challenge we face; the disruption of supply chains during the Covid pandemic and, more recently, the extreme rise in the cost of almost all building materials show how dependent construction projects are on external factors, especially when they rely on raw materials derived from fossil-based sources or that must be imported. The extraction of raw materials also has further social and ecological implications, leading to excessive exploitation of people and the environment. How can we then stop extracting new raw materials and instead use existing raw materials from the urban mine? In addition, demographic change has contributed to a shortage of skilled workers. The increasing academization further compounds the problem in trades that do not require an academic degree but are vital and irreplaceable in the construction industry. How can we still build for more people with a smaller skilled workforce?

In future, we will need to make *better* use of the available skilled labour, to use materials that have a *better* impact on the climate, and to make *better* use of materials that already exist through urban mining.

With respect to the last of these objectives, how much potential lies in the stock of existing buildings in Germany? According to the Federal Environment Agency, the volume of building materials contained in existing housing and residential buildings in Germany amounted to 10.1 billion tonnes in 2010, of which 4.5 billion tonnes were concrete, 247 million tonnes wood and 106 million tonnes metal.[3] What happens to these materials at the end of a building's useful lifetime? Again, the FEA reports that in 2018, some 73.9 million tonnes of construction waste and road debris were produced in Germany, of which 59.7 million tonnes were recycled. Only 15.8 million tonnes were "used as high-quality aggregate in the production of asphalt and concrete",[4] which reveals that the high-quality reuse of existing building materials is still relatively small. While the practice of crushing material from demolished buildings makes it reusable for aggregate, it permanently removes it from higher value reuse scenarios. We must therefore find ways to reuse entire components more effectively and at a greater scale than is currently the case. Digital deconstruction and reuse strategies offer the potential not just to retain materials used in building components for future life cycles but also the grey energy originally used to produce these components.

How can such digital methods potentially assist in the reuse of materials such as wood, concrete and steel? For all three of these material groups, digital innovations in the field of photogrammetry allow the creation of a digital twin. The geometry of a building is captured, or existing planning documents are validated as the basis for an algorithmic deconstruction planning. In this way, elements can be sawn, for example, to sizes that permit the reclaimed components to be sensibly reused in future projects while also allowing the building to be optimally dismantled and broken down into its individual constituents.

Using digital image capture and inspection methods, reclaimed steel sections can be quality assessed to determine any existing deformations or damage that could affect their residual load-bearing capacity for future projects. Alongside their reuse as traditional steel sections, digital manufacturing techniques such as robotic welding and 3D printing can potentially make them available for a broader range of reuse scenarios.

Recovered concrete elements can be requalified in a similar way. Here the focus lies on non-invasive means of analyzing the position and extent of reinforcements in a concrete component to determine how it can be reused in future. This step would create another digital twin, this time at the component level, which serves as a basis for further processing. Smaller optical flaws and cracks can be closed, while large defects can be repaired using robotic additive techniques. Damaged areas can be robotically removed so that intact sections can be reused. Equipping the harvested concrete parts with reversible connection details enables the transformation of in situ concrete structures into modular reusable building components.

1 United Nations, *United Nations Environment Programme. 2020 Global Status Report for Buildings and Construction: Towards a Zero-emission, Efficient and Resilient Buildings and Construction Sector*. Nairobi, 2020, https://globalabc.org/sites/default/files/inline-files/2020%20Buildings%20GSR_FULL%20REPORT.pdf.

2 Federal Environment Agency, "Abfallaufkommen", 13 October 2022, https://www.umweltbundesamt.de/daten/ressourcen-abfall/abfallaufkommen.

3 G. Schiller, C. Deilmann, K. Gruhler, P. Röhm, J. Reichenbach, J. Baumann and M. Günther, *Ermittlung von Ressourcenschonungspotenzialen bei der Verwertung von Bauabfällen und Erarbeitung von Empfehlungen zu deren Nutzung*. Federal Environment Agency, Texts, no. 56/2010, p. 72, https://www.umweltbundesamt.de/sites/default/files/medien/publikation/long/4040.pdf.

4 Federal Environment Agency, "Bauabfälle", 8 June 2021, https://www.umweltbundesamt.de/daten/ressourcen-abfall/verwertung-entsorgung-ausgewaehlter-abfallarten/bauabfaelle.

Methods already used in modern sawmills, such as computed tomography scans and digital yield optimization per log, can in future be applied to assess the reusability potential of timber elements. Other digital design and fabrication concepts can potentially utilize smaller timber elements with varying cross-sections, for example, by using robotic additive techniques to assemble them into new components. Hybrid construction methods using mono-material robotically nailed scrap wood in combination with earth- or cellulose-based materials offer a further way of broadening the range of applications of reclaimed timber materials.

In preparation for a future circular reuse of these components, the data generated during their digital reclaiming process can be used for quality assurance and crosslinked in databases for future design processes.

The approaches described here illustrate both the breadth of possible applications as well as the need for further research into digital reuse strategies. For example, can reversible connections milled into reclaimed concrete components sustain the loads that occur at the joints? Or, can internal reinforcements be localized with enough precision to be able to reliably predict their structural load-bearing capacity?

The articles in this chapter illustrate how a digital transformation in the construction industry can provide *better* concepts to counter the shortage of skilled workers through human-machine collaboration, and how computational design and fabrication processes can enable a *better* and scaled use of wood as a resource in construction.

COLLA-BORATIVE DIGITAL BUILDING

Commentary by
Kathrin Dörfler

In the building construction context of architecture, there is no conceptual or intellectual separation between the architecture we produce and the techniques we use to produce it. As digital technologies have become indispensable to the discipline and practice of architecture, the ability to design and innovate with technology has also become fundamental for architectural designers. Finding a common path to a sustainable future is not just an ecological, technological or economic project, but above all a cultural one.

Digital technologies provide powerful tools for understanding complex systems and tackling fundamental challenges. We have seen how computational methods, robotics and machine learning in architecture, engineering and construction can perform certain tasks that humans cannot, or that they do not wish to do. Developments in the fields of construction robotics, additive manufacturing and materials technology over the past two decades in particular have shown the potential for efficient, resource-conserving and highly rationalized and customized workflows.[1] But digital technologies and machines alone are not enough to address the challenges of labour shortages, efficient use of resources and construction quality. Although human intervention is often crucial for the success of digitally-enabled construction processes – to make decisions, intervene in processes, reprogram machines, trigger actions or make necessary adjustments in response to unforeseen events – research in this area seems focused almost exclusively on developing fully autonomous processes that reduce human intervention: that is, on replacing humans with machines rather than creating process-specific synergies between them.[2, 3] In the human-machine interaction context, it is widely agreed that greater autonomy implies less interaction between humans and machines and less human intervention in machine processes. A lot of research is therefore directed towards maximizing the autonomy of machines so that it becomes possible to dispense entirely with human intervention.

There is, however, also a positive correlation between autonomy and interaction or collaboration! Actual collaboration between humans and machines can only be achieved when machines have the greatest possible autonomy, that is when machines and robots have the ability to fundamentally understand their context and to react to it.[4, 5]

If digital technologies are combined with human knowledge and intuition in a purposeful way, by embedding human cognitive abilities in digital processes and, conversely, supporting human decision-making processes with machine intelligence, it is conceivable that we would have a greater impact on the great challenges of our time.[6] Instead of pursuing concepts of full automation, we could negotiate ways in which machines can meaningfully contribute to relieving the problem of labour shortage and to sustainable construction practices in direct collaboration with humans, starting with designers and planners and ending with construction workers, in a decentralized and resilient modus operandi. To bring together the best of their complementary skills and strengths, we could "build" on combinations of people and machines, combining the speed and accuracy of machines and their ability to process large amounts of data with our creative and flexible skills as humans to address and tackle the fundamental problems of our time through collaboration.

Further Reading

▶ Human-machine relationship, "Occupant-centric Building Control", p. 84
▶ Flexibility, "Architecture in Large Quantities", p. 132
▶ Competence building, "Building Capacity and Knowledge in the Local Economy", *Circular Construction and Circular Economy*, p. 38

1 F. Gramazio, M. Kohler and J. Willmann, *The Robotic Touch – How Robots Change Architecture*. Zürich: Park Books, 2013.

2 T. Salmi, J. M. Ahola, T. Heikkilä, P. Kilpeläinen and T. Malm, "Human-Robot Collaboration and Sensor-Based Robots in Industrial Applications and Construction", in Henriette Bier (ed.), *Robotic Building*, Springer, 2018, https://doi.org/10.1007/978-3-319-70866-9_2, pp. 25–52.

3 L. Atanasova, D. Mitterberger, T. Sandy, F. Gramazio, M. Kohler and K. Dörfler, "Prototype as Artefact – Design Tool for Open-ended Collaborative Assembly Processes", in *ACADIA*, 2020, pp. 1–11.

4 J. M. Beer, A. D. Fisk and W. A. Rogers, "Toward a Framework for Levels of Robot Autonomy in Human-Robot Interaction," *J. Human-Robot Interact.*, vol. 3, no. 2, 2014, https://doi.org/10.5898/jhri.3.2.beer, p. 74.

5 I. X. Han, F. Meggers and S. Parascho, "Bridging the collectives: A review of collective human–robot construction," *Int. J. Archit. Comput.*, vol. 19, no. 4, 2021, https://doi.org/10.1177/14780771211025153, pp. 512–531.

6 D. Mitterberger, L. Atanasova, K. Dörfler, F. Gramazio and M. Kohler, "Tie a knot: human–robot cooperative workflow for assembling wooden structures using rope joints", *Constr. Robot.*, vol. 6, no. 3–4, 2022, https://doi.org/10.1007/s41693-022-00083-2, pp. 277–292.

PARAMETRIC DESIGN-TO-FABRICATION PLATFORMS FOR SCALED INDUSTRIAL IMPLEMENTATION

The Convergence of Technologies in Mass Timber Construction

Article by Oliver David Krieg, Kristin Slavin and Oliver Lang

The architecture, engineering and construction (AEC) industry is facing unprecedented challenges caused by an ever-increasing density in urban areas and an intensifying need for sustainable solutions in the face of global warming. Although technological innovation holds the potential to solve these challenges, our industry has failed to respond quickly enough. In fact, the AEC industry is one of the slowest to innovate and one of the most difficult to disrupt. It is characterized by fragmentation between disciplines, within disciplines, and between projects. Most importantly, although most buildings share a common logic or many of the same building parts, our industry sees each project as a unique and service-based, one-off delivery.

The AEC industry can be described as an inter-organizational network. As such, the connections and interfaces between actors are not controlled by a single entity but rather by a common and sometimes informal agreement. Since this network behaviour makes it difficult for a single entity to change these interfaces, companies instead focus on optimizing their own operations within, thereby disincentivizing change. At the same time, the demand for urbanization and urban densification has led to a highly formulaic and unsustainable approach of real estate development models based on quick monetary investment return without a desire for quality or longevity, or any accounting of the long-term risk associated with current carbon-intensive construction practices. The resulting slow adaption of new technologies, coupled with pressing ecological, economic and liveability challenges, urgently needs to be addressed. Instead of innovating on one specific interface or technology, a more holistic approach to the design, engineering and delivery of buildings is needed.

Recent technological developments in digital design processes, manufacturing innovation and data processing promise to offer solutions to this challenge. Experimentation both in academia and industry in computational design and digital fabrication in the early 2000s have produced a generation of architects, engineers and designers with a strong knowledge base of manufacturing and software technologies, which can help us make data-driven decisions and reintegrate the design and building process. This, in turn, has resulted in numerous approaches to the industrialization, and to some extent, the productization, of architecture. When we start to think about buildings as products rather than artefacts of services provided, we start to reflect on design, function, materiality and manufacturing as a holistic and vertically integrated process. And this change is timely. Major cities across the world are implementing stricter sustainability targets, forcing the AEC industry to think more holistically about materials, manufacturing and building operations. Vancouver, for example, recently enacted the "Greenest City Action Plan" and the "Climate Emergency Action Plan" to incentivize, and soon require, carbon-neutral buildings. To achieve these new policies, we need accurate sustainability data embedded into the design process and a deep knowledge of the materials and processes that go into the making of a building.

Intelligent City is a technology-enabled urban housing company. Through the convergence of architecture, mass timber construction, parametric software and automated prefabrication, the company productizes multi-storey buildings for urban densification. When the entire building becomes a product, all systems and components within a building need to be designed and engineered for manufacturing and assembly. To make such an approach affordable and scalable, the company has developed a parametric platform that combines all building systems under a technological umbrella.

PRODUCT APPROACH TO DESIGN AND CONSTRUCTION

When we talk about productizing buildings, we are referring to the way that we systematize buildings into a set of typologies, code classifications and markets, within the boundaries of what can be manufactured. When buildings become products, they allow us to develop repeatable systems that enable the scale and consistency needed to drive down cost while providing higher quality through tighter tolerances and precision manufacturing. At the same time, standardized processes can allow for adaptation and customization, responding to site conditions and a wide variety of customer design needs without sacrificing the performance of the building or the speed of the process. We refer to this as mass customization.

1
One of the buildings Intelligent City is working on in 2023.

The systemization of the product definition and building systems also enables a parametric design process based on the design space defined by the product definitions. Without known boundaries and building systems, parametric design will be limited to early planning stage explorations. Integrating a high level of detail about the product into software allows us to take the digital process from conceptual design through to manufacturing in a comprehensive and accurate manner. This definition and integration is the paradigm shift from traditional construction to the platform approach.

PARAMETRIC PLATFORMS THROUGH VERTICAL INTEGRATION

Parametric design is a process that encodes each design decision as a parameter, thereby defining the relationship between input and output in the form of an algorithm. Parametric design becomes generative when applied in pursuit of the optimization of the design results. By integrating design control and analysis, an interactive work environment can be created that allows for quick design iterations and optimization of building performance, cost efficiency or sustainability.

While parametric design has mainly been used for extravagant projects such as museums or large towers, we argue that there is an untapped potential to leave behind the formalism of the last decades and instead enable buildings that are low-carbon, high-performance and far more liveable. Systematic construction and prefabrication do not have to follow a one-fits-all approach. Parametric software fundamentally enables interactions between product, building platforms and manufacturing. This is where a parametric design workflow becomes a platform-based approach.

In other industries, the term "platform-based design" describes a method for the development and integration of complex products that share compatible hardware or software. It is an inherently interdisciplinary process and requires a close integration of design, engineering, and manufacturing. The result is a general knowledge base within a company on which variants of the same solution can be realized.

However, in most industries, such platforms are not as flexible or customizable as is required in the construction industry. Instead of relying on fixed dimensions or a standardized set of building parts, a "parametric platform" describes a platform-based approach that is defined by parameters that can be changed and combined in different ways. In order to achieve such a holistic concept, all building systems and components need to be pre-engineered. Especially for multi-storey housing, the interaction of many of these

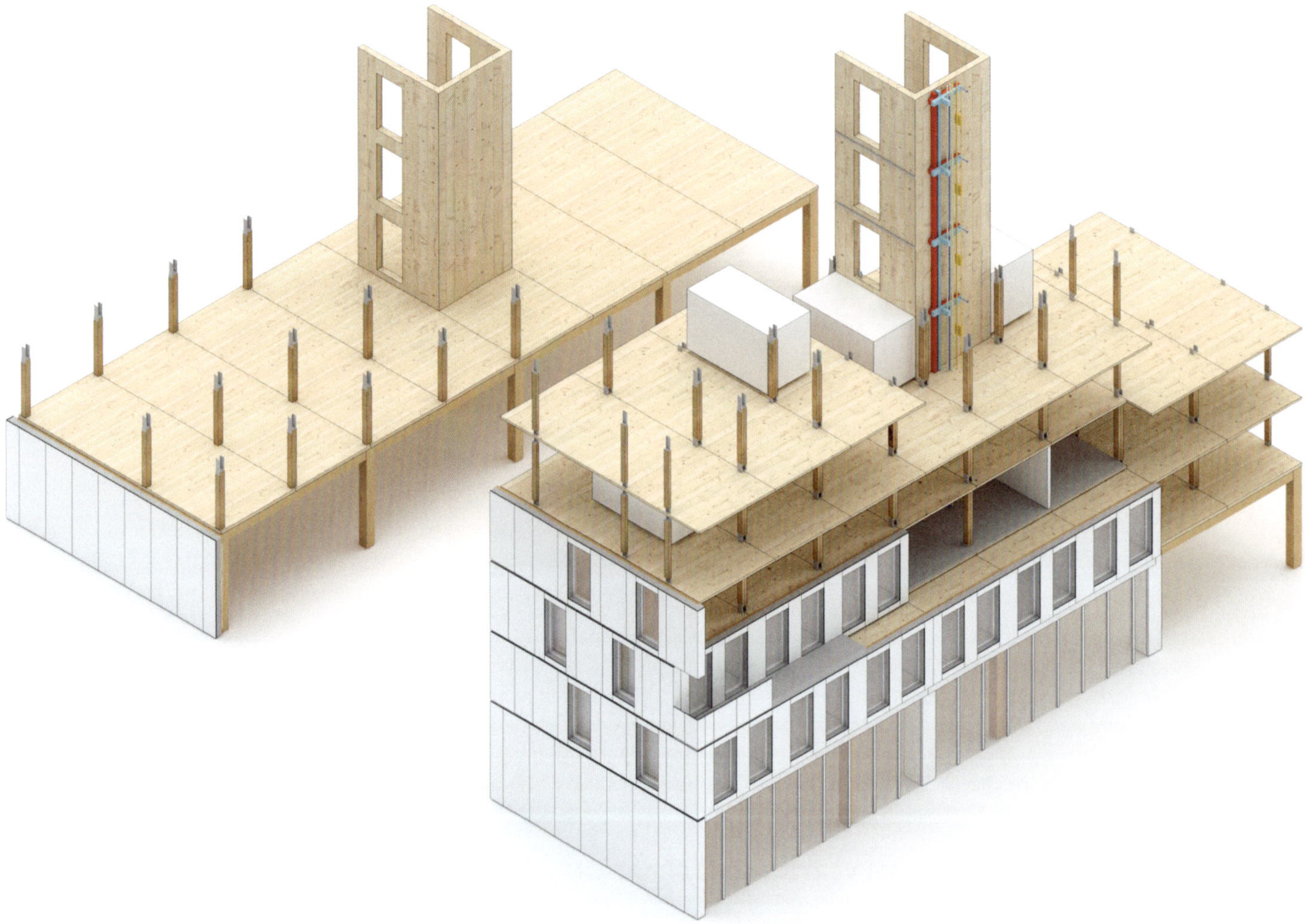

2

Intelligent City's mass timber building platform consists of adaptable floor cassette panels, high-performance envelope panels and other components such as lateral cores, service shafts and accessories.

components must be understood upfront and integrated into the logic of the platform. Only then can the platform be used to create variations without any additional effort and become a scalable solution that can be applied across many different cities.

At Intelligent City, we developed such a parametric platform for 4–18 storey mass timber urban housing, compliant with current mass timber high-rise regulations in Canada and the USA. At this height, mass timber buildings excel not only because of their economic competitiveness over concrete and steel, their structural performance and fire safety, but also for their possibility to create neighbourhoods that have the right density for public infrastructure, resilient local communities and connectedness. A well designed but parametrized product (e.g., apartments and buildings) would raise the level of liveability and quality, also regarding materials such as exposed mass timber ceilings.

The company's mass timber building system consists of customizable hollow-core floor cassettes with preinstalled services and high-performance facade envelope panels that can be Passive House certified. All building components are based on an interdisciplinary development approach with product-thinking at the heart. They encompass mass timber construction details, prefabrication and manufacturing automation principles, logistics and supply chain issues. Considerations of structural requirements for different heights, seismic cores or service shafts were integrated into the development process. New production workflows using industrial robots to automatically assemble large building parts allow for a higher degree of adaptability as well as assembly speed and quality.

3

Photograph of a prototype building showing the timber structure and envelope systems.

The integration of the parametric design process, the building systems platform and manufacturing automation enables a design system within which building variations can be explored and analysed, optimized and costed. Knowledge about all critical project data from the earliest stages of the design allows a highly informed decision-making process and the generation of a completely detailed virtual building from all data points, with clear manufacturing code and assembly instructions.

Such a systematized approach to certain building typologies within a parametric design environment is only possible if the entire process from design to delivery can be controlled. This final step from systematization towards productization requires vertical integration of design and manufacturing and enables an ecosystem of product-oriented companies that deliver holistic, proven solutions. The combination of seemingly opposing ideas of repeatable and scalable architecture and construction, based on mass timber, promises to provide the breakthrough innovation our industry so desperately needs.

ROBOTIC MASS TIMBER MANUFACTURING

The key to this breakthrough innovation lies in the vertical integration of disciplines under the umbrella of a parametric platform, which heavily involves design for manufacturing and assembly (DfMA) principles as well. While many available services outsource the manufacturing or focus solely on design, Intelligent City bridges this gap by directly engaging in prefabrication, thereby connecting manufacturing possibilities, materialization, engineering and design.

Timber construction is a great fit for prefabrication due to its machinability and relatively low weight, resulting in ease of transportation and assembly on site when compared to steel or concrete. Mass timber offers structural and fire safety advantages compared to timber frame construction, however, the sizes and weights of elements are typically outside of what humans can work with. This construction method therefore emphasizes the need for advanced manufacturing technologies, such as robotic manufacturing, that allow for a reconceptualization of building parts and processes.

In order to enable the level of customization described above, manufacturing technologies have to be developed in conjunction with the building systems. For example, the arrangement of cross laminated timber (CLT) panels and their connections was conceived not as a single process but rather as a process logic to be executed by similar but mass customized robotic processing steps. Contrary to traditional CAD/CAM processes, where the geometry of a building part is imported into specialized software for machine code gener-

4

Intelligent City's pilot plant in Delta, BC.

ation, the company's design-to-fabrication workflow seamlessly transitions from a design model to a manufacturing model. This is where parametric design becomes parametric manufacturing.

Intelligent City has developed robotically assisted assembly lines for its mass timber floor cassettes, columns and envelope panel system. The degree of automation responds to where customization and repetition are needed. While some assembly steps remain manual because they require more dexterity, others require precision or heavy lifting and are therefore automated. Our pilot plant in Delta, BC, can output building components for more than 400 apartments per year. The company is working on its expansion with larger factories and a higher degree of automation in a number of cities.

CARBON-NEUTRAL BUILDINGS, DISASSEMBLY AND RETROFIT

One of the most important aspects of prefabricated mass timber is its potential for carbon-neutral buildings. No other building material can help us deliver life-cycle carbon-neutral urban housing at scale. In a life cycle comparison, mass timber Passive House certified buildings have shown to be carbon-neutral, resulting in 2,940 kg CO_2e/m^2 less emissions than comparable concrete buildings with code-compliant energy performance over their entire life cycle. Neither prefabrication nor Passive House certification alone can achieve a result comparable to this vertically integrated productized approach.

Offsite construction enables both a full accounting of the materials we use to fabricate our buildings and a process of continuous improvement through procurement as additional low-carbon materials come to the market. When producing building components in a factory based on an accurate digital model, we know precisely the quantity of materials needed for the component and can therefore significantly reduce waste in the process. We also have a predesigned system and can improve the system's carbon efficiency over time by continuing to optimize the design and finetune manufacturing processes. Finally, there is an opportunity to include the global warming potential as one criteria in the procurement process in addition to the typical performance, financial and availability considerations. Rather than specifying a low-carbon material and then learning what is available or cost-effective at the time of construction, we can evaluate all our materials in advance and proactively change our material when we discover a performance-equivalent, lower-carbon option.

A more automated assembly process with robotics and other machinery also allows us to maintain the tight tolerances and precision needed to achieve Passive House performance in building operation. In contrast to traditional on-site assembly, we pre-test and certify our components to reduce the risk of compliance problems in construction and increase the confidence of the customer. By ensuring the envelope performance before the building is built, we can confidently reduce other systems, such as mechanical ventilation, in the building, providing a right-sized, optimized solution without compromising comfort.

Another important aspect of prefabrication and on-site assembly of large building components is their potential for disassembly and recycling. The parametric design process takes the environmental data and reports the impact of the building as it is being designed rather than as a post-design study such as current life cycle assessments (LCAs) are done today. LCAs are currently completed once a building has a high level of design detail, and therefore a low level of design adaptability, because the construction details and specifications are critical to determining accurate quantities and global warming potential inputs. With predesigned building systems, we already have that level of detail before the project even starts, and the parametric design process adapts those systems to fit the project needs, allowing the global warming potential (GWP) information to adapt in real time with the building design. This allows customers to make critical decisions regarding their projects with the environmental impact in mind, rather than relying on the knowledge of a fragmented team and hoping for the best.

Although our envelope panel system is part of our ecosystem of building components, it can also be employed for retrofit. A different set of connectors is used to equip concrete or other mass timber structures with this envelope panel system. For retrofitting, the existing building structure is scanned and translated into our 3D modelling environment. Then, our design engine picks up the envelope area and populates it with the envelope system, following the same segmentation rules as for newly constructed buildings.

This kind of integrated and parametric thinking enables scalability to reach national and international markets. This capability is key for a new technology to take a foothold in the AEC industry. While we respond to local needs, we must think global. It is in the combination of an adaptable platform with a parametric software system and manufacturing automation that this can be achieved.

Further Reading

▶ Modular construction, "The Urban Village Project", *Circular Construction and Circular Economy*, p. 122
▶ Design for disassembly, "The Urban Mining and Recycling (UMAR) Unit", *Circular Construction and Circular Economy*, p. 142
▶ Circularity, "Circular Construction Over Again", p. 142

Less

LESS

Refocusing on the Potential of Architecture

Introduction to Clean Energy Transition by Andreas Wagner

Rapid advancements in the building services sector in the 20th century, especially after the Second World War, opened up more and more often entirely new scenarios for air-conditioning that until then were undreamt of. In principle, it became possible to build almost any kind of building anywhere in the world and to adjust its indoor climate at will, regardless of the prevailing climatic conditions outdoors. It is from this unconstrained standpoint that corresponding norms and standards were determined, which gave rise to an international benchmark for what was considered as a comfortable indoor climate.

In the process, however, architecture became detached from the climatic conditions of its location. Traditional patterns of climate-appropriate building were no longer relevant as site-specific climate factors did not need to be considered in the design of an indoor climate, whether the intention was to actively leverage them or to minimize their negative effects. Instead, it became possible to build fully glazed buildings in cold continents far from the equator and also in tropical climes – thanks to omnipotent modern HVAC systems.

That this entailed the consumption of immense quantities of energy was given scant consideration at the time because of the seemingly unending supply of energy from coal, oil, gas and uranium. Only after the energy crises of the 1970s and the reports published by the Club of Rome and others, did a shift slowly come about: an awareness that not everyone on Earth has the same access to energy resources and that their availability is finite. To this came, in the early 2000s, an increased awareness of our own contribution as humans to climate change through the consumption of energy and the combustion of fossil fuels. Because construction is a major contributor to both aspects, it is imperative that we fundamentally rethink our activities in this sector on many levels.

In the design of indoor climates, a stronger focus on the principles of climate-appropriate building is therefore necessary, in which indoor climate issues can be resolved by predominantly architectural means. By ingeniously combining tried and tested design concepts and construction details that utilize the principles of building physics, we can create integrated building and energy concepts with a high standard of indoor comfort without requiring extensive building services, and in turn minimize greenhouse gas emissions resulting from building operation. Technological innovations can work in tandem with and further develop climate-friendly design, for example through the use of selective glazing for reduced solar radiation input or of phase-change materials that can increase the thermal inertia of lightweight forms of construction. Digitalization can also make important contributions, for example in the form of intelligent systems that predictively control HVAC systems or passive cooling mechanisms based on weather forecasts or that involve the occupants in indoor climate control by exchanging relevant information with them.

The assessment of energy consumption in buildings and energy-related emissions must be expanded to also consider the grey energy required for the production and manufacture of building elements and similarly of building services equipment. Seen against the broader perspective of the entire life cycle of a building, passive cooling strategies that use significantly fewer building services once again represent an attractive alternative. In this context, simpler, low-tech construction methods that are both circular and make use of natural building materials become viable (once again). These are in themselves nothing new: it is just that regionally specific construction methods using traditional artisanship joining techniques and predominantly local resources from closed material economies have long been displaced or supplanted by more advanced technological methods which in turn have arisen in response to normative requirements, cost concerns and industrial production methods. At the same time, one must be wary of propagating "simple building" as a universal remedy: it is important to carefully examine where simpler constructions are a sensible option and where innovative technologies can viably benefit a building's sustainability. The objective is therefore the sustainability-oriented design of efficient architecture with lean and intelligent building technology.

To come back to the aspect of comfort mentioned at the outset, we now know that a standard indoor climate that is achieved independently of the outdoor temperature is by no means a guarantee for user satisfaction and well-being. Building occupants will also find buildings without air conditioning comfortable, even to a certain extent at higher temperatures – provided that they have a means of being able to actively intervene in controlling the indoor climate, be that by interacting with the building (e.g., opening windows or operating sunshades), by ways of adapting personally (e.g., changing their clothing) or by employing so-called personal comfort systems (e.g., a table or ceiling fan, or a chair with heating/cooling functions). Since the early 2000s normative standards have adapted accordingly through the introduction of an adaptive comfort model – now "less is more" also signals a step towards greater sufficiency.

These considerations are the background for the discussions in this chapter and corresponding examples of potential applications.

SUSTAINABLE ARCHITECTURE IN THE EFFICIENCY TRAP?

Commentary by Thomas Auer

For some time now, sustainability has been elevated to the ranks of credentials to aspire to in the race to build taller, faster and better. For decades, architecture has set its sight on superlatives, which often take the form of grand gestures: the tallest, skinniest or most sustainable high-rise, the most intelligent facade, the tallest wooden structure ... the list is endless. Ambitious as they are, one must ask whether such projects have really made buildings more sustainable, even when they stake their claim on sustainability. Grand gestures invariably consume extraordinary quantities of resources. The contribution they make to the challenges of our time is therefore questionable.

Hardly a month goes by without a new building being lauded as supposedly the most sustainable building in the world. Often the reasoning is quite arbitrary. High-rise buildings made of concrete, steel and glass are praised for their use of cutting-edge smart building technology, the assumption being that this maximizes their energy efficiency. The fact that such building control technology has no effect on the amount of carbon used to construct the building, or on the fact that "glass buildings" heat up disproportionately, requiring corresponding cooling, is ignored entirely. Technological efficiency is used here as a vehicle to justify what are often questionable approaches. Typically, some form of comparison is cited as confirmation: a building performs X% better ... but better than what? Seen in this light, switching from a diesel SUV to a hybrid SUV would also seem advantageous. At the same time, experience has shown that complex control systems often fail to deliver in practice what they promise in theory. In the literature, the "performance gap" of modern, efficiency-optimized office buildings varies between 30% and 70%,[1] and in multi-storey housing we are also seeing an increasing performance gap as energy efficiency increases.

The closer we look at it, the more it becomes clear that energy efficiency alone is not sufficient as a model for sustainability, when seen from a holistic perspective. Instead of efficiency-driven superlatives, we need a different model for sustainable architecture. A potential counter model is the principle of "building simply",[2] i.e. building with thicker walls, smaller windows, and higher ceilings – none of which are driven by current efficiency models. Although this approach only just complies with the minimum energy requirements given in the Buildings Energy Act, a life cycle assessment for a 100-year period reveals that such houses are on par with the Effizienzhaus-40 standard, which stipulates 60% better energy efficiency compared to the minimum requirements; and that is without factoring in the performance gap often seen in high-tech approaches. When considered across the life cycle of a building, building simply is therefore arguably a better strategy than approaches that strive solely to optimize efficiency.

Even when in future derived from 100% regenerative sources, energy is and remains without doubt a valuable resource that must not be wasted. However, architecture cannot be reduced to a formula; it must always be balanced and appropriate. Focusing purely on energy efficiency, as has been the case for decades, is a dead-end approach. The German federal government's "Efficiency First"[3] philosophy cannot provide us with meaningful answers that are applicable to the diverse breadth of architecture that constitutes our building culture. Not only that: it can also even lead us in the wrong direction – as described above with the example of smart glass skyscrapers.

Efficiency serves as a driver for the technical upgrading of buildings – both where heating, ventilation and air conditioning systems are concerned, as well as monitoring and control technology. There is certainly potential in digitizing building operations. For example, the grid connectivity of buildings will become more relevant where building operations are more closely coupled to the availability of renewable energy sources. By contrast, a lighting fixture that knows my preferred lighting levels and switches on as soon as I enter the room offers no real added value and may conversely increase energy consumption.

Making our built environment more sustainable is one of the greatest challenges of our time. The race for efficiency of the past decades cannot adequately respond to this. Rather than striving for superlatives, we must focus on appropriateness and balanced approaches, and on aesthetics rather than grand gestures. In architecture, true sustainability also involves a certain humility.

1 M. Norbert Fisch, Stefan Plesser and Carsten Bremer, *Abschlussbericht zum Projekt "EVA – Evaluierung von Energiekonzepten für Bürogebäude"*, TU Braunschweig: Institut für Gebäude- und Solartechnik (IGS), 2007.

2 Einfach Bauen (2023). Research project at the TU München, https://www.einfach-bauen.net/.

3 Was bedeutet eigentlich "Efficiency First"?, Energiewende Direkt, 2016, Federal Ministry of Economic Affairs and Climate Protection, issue 23/2016, https://www.bmwi-energiewende.de/EWD/Redaktion/Newsletter/2016/23/Meldung/direkt-erklaert.html.

Further Reading

- ▶ Building simply, "Less – Refocusing on the Potential of Architecture", p. 58
- ▶ Efficiency, "Better – Efficiency in the Construction Industry", *Circular Construction and Circular Economy*, p. 30
- ▶ Resource costs, "Principles of Circular Construction", *Circular Construction and Circular Economy*, p. 22

CONTROLLED NATURAL VENTILATION SYSTEMS FOR NON-RESIDENTIAL BUILDINGS

Case Study by Matthias Rudolph

Air is vital for our sustenance – the average person imbibes around 1 kg of food and 2-3 kg of liquids daily but inhales the equivalent of 15 kg of air. This quantitative comparison alone shows how important the role of good air quality is for our health and wellbeing. Before we even start considering how we ventilate spaces, a baseline must therefore be that interiors should be as free from pollutants as possible – and for this we must use building materials that cause low to no pollution. Ventilation must then only serve the purpose of removing moisture along with emissions produced by people themselves. According to current standards,[1] an air change rate of around 25 to 36 m^3/h per person is required to keep carbon dioxide levels below 1,000 ppm for rooms used for normal indoor activities.[2] The concentration of carbon dioxide in the air serves as an indicator of indoor air quality. Similarly, most odours are assumed to be caused by people.

In short, interiors need to be ventilated. The question is: how do we create healthy air conditions, what technical means does this entail and how much energy do they consume? The following discussion and the two case studies presented here demonstrate the advantages of controlled natural ventilation systems for non-residential buildings.

MECHANICAL VENTILATION – A THEORETICAL PROMISE

According to calculations in line with the German Buildings Energy Act,[3] mechanical ventilation combined with heat recovery (MVHR) is able to ensure good air quality in an energy-efficient way, and therefore satisfies user demands in both respects. However, various studies have shown that what seems plausible in theory is rarely the case in practice. The research project Evaluation of Energy Concepts (EVA)[4] monitored the performance of multiple office buildings that employ both natural ventilation and mechanical ventilation and came to the conclusion that mechanically ventilated buildings consume approx. 30 % more energy in operation than naturally ventilated buildings to achieve a comparable level of air quality.

This performance gap can be attributed, among other things, to the theoretical assumptions that underpin the calculation of energy demand in the Buildings Energy Act or DIN V 18599.[5] For example, the standards assume a regular pattern of occupancy for office buildings in which workers arrive in the morning, leave in the evening and occupy office spaces according to a predefined profile. Ventilation systems start operating before work begins and continue running after hours to ensure good indoor air quality at the start of the day and to cater for people working late. The result is that many office spaces are consistently over-ventilated as these models no longer correspond to current working practices. Reliable digital communications and hybrid working arrangements with partial working from home have caused the occupancy patterns of office buildings to change: workplaces are now increasingly for analogue in-person communications and are no longer fully occupied all day.

To counter the problem of over-ventilation, room-mounted CO_2 sensors can be installed that monitor indoor air quality and regulate the amount of outdoor air influx as required. This does, however, require more technical services in the form of volume flow controllers, sensors and control systems – i.e., the use of technology to solve a problem caused by technology. Such systems also require long-term maintenance and servicing and must themselves also be monitored for malfunctions, along with corresponding mitigation measures. The added expense of variable air volume-flow systems is often also prohibitive and such systems are therefore only rarely installed.

KonLuft, a research project on the potential of controlled natural ventilation completed in 2016, revealed that even in regular malfunction-free operation, the primary energy demand for electricity, heating and cooling of a MVHR is significantly higher than that of a controlled natural ventilation system. A corresponding life cycle assessment also shows that the additional effort for production and recycling as well as the electricity costs for the operation of an MVHR system are not offset by the ventilation heat saved over the duration of its operation.[6]

Studies have also shown that mechanical ventilation systems do not always satisfy indoor comfort expectations. In naturally ventilated buildings, user satisfaction is consistently higher.[7, 8, 9]

1 Arbeitsstättenverordnung – ArbStättV, Abschnitt 4 ASR A3.6, Technische Regeln für Arbeitsstätten Lüftung (ASR A3.6), issued January 2012, last amended GMBl 2018, p. 474.

2 German edition of EN 16798-1:2019, Energy performance of buildings – Ventilation for buildings – Part 1: Indoor environmental input parameters for design and assessment of energy performance of buildings addressing indoor air quality, thermal environment, lighting and acoustics – Module M1-6.

3 Gesetz zur Einsparung von Energie und zur Nutzung erneuerbarer Energien zur Wärme- und Kälteerzeugung in Gebäuden (Gebäudeenergiegesetz – GEG), Artikel 1 G. v. 08.08.2020 BGBl. I S. 1728 (Nr. 37); last amended in Artikel 18a G. on 20/07/2022 BGBl. I p. 1237, valid from 01/11/2020; FNA: 754-30 Energieversorgung.

4 Stefan Plesser, Ernesto Kuchen and M. Norbert Fisch, "Ergebnisse einer Evaluierung von Energiekonzepten für Bürogebäude und Schlussfolgerungen für die Energieeffizienz und das Raumklima", *Bauphysik*, 30, 2008, 6, p. 389 ff., https://doi.org/10.1002/bapi.200810050.

5 DIN V 18599-1:2018-09, Energy efficiency of buildings - Calculation of the net, final and primary energy demand for heating, cooling, ventilation, domestic hot water and lighting.

6 KonLuft – Energieeffizienz von Gebäuden durch kontrollierte natürliche Lüftung, Abschlussbericht, Hochschule für Technik Stuttgart, 2016, Prof. Dr. habil. Ursula Eicker, Dr. Tobias Erhart, M.Sc., Dipl.-Ing. (FH), Dipl.-Phys. Daniel Gürlich, M.Sc. Maximilian Haag, Dr. Tobias Schulze, Dipl.-Ing. (FH), Document number: 122-004-13P V1.2, funded by the BMWi.

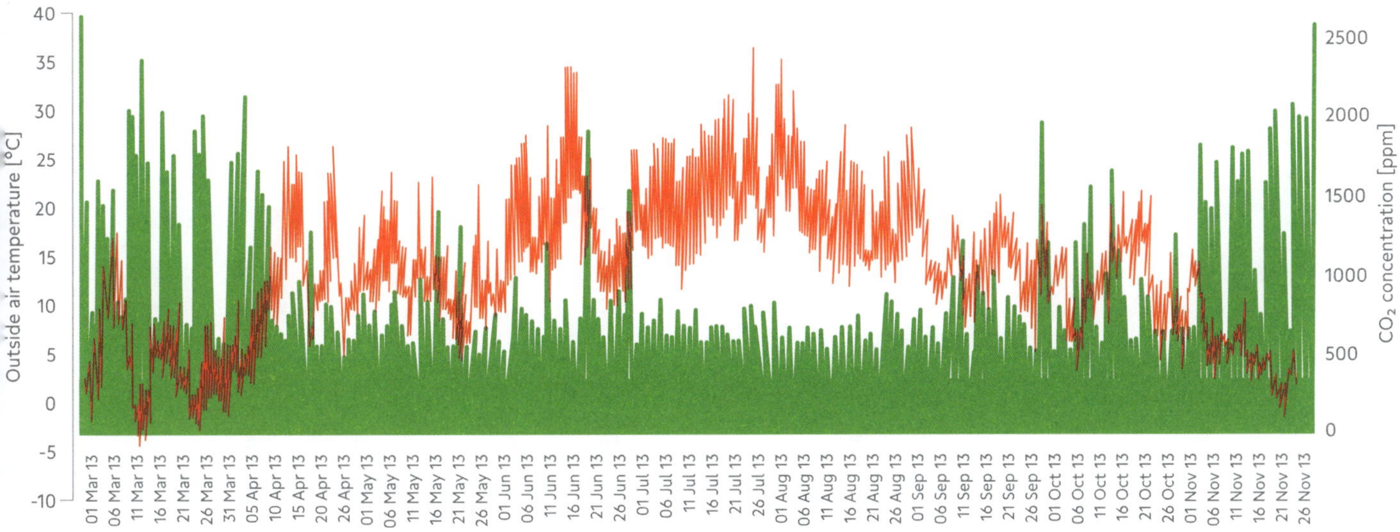

1

CO_2 content of indoor air (as an indicator for air quality) and outdoor temperature over the course of the year (January to December) in a window-ventilated group office.

CO_2

Temperature

HOW CAPABLE IS NATURAL VENTILATION?

User satisfaction levels are generally high for natural ventilation systems as long as (and because) users can determine them and act for themselves. Those who have an office of their own can adjust the opening cross-section of the window and the duration of ventilation to their personal needs. In smaller shared office spaces, people can generally reach a consensus on the degree and duration of ventilation. In open-plan offices it becomes more complex as both short, intermittent bursts of and "gentle", continuous ventilation with tilted windows produce flows of cold air that can cause discomfort by draught, even to those seated further from an open window, and who have less influence over the pattern of ventilation. Such discomfort can mean that spaces are ventilated less frequently, especially during cold times of the year, and this also results in persistently low levels of air quality. The only positive effect is then reduced heat loss.

Fig. 1 shows how the pattern of air quality (hourly levels of CO_2) in a window-ventilated office in Stuttgart in 2013 changes with outdoor air temperature over the course of a year.

If people ventilate less during the cold seasons of the year, is it at all possible to achieve good comfort levels and air quality levels using natural ventilation systems? This problem of conventional window ventilation can only be effectively solved by a carefully planned controlled natural ventilation strategy. One possible approach is to employ a basic level of controlled, draught-free natural ventilation with additional, tolerably short, intermittent bursts of ventilation. Another is to use part of the interior as a buffer space that is replenished with fresh air when not in active use.

There are certainly situations in which mechanical ventilation is a good means of ensuring indoor air quality. However, comparisons have shown that natural ventilation is in many cases the better choice. Well-designed natural ventilation systems enjoy high user satisfaction, can provide good air quality year-round, avoid the problem of over-ventilation and in turn minimize energy consumption. Because they make less use of technology, they are also generally more robust and have lower subsequent maintenance and servicing costs.

The following two case studies demonstrate possible approaches and how these can be incorporated into the architectural concept. The first project discusses the refurbishment of an office building from the 1970s for DAV in Munich, which employs a hybrid concept of continuous ventilation using natural air recirculation via the facade, while also providing sound insulation. The second project – the ANOHA Children's World in Berlin – is a house-in-house concept that utilizes the outer building as a thermal buffer and fresh air reservoir.

7 Hummelgaard et al., "Indoor air quality and occupant satisfaction in five mechanically and four naturally ventilated open-plan office buildings", Technical University of Denmark, 2006; *Building and Environment*, 42, 12, 2007, pp. 4051–4058.

8 Vivian Loftness, Volker Hartkopf, Lam Khee Poh, PhD students Megan Snyder, Ying Hua, Yun Gu, Joonho Choi, and Xiaodi Yang, Carnegie Mellon University Center for Building Performance, "Sustainability and Health are Integral Goals for the Built Environment", Healthy Buildings 2006, Lisbon, 4–8 June 2006.

9 Minyoung Kwon, Hilde Remøy, Andy van den Dobbelsteen and Ulrich Knaack, "Personal control and environmental user satisfaction in office buildings: Results of case studies in the Netherlands", *Building and Environment*, 149, 2019, pp. 428–435.

2

DAV Headquarters, Munich. The four-storey west and east facades have a 1.5-m-wide outdoor layer in front of the building skin for planting and maintenance.

CASE STUDY 1: DAV HEADQUARTERS, MUNICH

The client acquired an existing building from the early 1970s and, together with Element · A Architekten from Munich and hiendl_schieneis architektenpartnerschaft from Augsburg, converted and extended it according to ecological principles for use as their new federal headquarters. By refurbishing an existing structure rather than building anew, the construction resulted in fewer greenhouse gas emissions, and carbon could remain bound in the structure for the long term. Simulations of the impact of shading from surrounding buildings and vegetation were conducted for each respective area of glazing, and showed that extensive sections of the glazed facades did not need additional external shading.

The design team sought a low-tech approach to the air-conditioning and ventilation. The goal was to develop a natural ventilation concept that would provide very good acoustic and thermal comfort indoors despite high levels of traffic noise from a nearby motorway and fluctuating high wind forces caused by the adjoining high-rise buildings.

The solution entailed modifying the design of the wall parapet construction, which was consistently applied in all the office areas. Using a passive, sound-damping trickle vent element, outside air can flow at a constant rate into the building regardless of the pressure differential between inside and outside. Trickle vents are usually mounted just above a window but given the Alpine hinterland of Munich, this would have resulted in cold air draughts. Preheating the air via the built-in convector would have run the risk of freezing in the event of a malfunction, causing more significant damage. Instead, the trickle vents were incorporated into the walls close to the ground. An intake close to floor level allows incoming cold air from outdoors to mix passively with indoor air before being heated by the integral facade convector. This requires no electrical energy, instead employing the stack effect induced by the convector, which causes warm air to rise, drawing in both air from the room and from outside – resulting in an entirely passive, self-regulating natural system (Fig. 3).

In normal use, this stack effect draws in outdoor and indoor air at floor level and

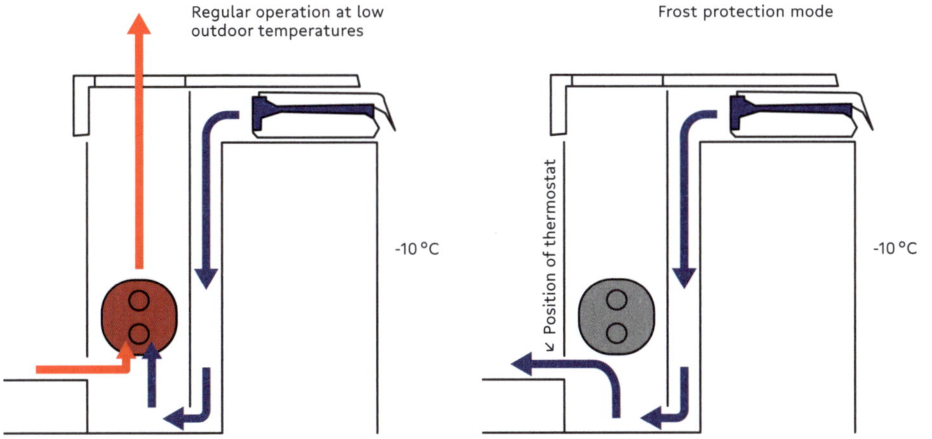

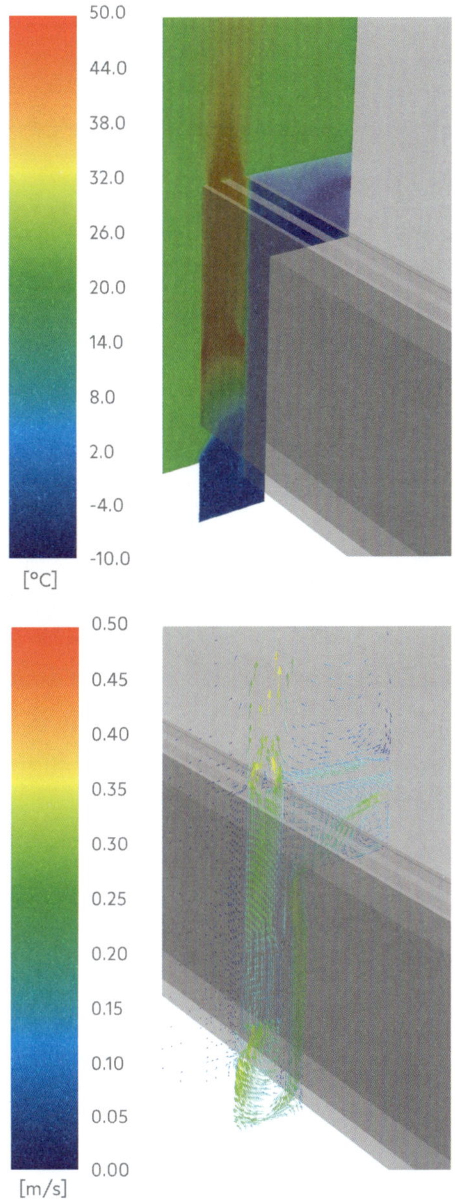

warms it, avoiding the problem of cold feet. The remote sensor of the thermostat measures the air temperature at the base of the convector shaft and controls the room temperature accordingly. When heating is not required, the preset room temperature can be lowered, and the convector deactivates. Due to the density difference, incoming cold from outside then flows not through the convector into the room, but passes via the floor-level opening over the thermostat, thereby activating the frost protection mode.

The functioning principles and operation cases of this configuration were verified using computational fluid dynamics simulations. Fig. 4 (top) shows the air temperature in a vertical section of the window parapet. In the lower area, the indoor air flow at 20 °C preheats the incoming outdoor air at -10 °C so that frost temperatures do not occur, and the resulting mix of fresh air and room air is drawn draught-free into the room via the convector. Fig. 4 (bottom) shows that the inward flow direction of the cold air is drawn upwards at the base of the parapet element where it mixes with indoor air from the room.

The dimensioning of the vents in the facade and of the centrally located vertical ducts for air extraction is informed by the principle of night-time cooling in summer. In this building, a hybrid ventilation approach is employed during the summer months to ventilate the building at night. Cool air passes over the exposed concrete ceilings drawing out accumulated heat to passively ensure good daytime thermal comfort on hot days. If required, ceiling fans provide increased air movement and user comfort. Fig. 5 shows a cross-section of the window parapet and sill (bottom) along with an installed element with the inspection cover removed (top).

Exhaust air is extracted centrally in shafts and discharged via exhaust fans through the roof. This system repurposed the existing vertical shafts of the previous mechanical ventilation ducts.

The project demonstrates that even in sub-optimal conditions with traffic noise and difficult wind conditions, natural ventilation concepts can still be a profitable alternative to exclusively mechanical ventilation systems. As fresh air enters via the shortest possible route, there is no ductwork that needs regular cleaning and takes up space in the interior. There nevertheless remains potential for further low-tech optimization: the peripheral trickle elements in the facade have motorized controllers and the exhaust air extraction is fan-driven. A next step could involve making the air outlets of the trickle vents manually operable with a lever or similar that indicates its open or closed state visually to the user. Exhaust air extraction could be driven naturally for much of the year, and as outdoor temperatures rise, waste heat from IT equipment could be used for the buoyancy effect in the vertical shafts.

3 ↖

Principle of outside air entering the building and being preheated passively. Facade section of parapet element showing the trickle vent and the convector.

Left: **Regular operation at low outdoor temperatures.**

Right: **Frost protection mode – cold air flows along thermostat and convector is activated.**

4 ↑

Computational Fluid Dynamics (CFD) simulation.

Top: **Temperature distribution of the parapet element at an outdoor temperature of -10 °C;**

Bottom: **Air velocity flow distribution.**

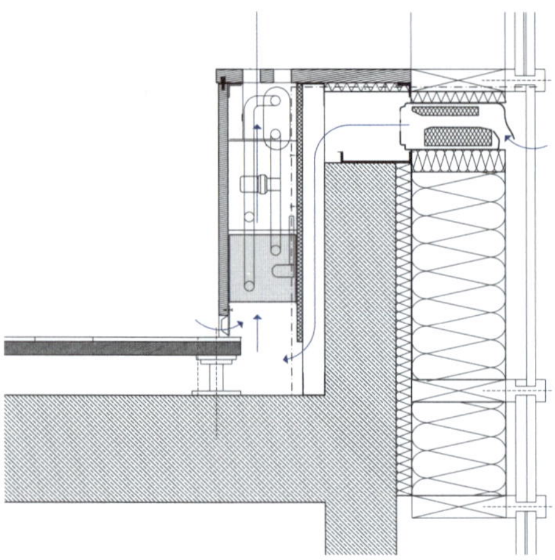

5

Passive trickle element with preheating via facade convector.

CASE STUDY 2: ANOHA – THE CHILDREN'S WORLD OF THE JEWISH MUSEUM BERLIN

Opposite the Jewish Museum in the Kreuzberg District of Berlin is a large hall that was formerly a wholesale flower market. It has since been converted for the Jewish Museum by the architects Olson Kundig from Seattle and Architekturbüro Engelbrecht from Berlin. Inserted into the rear, western part of the hall is a modern interpretation of Noah's Ark, or ANOHA for short, as a house-in-house project (Fig. 6). The centrepiece of the new children's world of the Jewish Museum is a 7-m-high round structure made of domestic spruce with a diameter of 28 m that serves as a soft counterpart to the rugged reinforced concrete skeleton frame shell of the hall (Fig. 7).

The ANOHA takes a consistent low-tech approach to its climate design concept. Instead of mechanical ventilation, it draws in fresh air naturally from the volume of the hall. The concrete structure has a large thermal mass that balances out fluctuations in the outdoor temperature, so that indoor temperature variations are less pronounced. The hall has no extra heating and is only passively warmed by waste heat from installations and exhaust air. The ANOHA itself has underfloor heating, which can also be used as underfloor cooling in extreme summer temperatures.

The large volume of the hall interior serves effectively as a fresh air repository.

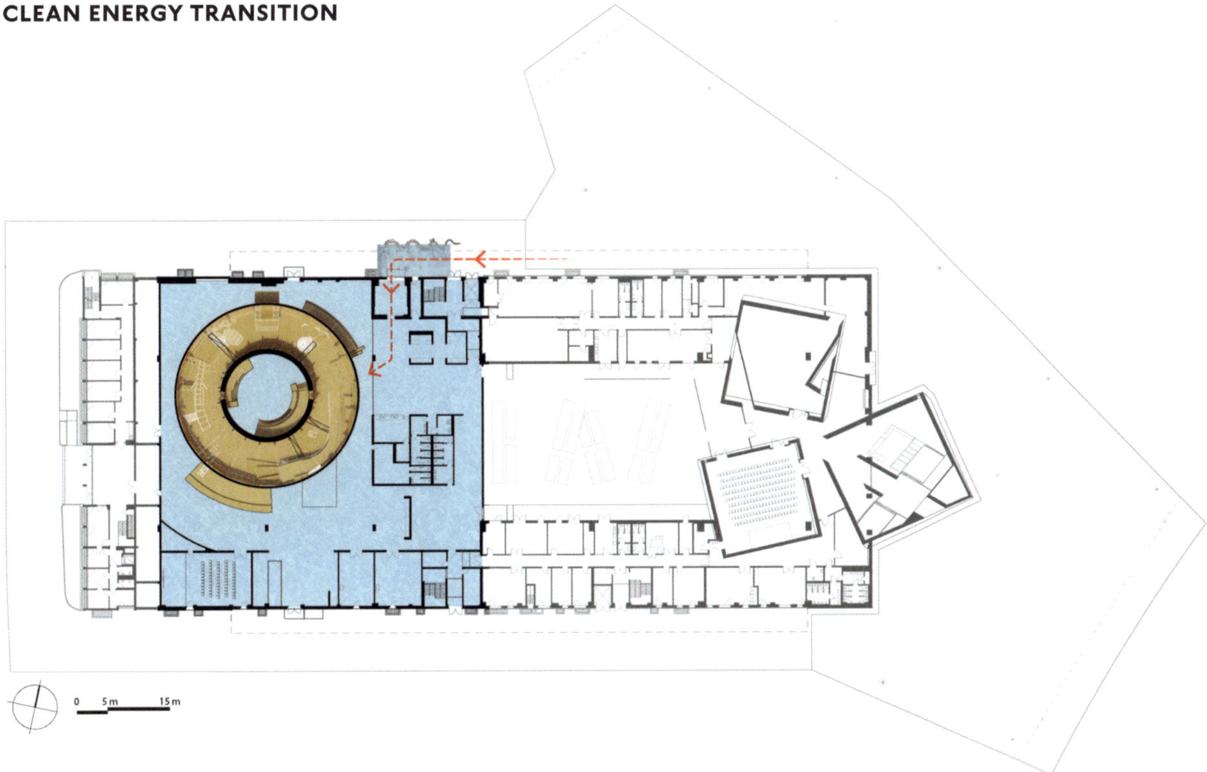

6

Floor plan of the ANOHA Children's World in the existing hall.

Controlled vents in the roof ensure good air quality at all times and provide a continuous flow of air in the roof area of the ANOHA (Fig. 10). A significant element for the ventilation and air-conditioning concept are the large ceiling fans mounted inside the arc below the ceiling intakes (Fig. 11). At a diameter of 2.4 m, they rotate slowly and practically noiselessly, mixing incoming cool air from the hall in winter with rising warm air inside the ANOHA without causing uncomfortable draughts or needing additional reheating of incoming air. In addition, they distribute air throughout the ANOHA space, improving thermal comfort during the warm summer months.

Smoke tests conducted on site in spring 2022 confirmed the design calculations: the combination of naturally ventilated air intakes and ceiling fans mounted beneath them ensures sufficient preheating of the incoming air from the hall and prevents draughts. Fig. 8 shows how indoor room air (enriched here by a fog generator) mixes with the incoming hall air.

In addition to its function as a fresh air reservoir, the hall also acts as a temperature buffer, cooling incoming outdoor air during the summer months. Temperature measurements for the week of 25 August 2016, for example, reached 35 °C while indoor air temperatures in the upper area of the hall topped out at 27 °C. Even when taking into account additional internal loads of 10 W/m² due to lighting and the thermal contribution of people, the risk of overheating is very limited. With no active cooling in the ANOHA, thermal simulations showed operative room temperatures only exceeding 26 °C for 113 hours of use time of an entire year (Fig. 9), and that is without considering the cooling effect of increased air movement produced by the ceiling fans.

This case study shows that by leveraging the large spatial volume of the existing building, it was possible to implement integrated passive cooling and ventilation strategies. Specifically, the house-in-house configuration in a large existing hall that can serve as a fresh air reservoir and thermal buffer zone made it possible to achieve consistently high levels of air quality and thermal comfort all year round with only minimal use of technology. The combination of fresh air vents in the ceiling to the hall and ceiling fans to distribute and preheat incoming air by mixing it with room air provides a comfortable supply of air even at high occupancy levels and low outdoor temperatures.

Further Reading

▶ Air exchange, "Celebrating the Genius of Simplicity", p. 70

▶ Comfort, "Greenhouse Gas Emissions – An Appropriate Target, Design and Assessment Parameter", p. 82

▶ Adaptive reuse, "Deconstruction of Place, Acceleration of Waste", *Circular Construction and Circular Economy*, p. 52

8

Smoke test conducted to verify the natural ventilation concept.

Video: https://www.youtube-nocookie.com/embed/i8UDLeUdWh8.

7

ANOHA Children's World, house-in-house.

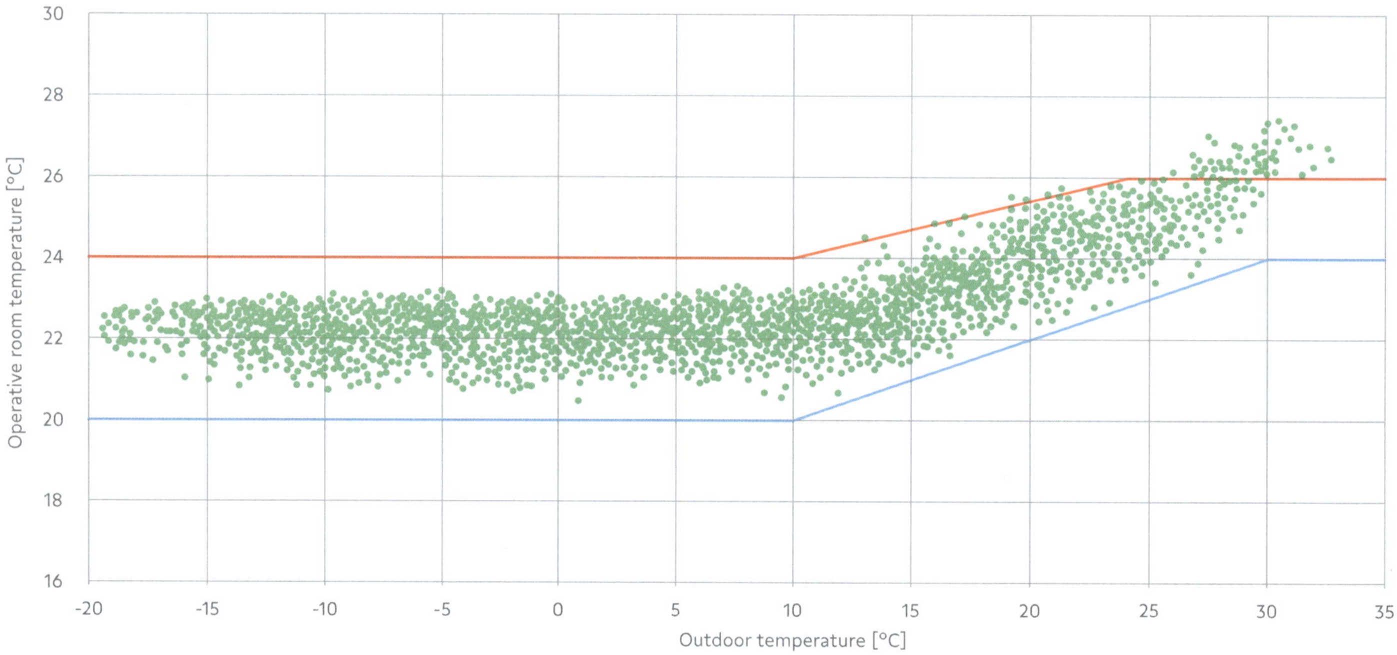

9

Annual temperature distribution of the operative room temperature in the Museum as a function of the outdoor temperature.

- Operative room temperature of museum
- Upper thermal comfort limit exceeded for 113 h
- Lower thermal comfort limit exceeded for 1 h

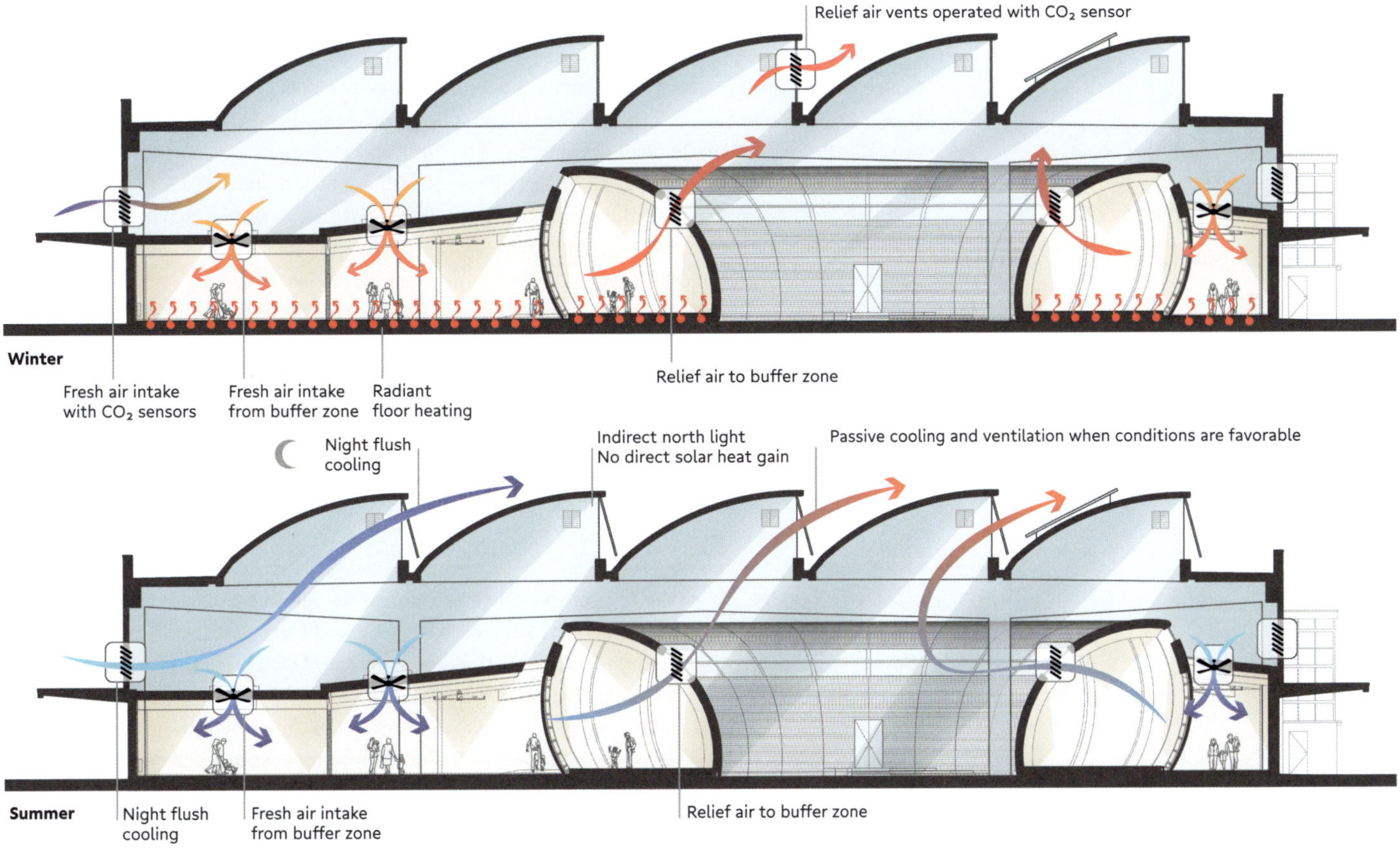

10 ↑

Air-conditioning and ventilation concept – operation in winter (top) **and summer** (bottom).

Unconditioned buffer zone of the hall

Exhibition area

11 ←

Air intake in the ceiling area and mixing of outdoor air and indoor air via the ceiling fans.

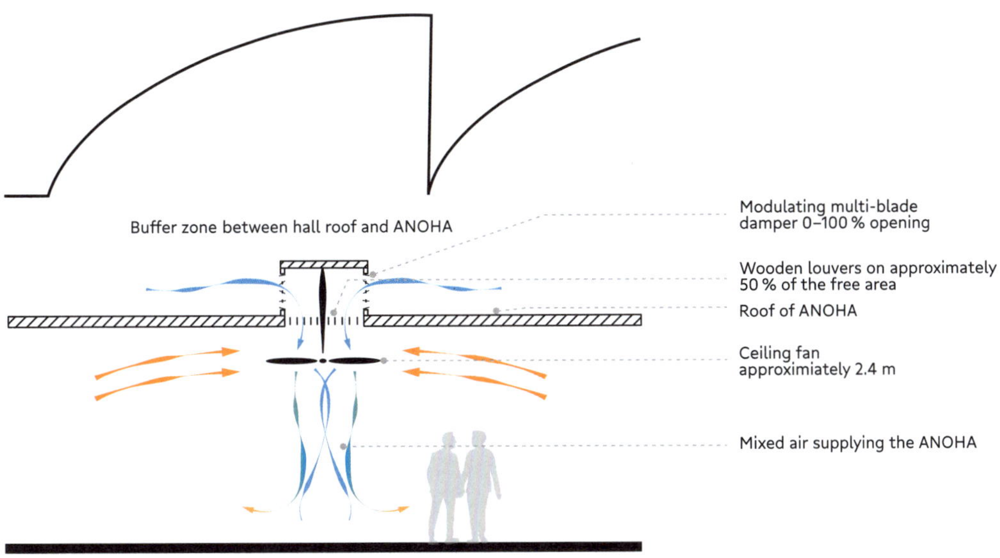

CELEBRATING THE GENIUS OF SIMPLICITY

The 2226 Concept by Baumschlager Eberle Architekten

Article by Benjamin Weber and Andreas Wagner

The 2226 concept by Baumschlager Eberle Architekten represents a radical proposal for minimizing building services through the design of high-performance architecture. Described by the architects as a "manifesto for sustainable building",[1] the 2226 concept provides high levels of indoor comfort – good air quality and a constant temperature range between 22 and 26 °C – without heating, air-conditioning or mechanical ventilation with heat recovery. The first 2226 project in Lustenau, Austria, built in 2013 as a mixed-use building (including a gallery, restaurant, offices, fitness studio and two apartments), was equipped with extensive sensors to assess its performance. The monitoring results confirmed that the building essentially behaves as simulated in advance.[2] In the meantime, four 2226 projects have been completed and several others are in development or under construction. The concept is thus the well-proven and has since also been applied to purely residential buildings.

Although the concept predominantly makes use of heat emitted by the residents and electrical appliances, its low-tech approach is by no means primitive. Rather, it demonstrates that challenges with regard to use and comfort, which are often met in traditional new buildings with more and more technical equipment, can also be solved through the building's architectural design: essentially the building becomes an elementary part of the indoor climate concept. Aside from high-quality architectural design, this concept requires a good cross-disciplinary understanding of the consequences of design decisions – for example with the help of high ceilings as a means to keep air exchange and thus ventilation heat losses low. It is in essence an "intelligent updating of architectural knowledge with modern planning tools".[3] In terms of its overall objective to obviate the need for conventional heating, the approach is comparable to the Passivhaus idea but unlike that concept, it does not employ a ventilation system with heat recovery and heat supply systems to warm incoming fresh air. Instead it chooses a different path.

For Baumschlager Eberle Architekten, this means employing several (still) rather unconventional approaches. The buildings are masonry constructions with separate load-bearing and insulating layers that result in wall thicknesses of 60 cm and more. It would be possible though to reduce the wall thickness with the help of a conventional external layer of insulation. While material usage is high, the construction is less susceptible to defects and has a longer service life; Baumschlager Eberle Architekten estimate a service life of up to 200 years. Room heights of 3 m and more and the largely open floor plan layout ensure effective natural ventilation, which is primarily computer-controlled but can also be overridden by the users. At present only residential projects have openable windows; all other 2226 buildings instead have openable ventilation flaps.

The main functioning principle of the building is a precise balance between heat gains (solar and internal), thermal storage mass and actual, user-controlled ventilation requirements. It is not possible to adequately represent the very high thermal mass or occupancy-dependent fluctuations in ventilation heat losses using current calculation and assessment methods.[4] Detailed dynamic simulations have therefore become an essential part of such planning. A further benefit of the overall robustness of the architectural concept and keeping technical services to a minimum is that this reduces the risks associated with incorrect building operation. Other high-tech buildings are often plagued by a "rebound effect" in which suboptimal user behaviour greatly compromises their energy efficiency.

The concept has since been transferred to the residential sector with the completion of the Apartment Building 2226 Graf in Dornbirn. Office buildings typically have consistent and predictable occupancy patterns and corresponding high internal loads, while the latter are significantly lower and in any case more uneven for the heat supply in residential buildings. Significant differences result from the number of occupants, the time they spend in the dwelling and the heat production, for example through cooking. To provide additional coverage, Baumschlager Eberle Architekten include so-called "backups" – that provide heat on demand where needed, which are powered by photovoltaic panels on the roof. Given the limited availability of PV-based power during the heating period, total solar coverage will obviously only be possible on balance over an extended period. In fact, the architects are

1 https://www.2226.eu/die-umsetzung/projekte-details/2226-emmenweid-schweiz/.

2 Matthias Hüttmann, "Haus ohne Heizung", *Sonnenenergie*, 3, 2016, pp. 37–41.

3 Ibid., p. 40.

4 See also Jakob Schoof, "Haus ohne Heizung: Bürogebäude von Baumschlager Eberle in Lustenau", *Detail*, 3 February 2014, https://www.detail.de/de/de_de/haus-ohne-heizung-buerogebaeude-von-baumschlager-eberle-in-lustenau-11703.

5 Energy Institute Vorarlberg, *Bürogebäude 2226 Lustenau (AT), Ökobilanz April 2021*, Dornbirn.

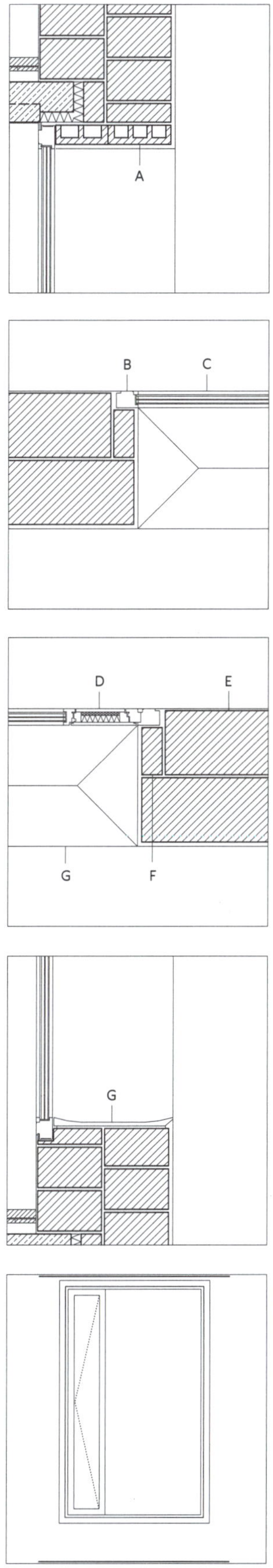

not dogmatic about eradicating building technology; rather they are interested in sensibly ascertaining "how much is enough".

Regarding the life cycle assessment of the building during production, the eco-index, global warming potential and primary energy consumption are lower than for a conventional building due to the long service life, low maintenance requirements and lean technical building equipment.[5] Only during operation an identical passive house would have a slightly lower global warming potential, but this can be compensated by electricity from renewable sources. To reduce material usage and achieve a better ratio of usable space to construction area, as well as a higher circularity and reuse or recycling ambitions, it seems worthwhile to investigate alternative construction methods.

Alongside these questions, the indoor climate concept could be developed further, for example by expanding self-imposed temperature limits according to usage zones in the building. For example, bedrooms or other rooms that are not in constant use do not have to be set at 22°C. Clever zoning of the floor plan may also make it possible to dispense with some of the aforementioned "backups". Last but not least, applying the concept to residential buildings implies that users may need to be involved more in the control and regulation of the building. This entails educating users on ideal consumption and use patterns and making them aware of how they themselves contribute to generating and using internal loads.

Either way, Baumschlager Eberle Architekten's concept is a refreshingly simple approach that, while complex in its planning, has so far proven itself admirably in practice. In striving for greater sustainability in construction, it refocuses attention on aspects of sufficiency and traditional building design strategies and – with the help of modern planning tools – employs carefully selected architectural means to improve and regulate indoor room climate.

1 ↑

Building 2226, the first building based on the 2226 principle by Baumschlager Eberle Architekten in Lustenau, Austria, completed in 2013.

2 ↗

Window and wall details of Building 2226 in Lustenau.

A Brick lintel
B Window frame, white fir
C 3-layer insulated fixed glazing
D Ventilation flap
E Load-bearing brick
F Insulating brick
G Window sill, sandstone

3 ↑

Office Building 2226 Emmenweid in Emmenbrücke, Switzerland, completed in 2018.

4 →

Left: **Interior view of a window of Building 2226 Emmenweid with closed ventilation flap;** Right: **Window with open ventilation flap.**

5 ↑

Apartment Building 2226 Graf in Dornbirn, Austria, completed in 2020.

6 ←

View of the windows of the Apartment Building 2226 Graf in Dornbirn.

Further Reading

▶ Heat recovery, "Controlled Natural Ventilation Systems for Non-residential Buildings", p. 62

▶ User comfort, "Greenhouse Gas Emissions – An Appropriate Target, Design and Assessment Parameter", p. 82

▶ Low-tech approach, "Sustainable Architecture in the Efficiency Trap?", p. 60

LESS

Digitally Customized Construction

Introduction to Digital Transformation by Moritz Dörstelmann

Demand for construction around the world continues unabated. The global population is still growing, peaking according to current forecasts in the second half of the 21st century. Despite the unequal distribution of opportunities, many of these people will succeed in improving their standard of living, which in turn will further increase construction activity. Since this coincides with the critical phase for avoiding climate tipping points within the same period, we need to quickly and significantly reduce emissions resulting from building activity while also finding qualitative ways to meet the construction demand to avoid the intensification of global distribution conflicts. Given the diverse sociocultural contexts around the world, this will inevitably take very different forms. As such, we face a common global problem for which there is no globally generalizable solution.

Obvious starting points are to incrementally improve existing building processes and materials, or to substitute them with alternative materials that cause lower emissions. For insulation materials and concrete, for example, there is great potential for short-term gains without fundamentally altering the existing modus operandi of the building sector. While this brings improvements, "business as usual" in a slightly modified form will not be enough. We also need novel low-emission building technologies. The key question here is how quickly can low-emission construction methods achieve a scale of implementation sufficient to bring significant climate benefits?

Exciting solutions to some of these problems can be found in the past. For centuries, regional building methods evolved that are adapted to local climates and use locally available materials. While a return to archaic ways of building and living is neither desirable nor feasible, whether in construction or in other sectors such as agriculture, we can transfer their qualities into the future with the help of advanced or even still-to-be-developed building techniques. Like their pre-industrial, artisanal counterparts, such building methods need to be low-energy and low-emission processes that harness natural and local materials flows. To combine these goals with the requirements of efficient building methods, we must find ways to digitally reinterpret regional and historical building methods that go beyond merely automating their steps.

Integrative computational design and fabrication processes have the potential to realize this on multiple levels. Computational generation and robotic implementation of complex material configurations can tap into the potential of high-resolution performative differentiation of building components that facilitates digital mass-customization approaches, but also significantly reduce the grey energy embedded within a structure through the load-adapted use of hybrid material systems. In addition, it becomes possible to close local material cycles and reduce emissions resulting from processing, transport and assembly by developing small-scale mobile production units for deployment in flexible, local mini-factories or by using mobile robotics directly on the construction site.

The combination of energy-efficient processing methods for simple materials and digital construction and fabrication technology can contribute significantly to reducing emissions in the construction industry. To put this into action within a realistic time horizon, we need both further applied research in the field as well as forward-looking, risk-tolerant entrepreneurship to rapidly bring such low-emission construction technologies to market.

BUILDING MORE WITH LESS MATERIAL

Integrative Computational Design and Construction

Commentary by Jan Knippers and Achim Menges

Over the course of the 20th century, we have seen modern construction systems become increasingly simplified to favour repeatable elements made of isotropic materials that are straightforward to use and to manufacture. Although these consume more material than necessary, they are still cheaper economically than investing additional cost and effort in optimizing material usage for building constructions.

An example of this is the ubiquitous flat concrete slab ceiling supported at regular intervals by columns: its flat underside makes it quick to produce but requires greater quantities of steel and concrete due to the concentration of loads at the points of support. Ribbed slabs or floor slabs supported by columns with mushroom-shaped crowns sustain the same loads with less material. Although these were once commonplace until the mid-20th century, they have since practically disappeared from use. They are simply not cost-effective to produce as the material cost of mass-producible reinforced concrete is comparatively cheap while labour costs for planning and manufacture have risen consistently.

The need to find ways to address climate change is now forcing us to rethink this paradigm. As soon as ecological costs are factored into the equation alongside economic costs, the situation changes: anisotropic materials, structurally articulated building elements and load-responsive structural forms then become more suitable. Today, such resource-optimized systems can only be produced cost-effectively using consistent, integrated digital design and production. No one single building system will be able to address all the challenges ahead: we will need low-carbon concrete construction methods for infrastructure projects as well as flexible timber construction systems for multi-storey buildings.

To progress beyond merely optimizing existing construction methods and to be more ecological, we need to invest in fundamental, open-ended research into computational design methods and robotic fabrication processes. The introduction of reinforced concrete some 150 years ago transformed the building industry. Now additive and autonomous processes have the potential to enable completely new approaches to building. Examples include the robotic filament winding of natural fibres or additive printing of bio-based matrix systems. While not all these methods may find their way into common building practice, we still need new approaches, and therefore also more fundamental research into climate-neutral ways of building.

Further Reading

▶ Efficient use of materials, "Strength through Geometry and Material Effectiveness", *Circular Construction and Circular Economy*, p. 72
▶ Reinforced concrete construction, "The Reuse Potential of Steel Profiles for Hybrid Multi-storey Construction", p. 116
▶ Natural fibres, "Digital Craft and Circular Construction", p. 110

Different

DIFFERENT

Rethinking System Boundaries for the Energy Transition

Introduction to Clean Energy Transition by Andreas Wagner

The energy transition is well underway – or so it seems based on the number of news features, articles and discussions that appear almost daily in the media. But how is it progressing? Where do we stand? As yet, unfortunately, the facts are not really promising – we lag so far behind the agreed climate targets that it seems the longstanding aim to limit global warming to 1.5 degrees is no longer attainable.

Why is that? The path has been agreed upon: most of the world acknowledges the need to be climate neutral by 2050 at the latest in order to maintain a tolerable global climate. Where there is no agreement, however, is who should make which contributions to this, as industrialized countries have long been living at the expense of the developing and emerging countries. In this context, the model of the 2,000-watt society conceived in Switzerland represents an interesting proposal for a form of global equity that – based on an average level of energy consumption of 17,520 kWh per person in 2010 – allocates every person in the world the same primary energy budget (and thus also the same emissions budget). If this demand can be satisfied in future using renewable energy sources, then we will have achieved an energy supply system that is sustainable across the board. Those consuming much higher levels of energy must accordingly make a greater effort to reduce consumption.

A further impediment to a faster energy transition is the comparatively slow implementation of pricing carbon emissions around the world. Had this been introduced earlier, more uniformly and with a more consistent rate of increase, along with accompanying emissions trading, then many of the current debates on subsidy programmes or exemptions for specific technologies would not be necessary. Indeed, the revenue this would have generated could have supported measures to increase energy efficiency and the use of renewable energies, as well as to cushion accompanying social inequalities.

In the context of the building sector, sectoral emissions budgets – in Germany at least – falsify the full contribution of buildings to total emissions. Currently, greenhouse gas emissions attributed to the building sector only include locally produced emissions, such as those arising from the combustion of fossil fuels to provide heat. This means one could achieve zero emissions by simply switching to electricity-based heating (along with corresponding thermal insulation improvements) because the energy consumption for generating electricity is allocated to the energy sector. This method of accounting by source also means that so-called grey emissions resulting from the production and transportation of building materials and elements are not attributed to the building sector but to the industrial production sector.

At least this accounting method, which is based on international agreements on emissions accounting, does not impact on those planning objectives that are addressed by pre-defined calculation procedures – today proof of primary energy demand for building services, in future also of greenhouse gas emissions over a building's entire life cycle – which focus on actual occurring energy flows in the building. Here too, though, primary energy indicators do not tell the whole truth. Current calculation methods do not include, for example, the energy consumed by lifts and household or office appliances. Likewise, electromobility can affect the electricity consumed by a building when it is equipped with a charging station.

We must, therefore, consider system boundaries at different levels – at the level of the building when planning integrated energy concepts (for example, where an electric vehicle can be considered an additional storage medium for self-generated solar power) and at the sector level when calculating the balance of greenhouse gas emissions. If we were to calculate balance according to the polluter pays principle – rather than the current point of source principle – it would rapidly show where and why changes are necessary and in turn stimulate corresponding technical innovations.

A good example of breaking down system boundaries is the P2G&H project described in this chapter. Here, green hydrogen is produced using surplus solar energy which in this project is not used to heat buildings because, in the long term, hydrogen will only be a niche application in buildings, as the need for hydrogen is much greater and more urgent in industry. The project instead employs waste heat from electrolysis to feed a district heating grid, thereby significantly increasing the overall system efficiency of the power-to-gas-and-heat concept. This synergy between green hydrogen production for industry and district heating is an excellent example of the much-vaunted sector coupling: a coordinated approach to different energy supply and demand concepts using different forms of energy and their conversion to create cross-sectoral integral energy concepts that serve both individual buildings and the entire neighbourhood.

Wind-to-heat systems represent a similar approach in which surplus electricity from wind turbines is converted to heat and put into district-level thermal storage. While these may prove to be interim solutions until sufficient infrastructure becomes available in the form of more efficient power grids and electrical storage capacity, such cross-sectoral solutions serve to reduce emissions instead of capping surpluses from renewable energy systems (and thus allowing them to go unused) when power grids are overloaded.

Another essential aspect for advancing the energy transition is digitalization. Here, too, progress has been too slow. Power grids are still unprepared to cope with the expected dramatic rise in heat pumps and photovoltaic systems, not just with respect to capacity but also the requisite intelligent smart-grid management systems. Broad adoption of new heating systems will only happen when appropriately transparent incentives are created for end customers to economically operate heat pumps and solar power systems. For this, buildings throughout the country need to be equipped with high-resolution smart meters that can respond to dynamically changing electricity tariffs depending on the respective supply of renewable energy. For the grid operators, these are also an essential prerequisite for incorporating bi-directional grid-serving strategies to avoid overloading the power grid.

The coupling of energy and digitalization can also be taken to a new level in the automated operation and regulation of buildings. New data modelling techniques and machine learning methods make it possible to better map and forecast the operating patterns of buildings and thus their energy performance with a view to improving energy efficiency. This can be extended even further to incorporate and model specific data captured from building users through mobile apps and smart watches, allowing their individual comfort needs to be incorporated into an energy-efficient indoor climate-control system. This chapter therefore also examines the intelligent linking of these two systems.

GREEN-HOUSE GAS EMISSIONS – AN APPRO-PRIATE TARGET, DESIGN AND ASSESSMENT PARAMETER

Commentary by
Thomas Lützkendorf and
Alexander Passer

An important aspect in building design is to minimize the energy demand for the operation of buildings and to limit the consumption of non-renewable primary energy to meet that demand. The aim is to supply buildings with energy that comes predominantly from renewable sources. Corresponding energy concepts thus also contribute to protecting natural resources, which is a central objective of the environmental dimension of a sustainable development. The task of protecting natural resources is as important as ever and is reflected in the EU's Energy Performance of Buildings Directive (EPBD) in the form of limits to the "total primary energy demand" of buildings.

In future, however, we need to go further and design buildings that can operate with little or no negative impact on the climate. Therefore, alongside protecting natural resources, a further important target is to design buildings with no operational greenhouse gas emissions (GHG), or at least with a (net-zero) balance of corresponding emissions.

Resource and climate protection thus become equal and complementary targets in building design. In a first step, the energy demand of buildings must be reduced – in line with the "zero-carbon-ready" approach of the International Energy Agency (IEA)[1] – to a level that allows them to be supplied with decarbonized energy immediately or in the medium term. In a second step, the energy supply must be ensured, preferably with energy from renewable sources. As such, it is no longer sufficient to evaluate and demonstrate fulfilment of these two targets using a single design and assessment parameter. Especially in the case of building concepts that claim to be climate-friendly or climate-neutral, the balance of greenhouse gas emissions should also be demonstrated.

The target value on the one hand – zero or net-zero greenhouse gas emissions as a contribution to climate protection – and the assessment criteria as well as the indicator on the other – the global warming potential over a 100-year horizon, measured in CO_2-equivalent emissions, which aggregates greenhouse gas emissions into a sum parameter – must form a unit. Information on the levels of useful, final and primary energy demand and/or consumption should therefore be supplemented by corresponding information on the level of greenhouse gas emissions resulting from their energy consumption during operation. Many European countries are currently discussing whether, when and how this should be implemented. France[2] and Denmark[3] have already introduced corresponding requirements.

The authors advocate that such targets are better described by a system of several requirement parameters. The degree to which the goal of "climate neutrality" has been achieved must be determined, evaluated and reported through an appropriate target, design and assessment parameter – the Global Warming Potential (GWP) mentioned above. Greenhouse gas emissions resulting from the operation of buildings thus become a sub-quantity of the increasingly requested indicator of the greenhouse gas potential or carbon footprint of buildings.[4] International standards already exist to define how these should be determined and declared.[5]

However, a combined assessment of overall energy efficiency ("energy performance") and the greenhouse gas emissions ("carbon performance")[6] is not the only recommendation. In future, it will also be a question of quantifying energy input and greenhouse gas emissions as comprehensively as possible by incorporating, for example, energy consumed by technical building systems including building automation, user-related energy use and emissions from refrigerants. Here, too, European and international standards already provide guidance.[7]

The significant improvements in energy performance in recent years have given rise to an additional effect: an increase in the relative and absolute importance of embodied energy and embodied emissions resulting from the production, construction and maintenance of buildings.[8] The aim is to quantify, evaluate and specifically influence the use of resources and the impact on the environment over the entire building life cycle through the application of life cycle assessment. The IEA EBC Annex 57[9] and IEA EBC Annex 72[10] projects, both already completed, provide a basis for this. Information on the level of greenhouse gas emissions over the life cycle of buildings is already required as part of current sustainability assessment systems, such as the EU LEVEL(s)[11] system, the EU Taxonomy and national

1 International Energy Agency (2021). Net Zero by 2050 – a roadmap for the global energy sector. Revised version October 2021, https://iea.blob.core.windows.net/assets/deebef5d-0c34-4539-9d0c-10b13d840027/NetZeroby2050-ARoadmapfortheGlobalEnergySector_CORR.pdf.

2 Réglementation environnementale des bâtiments neufs (RE2020), Ministère de la Transition écologique (MTE), 2020, https://rt-re-batiment.developement-durable.gouv.fr/IMG/pdf/guide_re2020_dhup-cerema.pdf.

3 BR18 (bygningsreglementet.dk); https://www.oneclicklca.com/baeredygtighedsklassen-low-carbon-targets-for-denmark-construction/.

4 ISO 14067: 2018.

5 ISO 16745-1: 2017 and ISO 16745-2: 2017.

6 https://www.construction21.org/articles/h/carbon-performance-a-necessary-complement-to-energy-performance-eu-buildings-policy-should-address-the-carbon-footprint-of-construction-says-bpie.html.

7 EN 15978-1 (in development) and ISO 16745-1: 2017.

8 M. Röck, M. R. M. Saade, M. Balouktsi, F. N. Rasmussen, H. Birgisdottir, R. Frischknecht, G. Habert, T. Lützkendorf and A. Passer, "Embodied GHG emissions of buildings – The hidden challenge for effective climate change mitigation", *Applied Energy*, 258, 2020, https://doi.org/10.1016/j.apenergy.2019.114107.

9 Annex 57 – Evaluation of Embodied Energy and CO_2eq for Building Construction, 2014, International Energy Agency, Energy in Buildings and Communities Programme, http://www.annex57.org.

funding programmes. The draft of the above-mentioned EU EPBD stipulates that greenhouse gas emissions in the life cycle of buildings will in future be additionally stated in the energy performance certificate. Further work is also being undertaken on ways to implement these approaches in planning and legislative processes, including a new IEA EBC Annex 89.[12] The authors encourage support for these objectives. The identification, assessment and targeted influencing of greenhouse gas emissions, initially during building operation, but then also over the entire life cycle of a building, makes an important contribution to achieving climate neutrality for buildings and the building stock and thus to sustainable development.

Further Reading

▶ Greenhouse gas emissions, "The Clean Energy Transition in the Context of Sustainability", p. 20

▶ Life cycle analysis, "The Economy of Urban Mining", *Circular Construction and Circular Economy,* p. 80

▶ Embodied energy, "Principles of Circular Construction", *Circular Construction and Circular Economy,* p. 22

10 Annex 72 – Assessing Life Cycle Related Environmental Impacts Caused by Buildings, 2016-2023, International Energy Agency, Energy in Buildings and Communities Programme, https://annex72.iea-ebc.org.

11 Level(s) – European framework for sustainable buildings, 2021, European Commission, https://environment.ec.europa.eu/topics/circular-economy/levels_enu.

12 Annex 89 – Ways to Implement Net-zero Whole Life Carbon buildings, 2023-2027, International Energy Agency, Energy in Buildings and Communities Programme, https://www.iea-ebc.org/projects/project?AnnexID=89.

OCCUPANT-CENTRIC BUILDING CONTROL

The Role of Occupants in Building Operation

Article by Matthias Berning

The divergent goals of balancing occupant needs and comfort with resource consumption describe an inherent conflict in building operation. In a modern commercial building, this is addressed by a Building Management System (BMS) that monitors and controls the different services in the building, including lighting, heating, ventilation and air-conditioning/cooling, as well as their energy consumption. Traditionally, these systems are configured on preset static temperature setpoints and scheduled setbacks, defined during the planning phase and sometimes adjusted during commissioning, but normally not during ongoing operation. Although the settings rely on existing industry standards and some input from prospective tenants, they rarely match with the real utilization of the building. Given the diverse and dynamic nature of occupants' needs and expectations, this is not surprising, however, it leads either to partly inefficient operation or a decrease in user satisfaction. In a way, occupant behaviour is regarded as a disturbance in classical building control, as the main obstacle to reaching truly optimal building operation. The ensuing energy performance gap (the difference between planned/simulated and real energy consumption) is even attributed increasingly to the tenants, even though more focused research is needed to understand this effect.[1]

Ultimately, buildings are constructed to be used by people, for living, working or other purposes. Accordingly, Occupant-Centric Control (OCC) should strive to respond in realtime to their presence, preferences and intents. In this way, energy is only used when and where needed to heat, cool or illuminate a given space, with the target of reaching the desired level of comfort. OCC can reduce overall energy use by sustaining the dynamic balance between occupant needs and resource consumption. On a small scale, this concept has already been implemented in Building Automation Systems (BAS), e.g., by turning on lights only when people are present and there is no or insufficient natural illumination.

Scaling this approach to the indoor environment as influenced by Heating, Ventilation and Air Conditioning (HVAC) is more challenging. These systems usually supply larger zones or even the whole building, including multiple rooms and a larger number of occupants. On a temporal scale, it might take more than an hour to transition from idle operation to an intended setpoint, requiring predictive control to reach energy savings. Additional thermal comfort factors include environmental conditions such as air velocity, temperature gradients or spatial asymmetries and the different seasons, as well as personal factors like activity and clothing level. To solve this challenge, OCC requires additional sensors combined with occupants' preferences, either expressed explicitly via user interfaces or inferred through data-driven analysis of building interactions (Fig. 1). First studies on OCC showed potential energy savings of 20 % and more.[2] Integrating more detailed occupant models in combination with appropriate control strategies should yield even better results.

INPUTS FOR OCCUPANT-CENTRIC CONTROL

There are multiple sources of information about building occupants. Each of them provides different levels of granularity and features individual strengths and weaknesses. The granularity of information can be described in two dimensions. One is spatial resolution, indicating whether the information can be mapped to individual control zones or only to the building as a whole. The other dimension refers to the type of occupant information[2] (as illustrated in Fig. 2) and is either related to occupancy or thermal comfort. Occupancy considers occupant presence, count and individual position of people, while comfort modality can be further divided into personal conditioning and the collective preferences based on different strategies.

Existing sensors of BAS provide feedback for the HVAC control and enable its basic functionality. The most common types are temperature sensors, ideally multiple sensors per zone. Additional indoor environmental sensors report relative humidity and CO_2 concentration for ventilation control. All of these are also indirect indicators for the presence and number of persons in a certain zone. More information can be gathered from binary sensors on windows and doors and from user interfaces like thermostat controls or light switches

1 Ardeshir Mahdavi, Christiane Berger, Hadeer Amin, Eleni Ampatzi and Rune Andersen, Elie Azar, Verena Barthelmes, Matteo Favero, Jakob Hahn, Dolaana Khovalyg, Henrik Knudsen, Alessandra Luna Navarro, Astrid Roetzel, Fisayo Sangogboye, Marcel Schweiker, Mahnameh Taheri, Despoina Teli, Marianne Touchie and Silke Verbruggen, "The Role of Occupants in Buildings' Energy Performance Gap: Myth or Reality?", *Sustainability*, 13, 2021, https://doi.org/10.3390/su13063146.

2 Wooyoung Jung and Farrakh Jazizadeh, "Human-in-the-loop HVAC operations: A quantitative review on occupancy, comfort, and energy-efficiency dimensions", *Applied Energy*, 239, 2019, pp. 1471–1508.

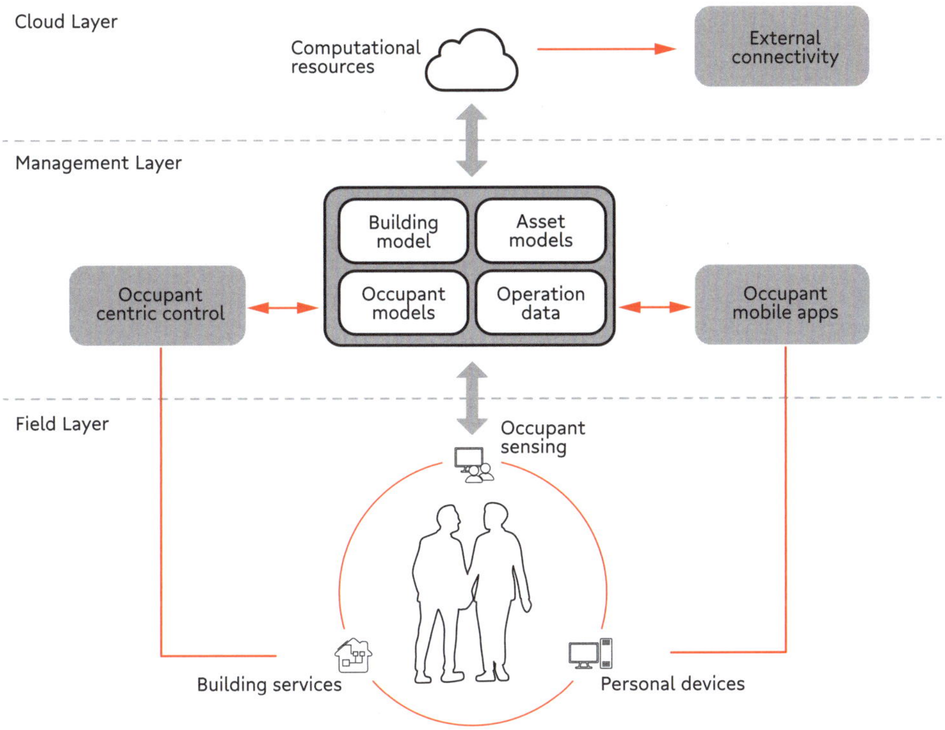

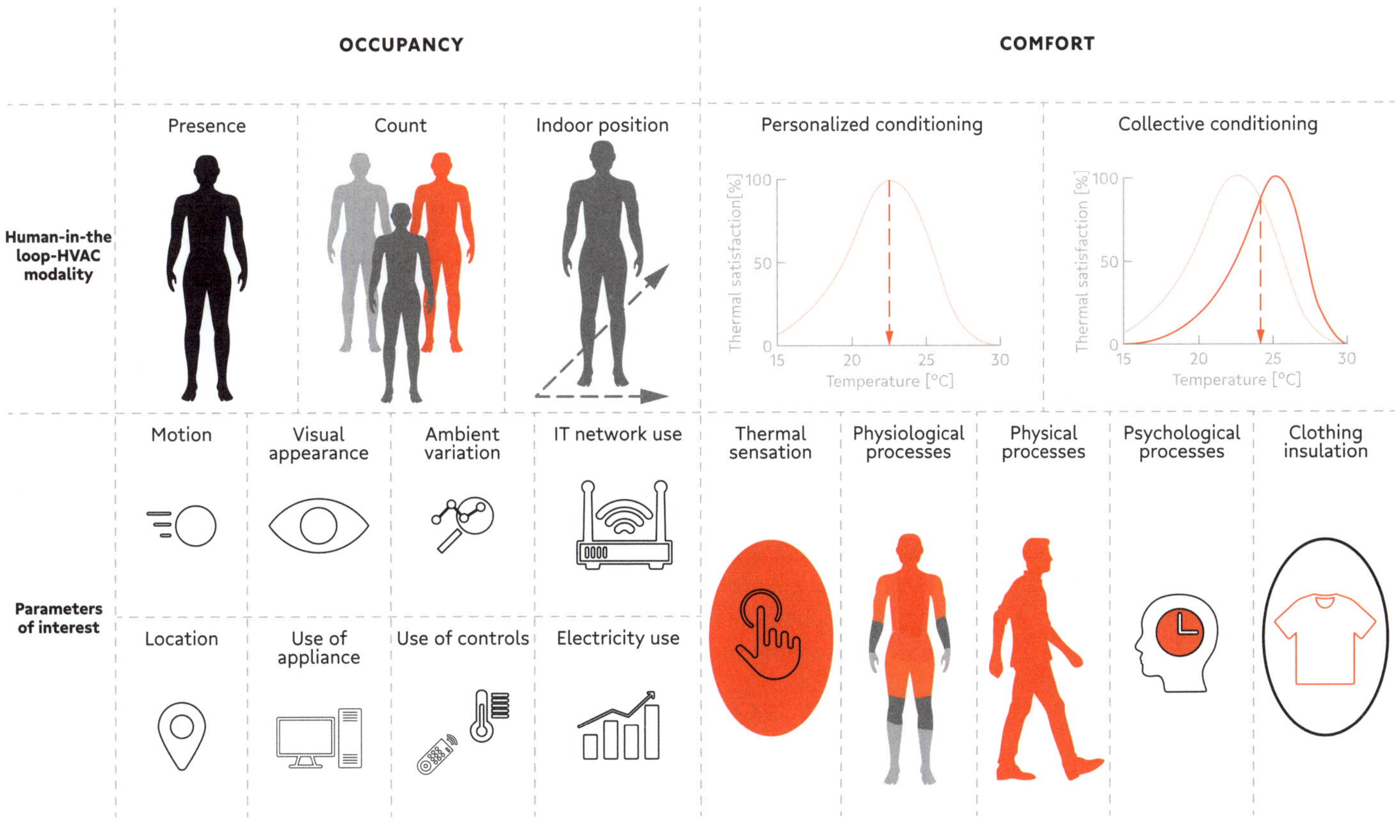

1

System architecture for data-driven occupant-centric building controls. The control system has access to multiple information sources and rich computational resources to optimize the building operation.

2

Human-in-the-loop HVAC modalities of occupancy and comfort along with their parameters of interest.

Based on: Wooyoung Jung and Farrakh Jazizadeh, "Human-in-the-loop HVAC operations: A quantitative review on occupancy, comfort, and energy-efficiency dimensions", *Applied Energy*, 239, 2019, pp. 1471–1508.

3

Mean accuracy of occupancy count as a function of time for a door counting sensor with 1.4 % counting error rate and different mitigation strategies.

- Symmetric error no reset $T_{correct}$ = 69.9 %
- Discard negative occupancy $T_{correct}$ = 82.2 %
- Reset at empty room $T_{correct}$ = 98.0 %

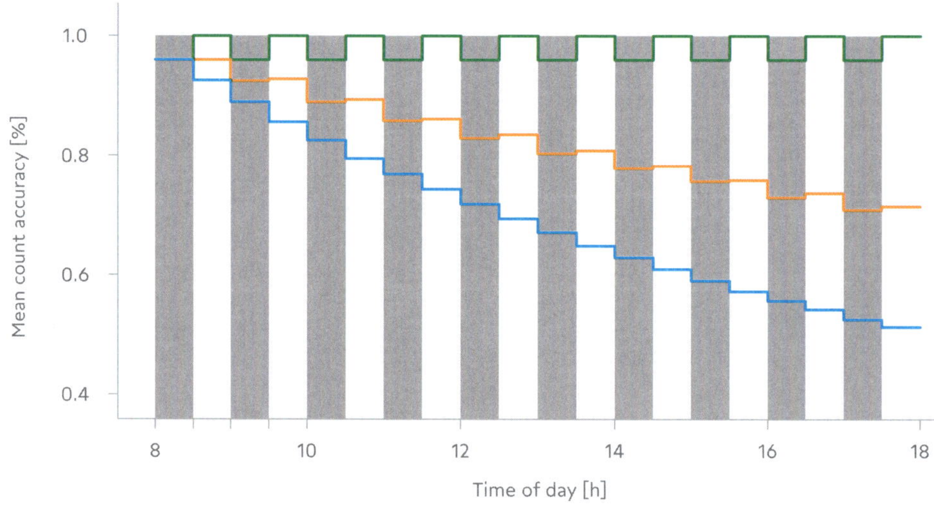

and dimmers. While it is more difficult to gather information about the number of persons present from building controls, their explicit interaction with these can show the intents and needs of occupants (e.g., heating the room or requesting fresh air).

Dedicated occupant detection and counting sensors are increasingly used to monitor occupants throughout the building. While regular motion detectors will only provide data about the presence in a certain field of view, doorway sensors can count the number of persons, and camera-based options can even report on their location within a larger space. Other common approaches include the counting of active electronic devices in a corporate Wi-Fi network and radar-based scanning with ultrasonic or electromagnetic waves. The right choice will depend on different factors, including cost, coverage and the preservation of the occupants' privacy.[3] Typically, explicit occupancy-counting sensors will exhibit a higher robustness and accuracy, but our long-term tests also revealed errors.

Such technical inaccuracies should be expected and mitigated in the control. Fig. 3 shows the plot of an overhead counting sensor in the doorway of a meeting room and its error probability over one simulated day. Even a very low error rate of 1.4 % per threshold crossing will result in a high probability to report an empty room as occupied, leading to energy wastage. Therefore, it is advisable to use counting systems that can track the entire zone, or at least use a conventional PIR detector to reset the count to zero when no one is present.

Occupants' personal devices, such as mobile phones and wearables, enable rich interaction and connectivity with the building infrastructure. This is already exploited in apps for occupants which allow them to reserve a shared desk, book a conference room or even provide input to the building controls. These digital user interfaces can be further employed in multiple ways to gather occupant preferences. Explicit manipulations of the temperature setpoint provide clear information on intent, but are often too infrequent to generate a user model. Incentivizing occupants to share their preference profiles is an option, using the personal device as a wallet and a medium to transfer this data. Other options include solicited feedback or just-in-time surveys. Strategically querying users regarding their personal comfort – on the smartphone, laptop or smartwatch,[4] and well balanced to not overload the user – will provide more timely feedback for the building control.

CONTROL STRATEGIES

Conventionally, a BMS will provide setpoints based on schedules and other inputs to a BAS, which in turn will use a control strategy to influence the available actuators (e.g., cooling valve, fan speed, damper opening, etc.) to reach a desired state. Today, most installed systems still rely on reactive strategies, including simple on/off sequencing or closed loop PID control, which only alter the current state after an event is detected. As described earlier, this is appropriate if the reaction is very fast, e.g., for lighting, but is less

3 Christian Groß, Reuben Borrison, Johannes Schmitt and Markus Aleksy, "Towards an Occupancy Count Functionality for Smart Buildings – An Industrial Perspective", in *2020 2nd IEEE International Conference on Industrial Electronics for Sustainable Energy Systems (IESES)*, Cagliari, Italy, 2020, pp. 331–336, https://doi.org/10.1109/IESES45645.2020.9210641.

4 Prageeth Jayathissa, Matias Quintana, Mahmoud Abdelrahman and Clayton Miller, "Humans-as-a-Sensor for Buildings – Intensive Longitudinal Indoor Comfort Models", *Buildings*, 10, 174, 2020, https://doi.org/10.3390/buildings10100174.

ideal when dealing with slow systems like HVAC operation. Using, for example, a control application to change the indoor temperature from a setback to a target setpoint after an occupant entered the room will either waste energy by preemptively reducing the difference between idle and target temperature, or will impact user comfort during the time it takes to reach the desired state.

Predictive control strategies strive to reach an optimum between energy consumption and user comfort. In the previous example, the BAS would anticipate the presence of a user based on a predictive model and precondition the room at an acceptable range when the user enters. These methods are characterized by a prediction horizon, which describes the timespan that the algorithm will have to look into the future, to determine an optimal series of control signals. This approach will vary according to the building and control targets. A well-known method is Model Predictive Control (MPC), which relies on a model of the system, the system inputs and potential disturbances. MPC will optimize the control output for all time steps within the prediction horizon, given the current and previous states as well as forecasted inputs. Depending on the size of the state space and the complexity of the optimization method, this method can become computationally expensive.[5] Even with current advances in data storage and processing, the tradeoffs for implementing MPC in BAS are quite limiting. Therefore, alternative approaches explore offloading the complex calculations into a higher-level system. Highly detailed deterministic models can be substituted with a surrogate, so-called black-box or grey-box models, which are data-driven approaches. Overall, acquiring and validating these models is one of the major obstacles in their widespread adoption. In the case of OCC for HVAC, the system will require a thermal building model, an HVAC system model and, crucially, one or multiple occupant models.[6] While the former two can be traced back to physical equations, given sufficient information, the latter must be inferred from behavioural data.

A different predictive control strategy is the Machine Learning (ML) approach of Reinforcement Learning (RL) trained in an active control system. The algorithm changes its control variables based on the current state and observes the end-to-end system behaviour. Based on the optimization goals, a score will be computed which is fed back to the algorithm. If the energy efficiency and/or occupant satisfaction goals are met, the algorithm will reinforce the latest behaviour. If by contrast it gets a negative rating, it will avoid this behaviour in similar situations and try something else. RL adapts to user behaviour without requiring any implicit modelling, however, the trial and error procedure can become quite unpleasant. As such, it is advisable to initialize these algorithms in a simulation environment – which will, again, require good models. Overall, the described algorithms can reach a similar performance as MPC, with different strengths and weaknesses.[7]

OCCUPANT MODELLING

Different types of occupant models vary according to the required outputs. Thermal comfort models describe the satisfaction or state of occupants in view of the environmental conditions of an interior space. Occupancy models aim to determine the presence of occupants in an individual space, or the number of occupants in a zone or building. The target of behavioural models is to predict the interaction with the building, e.g., opening a window or lowering the shading, usually driven by the need to restore comfortable conditions,[8] as shown in Fig. 4.

Historically, statistical modelling within a large number of systematic observations has been used when trying to identify a generic model as source of information. A well-known example is the Fanger model for thermal comfort, codified into building standards.[9] It defines the "Predicted Mean Vote" as an index to judge indoor environmental conditions. For interactions with the building and occupancy patterns, sequential stochastic models like Markov chains have been employed successfully. One drawback of the global statistical approach is the tendency to suppress occupant diversity and individual differences in buildings and assets. It can also lack flexibility, keeping it from adapting to disruptive changes in occupant behaviour. Therefore, forthcoming modelling approaches are based on Machine

5 Ján Drgoňa, Javier Arroyo, Iago Cupeiro Figueroa, David Blum, Krzysztof Arendt, Donghun Kim, Enric Perarnau Ollé, Juraj Oravec, Michael Wetter, Draguna L. Vrabie and Lieve Helsen, "All you need to know about model predictive control for buildings", *Annual Reviews in Control*, 50, 2020, pp. 190–232, https://doi.org/10.1016/j.arcontrol.2020.09.001.

6 "Occupant-Centric Sensing and Controls", in *ASHRAE Handbook — HVAC Applications*, Ch. 65, American Society of Heating, Refrigerating and Air-Conditioning Engineers, Atlanta, GA, 2019.

7 Phillip Stoffel, Laura Maier, Alexander Kümpel, Thomas Schreiber and Dirk Müller, "Evaluation of advanced control strategies for building energy systems", *Energy and Buildings*, 280, 2023, https://doi.org/10.1016/j.enbuild.2022.112709.

8 William O'Brien, Andreas Wagner, Marcel Schweiker, Ardeshir Mahdavi, Julia Day, Mikkel Baun Kjærgaard, Salvatore Carlucci, Bing Dong, Farhang Tahmasebi, Da Yan, Tianzhen Hong, H. Burak Gunay, Zoltan Nagy, Clayton Miller and Christiane Berger, "Introducing IEA EBC annex 79: Key challenges and opportunities in the field of occupant-centric building design and operation", *Building and Environment*, 178, 2020, https://doi.org/10.1016/j.buildenv.2020.106738.

9 ANSI/ASHRAE Standard 55, Thermal environmental conditions for human occupancy, American Society of Heating, Refrigerating and Air-Conditioning Engineers, Atlanta, GA, 2020.

Learning (ML), which focuses on the process of identifying underlying patterns in the given data and in order to reproduce these on demand.

Popular ML models for occupant behaviour comprise decision trees and related random forests and support vector machines and probabilistic graphical models. The large number of parameters of ML models can be initialized randomly or by transferring knowledge from a previous application. In the following training steps the parameters are adapted using a suitable algorithm, until the model has "learned" the relationship between the input and output data. The ensuing hypothesis is tested before use with a separate set of validation data. This automated process enables the use of local data for (re-)training and adaptation. The model can also be updated continuously over time using online learning.

While continuous learning is basically feasible for each time step, the training is quite resource-intensive, requiring a connection to external systems. The resulting models can provide very good predictions, but they usually lack explainability, i.e., it is hard to understand occupant needs or motivations from the final structure. Their performance also depends on the quality of the feature extraction, so that the input data needs to be preprocessed and selected manually to be effective.[10]

Recent advances in ML, known as Deep Learning (DL), are getting rid of these limitations by employing massive artificial neural networks with multiple layers. The first emerging layers are implicitly trained to interpret the raw input data in the most efficient ways. The following layers rely on the semantics encoded in the nodes of the neural network, producing intermediate representations and finally the model output. There are even more advantages of this subset of algorithms. Common models for this task, hidden Markov models and recurrent neural networks, more specifically the Long Short-Term Memory (LSTM) architecture, provide memory of varying depth in each node and can therefore encode temporal patterns from time-series data, which otherwise would exceed the depth of the model. Overall, these DL approaches can provide predictions with an accuracy of 90% and more.[11]

A drawback is that these benefits come at the cost of requiring massive amounts of training data and computation time. Current research aims to split this effort into multiple parts, teaching generic information about time series, building physics and causalities in a first step and subsequently feeding training data on a unique building for specialization. As ML is improving over time, it is likely that new algorithms will be found for occupant modelling as well.

SUSTAINABLE BUILDINGS ARE OCCUPANT-CENTRIC

It is expected that 90% of today's building stock will still be in operation by 2050. To reach net-zero goals, we need to improve the sustainability of the brownfield, which often operates without building automation and only simple HVAC control. Efficient building management including Occupant-Centric Operation is one of the key components along this path. The field is an active area of research and there are already concrete results. Overall, it is hard to determine the exact energy savings provided by a certain algorithm or modelling approach in a real deployment, since there are many confounding factors. As stated in the introduction to this article, field studies measured improvements by 20% and up to 70%, showing the huge spread in results.[12] While simulations are a useful tool for direct comparison, they often assume idealized asset conditions. In practice, even simple OCC measures, such as presence detection and modelling of zone-specific schedules, can significantly improve the building performance. Specific occupant models are also beneficial to inform building retrofits by feeding simulations and certification; they can be used to understand space utilization, canteen queues and electric vehicle charging behaviour in the parking lot.

In part driven by the COVID-19 pandemic, the occupancy profiles of buildings seem to be increasingly dynamic as people and companies change workplace models more frequently. Building services are expected to exchange information with the electrical network and other external systems, thereby adding more complexity. OCC relies on a connected BAS with a central management layer, which brings its own benefits. In our

10 Salvatore Carlucci, Marilena De Simone, Steven K. Firth, Mikkel B. Kjærgaard, Romana Markovic, Mohammad Saiedur Rahaman, Masab Khalid Annaqeeb, Silvia Biandrate, Anooshmita Das, Jakub Wladyslaw Dziedzic, Gianmarco Fajilla, Matteo Favero, Martina Ferrando, Jakob Hahn, Mengjie Han, Yuzhen Peng, Flora Salim, Arno Schlüter and Christoph van Treeck, "Modeling occupant behavior in buildings", *Building and Environment*, 174, 2020, https://doi.org/10.1016/j.buildenv.2020.106768.

11 Zhe Wang, Tianzhen Hong and Mary Ann Piette, "Predicting plug loads with occupant count data through a deep learning approach", *Energy*, 181, 2019, pp. 29–42, https://doi.org/10.1016/j.energy.2019.05.138.

12 Wooyoung Jung and Farrakh Jazizadeh, "Human-in-the-loop HVAC operations: A quantitative review on occupancy, comfort, and energy-efficiency dimensions", *Applied Energy*, 239, 2019, pp. 1471–1508.

13 Uwe Laudenklos, "How smart, thinking buildings can help people feel better", ABB Conversations, https://www.abb-conversations.com/2022/07/how-smart-thinking-buildings-can-help-people-feel-better/ (accessed 14 February 2023).

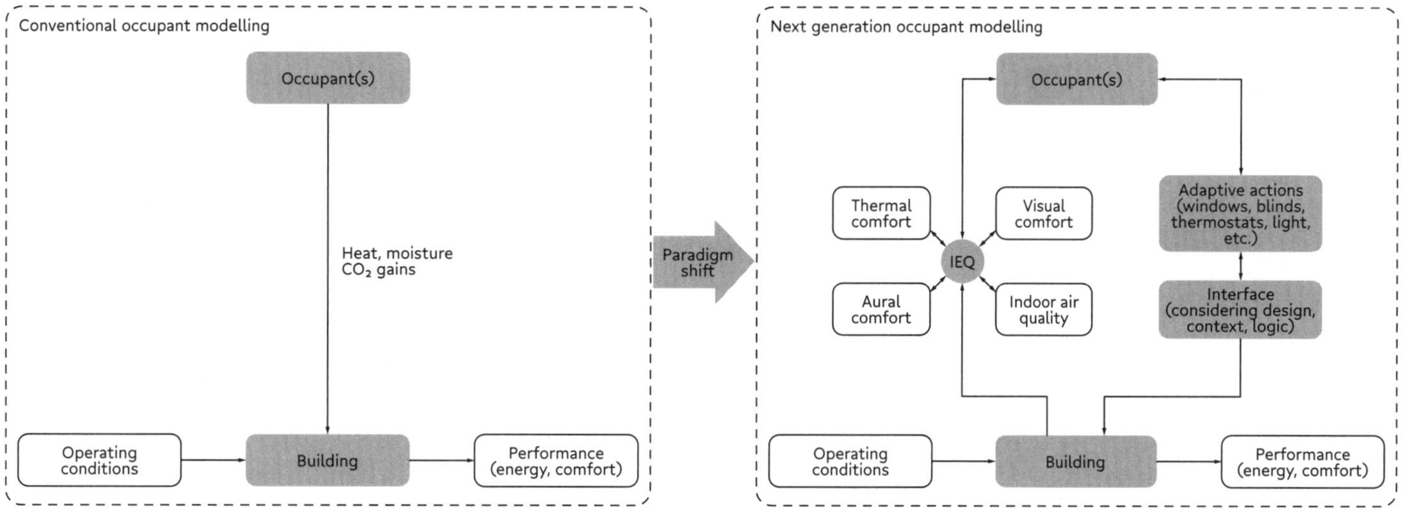

experience, retrofitting commercial smart building solutions can already provide efficiency gains of up to 30 %, achieved by rule-based automation and continuous monitoring and providing insight for manual optimization. The basic infrastructure of BAS provides transparency and flexibility to adapt operation and connect it to additional services for further analysis and optimization.[13] ML alone is no panacea. Instead, it needs to be conceived as a key component in a larger system. The combined application of data-driven optimization, cloud computing and distributed sensing is able to create sustainable places to meet, work and live.

Further Reading

▶ Comfort, "Controlled Natural Ventilation Systems for Non-residential Buildings", p. 62
▶ Passive systems, "Celebrating the Genius of Simplicity", p. 70
▶ User-centered planning, "Circular Construction Over Again", p. 142

4

Paradigm shift from occupants as passive participants in buildings to dynamic actors with multiple inputs and interactions.

Based on: William O'Brien, Andreas Wagner, Marcel Schweiker, Ardeshir Mahdavi, Julia Day, Mikkel Baun Kjærgaard, Salvatore Carlucci, Bing Dong, Farhang Tahmasebi, Da Yan, Tianzhen Hong, H. Burak Gunay, Zoltan Nagy, Clayton Miller and Christiane Berger, "Introducing IEA EBC annex 79: Key challenges and opportunities in the field of occupant-centric building design and operation", *Building and Environment*, 178, 2020, https://doi.org/10.1016/j.buildenv.2020.106738.

CLIMATE-NEUTRAL URBAN DISTRICT NEUE WESTSTADT, ESSLINGEN

The P2G&H Concept – Green Hydrogen with Waste Heat Utilization

Case Study by
M. Norbert Fisch

Green hydrogen has a key role to play in the drive to achieve the climate goal of net-zero greenhouse gas emissions and decarbonize the energy use of all consumption sectors. In the Neue Weststadt district of Esslingen in south-west Germany, the concept of P2G&H – Power to Gas and Heat – is being put to the test as part of an ongoing real-world laboratory project for a new "Climate-neutral Urban District". In this concept, green hydrogen is produced at the neighbourhood level close to the point of consumption and the waste heat it produces is utilized directly. The concept has been developed, planned and scientifically monitored – from implementation to the operation phase – by Steinbeis Innovation Center energyplus.

In 2010, the German Federal Ministry of Economic Affairs and Technology (BMWi) set out its plans for a transition to clean energy,[1] and the German government committed to ambitious targets to reduce greenhouse gas emissions[2] in its Climate Action Plan, in sync with the EU Green Deal.[3] To achieve these, the government will need to significantly ramp up the expansion of solar and wind energy farms: renewable energy production capacity will need to rise almost fivefold from the current level of approx. 110 GW (in Germany) to more than 500 GW by 2050 (Fig. 1).

This will cause a corresponding rise in surplus electricity output resulting from the fluctuating nature of renewable energy sources, which at present is non-usable. Rather than throttling overcapacity, as is currently the case, this surplus can be converted into hydrogen (Power to Gas, P2G) as a chemical energy carrier. Green hydrogen is therefore a key enabler of the clean energy transition. It can be used as a direct substitute for carbon fuels in many chemical processes, and, like natural gas, can be stored for extended periods of time without loss of capacity for later conversion back into energy – not only to cover dark lulls in renewable energy supply – through fuel cell CHP or gas turbine power plants.

Scientific studies confirm the central role that hydrogen has to play in the transition to a climate-neutral energy supply system. Over the coming two decades, green hydrogen will initially be used to advance decarbonization in industrial and mobility sectors, but from 2040 onwards its adoption in the building sector must also be accelerated if we are to reach the target of net-zero emissions. A study by Forschungszentrum Jülich on transformation strategies for the German energy system up to 2050 (FZJ, 2020)[4] predicts that hydrogen demand in Germany will reach 12 megatonnes (Mt) per year. Assuming that around half this hydrogen will be produced domestically, Germany will need to target an electrical output capacity of 50 to 60 gigawatts (GW) using electrolysis plants. A precondition for such green hydrogen production is that electrolyzers must operate during periods in which the proportion of renewable energy sources in the grid mix is as high as possible. With this approach, the mean number of full-load hours per year would lie between 4,000 and 5,000 hours. The waste heat that this level of hydrogen production would produce is estimated at around 110 terawatt hours (TWh) per year which, according to the BMWi in 2021, is roughly equivalent to the level of fossil-fuel fired district heating currently provided in Germany (approx. 104 TWh in 2020)![5]

From a strategic and economic perspective, the challenge is now to ramp up hydrogen production as efficiently as possible and to make best possible use of the potential of waste heat. The P2G&H concept follows exactly this principle. One approach is to construct decentralized electrolysis plants with a lower capacity (2–3-digit MW) close to customers of green hydrogen, for example in locations with good transport connectivity near urban conurbations. The resulting waste heat can then be efficiently used to supply local neighbourhoods using existing or newly constructed heat distribution networks. With this approach, the efficiency of hydrogen production can potentially be increased from approx. 55% to up to 85% (Fig. 2). In addition, producing energy and heat close to the point of consumption reduces transport distances and reinforces regional economic cycles.

1 Energy concept for an environmentally sound, reliable and affordable energy supply, Federal Ministry of Economic Affairs and Technology (BMWi), now the Federal Ministry for the Environment, Nature Conservation and Nuclear Safety (BMU) (28 September 2010).

2 Deutscher Bundestag, publication 19/13900, 2019.

3 European Green Deal: Commission proposes transformation of EU economy and society to meet climate ambitions, European Commission, 2021, https://ec.europa.eu/commission/presscorner/detail/en/IP_21_3541.

4 M. Robinius et al., "Wege für die Energiewende. Kosteneffiziente und klimagerechte Transformationsstrategien für das deutsche Energiesystem bis zum Jahr 2050", Schriften des Forschungszentrums Jülich, Energie & Umwelt Series, Vol. 499, 2020.

5 Energiewende Direkt, https://www.bmwi-energiewende.de/EWD/Redaktion/Newsletter/2021/03/.

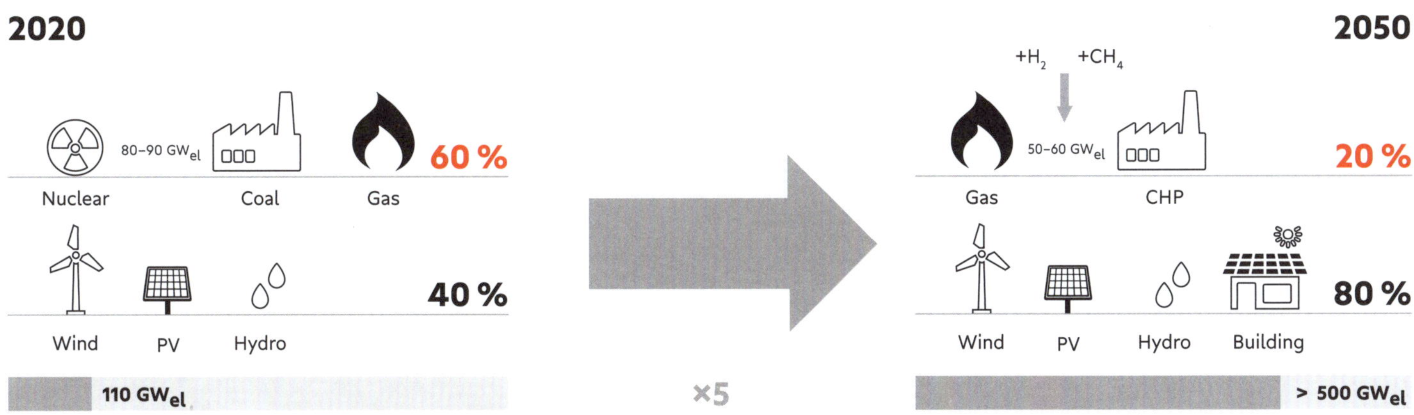

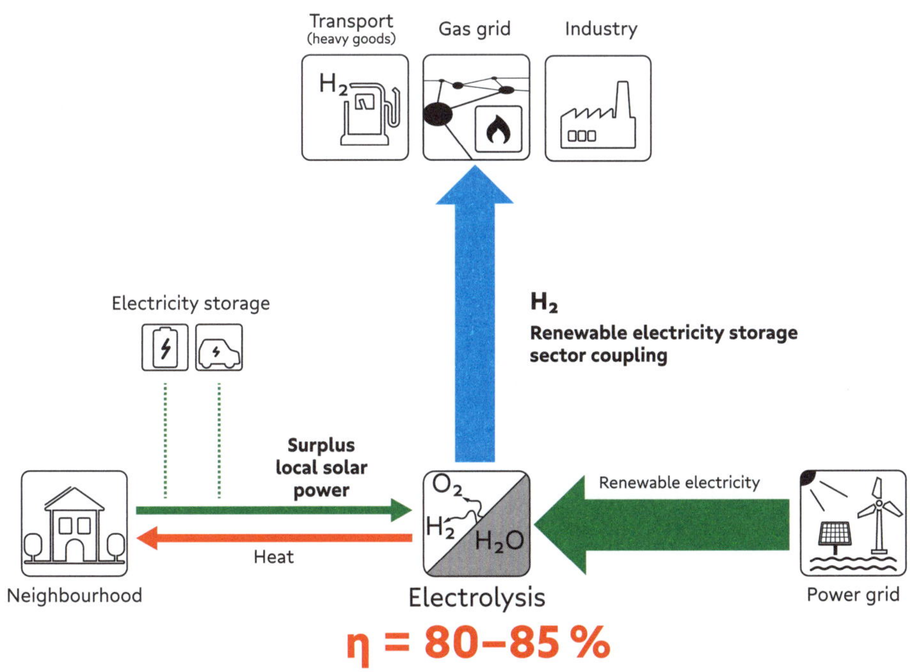

GREEN HYDROGEN

While hydrogen can be used as a substitute for fossil fuels, its full potential for mitigating climate change is only achieved when produced using renewable energy sources. This so-called green hydrogen is therefore the cornerstone of the P2G&H concept. To be compliant, the operators of electrolysis plants commit to producing green hydrogen, as per § 12i of the German Renewable Energy Sources Act from 14 July 2021 (BGBl. I, p. 2860), which stipulates that operators must undertake to use energy from renewable energy sources in Germany and to provide evidence in the form of guarantees of origin. The use of renewable energy minimizes the emissions burden of green hydrogen production. Supply agreements with regional wind and solar power plants, both existing and planned, are particularly suitable and additionally benefit local economies and in turn contribute to local acceptance.

The mode of operation of electrolysis plants as a component of the clean energy transition also benefits the energy system. To achieve net-zero emissions, it is necessary to flexibly control the integration of renewable energy power plants into the power

1

Necessary expansion of photovoltaic and wind energy capacities.

Based on: M. Norbert Fisch, 2019, lecture Zukunftsstadtkonferenz, Münster.

2

Conceptual approach of P2G&H – increased efficiency for the production and utilization of green hydrogen.

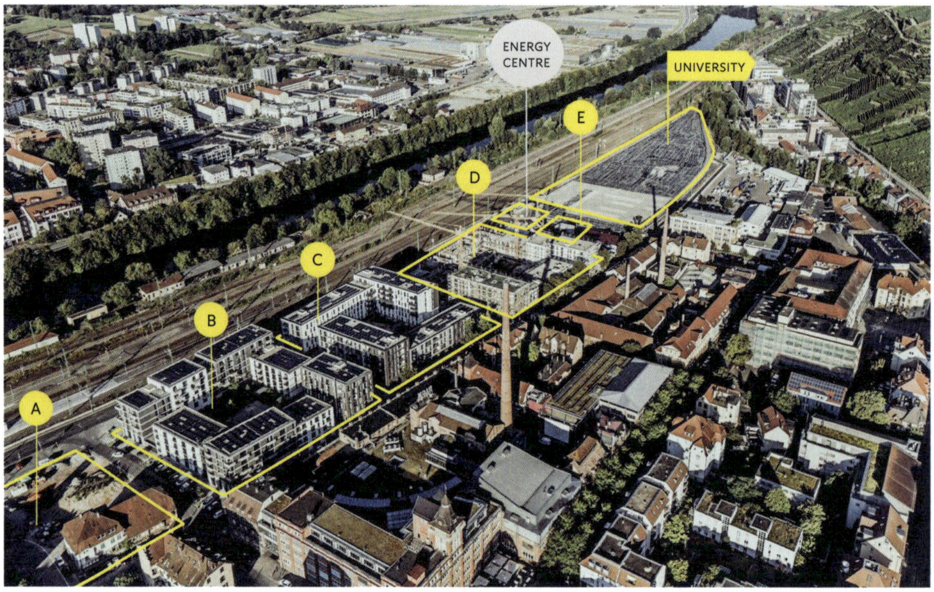

3

Neue Weststadt, Esslingen – residential blocks A to D, office tower E and university campus.

system. A study on the need for a new electricity market design commissioned by the BEE Federal Association for Renewable Energy in 2021[6] cites that electrolyzers can make a fundamental contribution to stabilizing the market and supply system in future by affording greater flexibility to the renewable energy market. The study concludes that the provision of an overall electrolysis capacity of up to 100 GW_{el} in Germany could strengthen the economic resilience and independence of the entire system.

A breakdown of electricity generation sources shows that in 2022 the greenhouse gas emission factor averages around 400 g/kWh in Germany. Assuming that electrolyzers are operated during periods with a high proportion of renewable energies, the emission factor falls to around 275 g/kWh for those periods.[7] With the increasing expansion of renewable electricity generation, the emission factors will decrease further. In a fully decarbonized electricity system, or if energy purchases are certified as being 100 % from renewable sources, the emission factor will eventually tend towards zero.

A FLAGSHIP PROJECT IN ESSLINGEN

Since 2016, an approx. 12 ha inner-city site in the Swabian town of Esslingen am Necker in south-west Germany has served as a real-world laboratory for researching the implementation of a clean energy transition. Conceived as a flagship project for climate-neutral urban districts, it is funded by the Federal Ministry of Economic Affairs and Climate Protection (BMWK) and the Federal Ministry of Education and Research (BMBF) as part of the "Solar Construction/ Energy-Efficient Towns" funding initiative.

A joint venture between the City of Esslingen as the lead applicant and 13 partners in total, the project is being funded with EUR 12 million between 2016 and 2024. The overall scientific and organizational coordination is provided by Steinbeis Innovation Center (SIZ) energyplus in Stuttgart. An interdisciplinary team of researchers (from the fields of technology and social sciences), practitioners, facilitators and public participators was brought together to address the broad range of sectors and technical aspects within the project.

The goal of the new climate-neutral urban district is to reduce its annual carbon emissions to less than 1 tonne per inhabitant for housing and mobility by utilizing waste heat from the local production of hydrogen. This also contributes to the city's goal to reduce carbon emissions across the city by a quarter. The new district will also play an essential role in the ongoing drive to achieve further climate goals.

The urban design concept developed by Lehen drei Architekten Stadtplaner SRL, Stuttgart, in 2013 encompasses four urban blocks (A to D) with a total of around 500 residential units and a mix of 70 % residen-

6 *Neues Strommarktdesign*, study commissioned by BEE e.V., 2021, https://www.klimaneutrales-stromsystem.de/pdf/Strommarktdesign-studie_BEE_final_Stand_14_12_2021.pdf. *New Electricity Market Design Study*. Abbreviated English-language synopsis: https://klimaneutrales-stromsystem.de/pdf/english/20211213_BEE_New%20Electricity_Market_Design_Study_Short_version_ENG.pdf.

7 Based on own calculations, SIZ energyplus, Stuttgart.

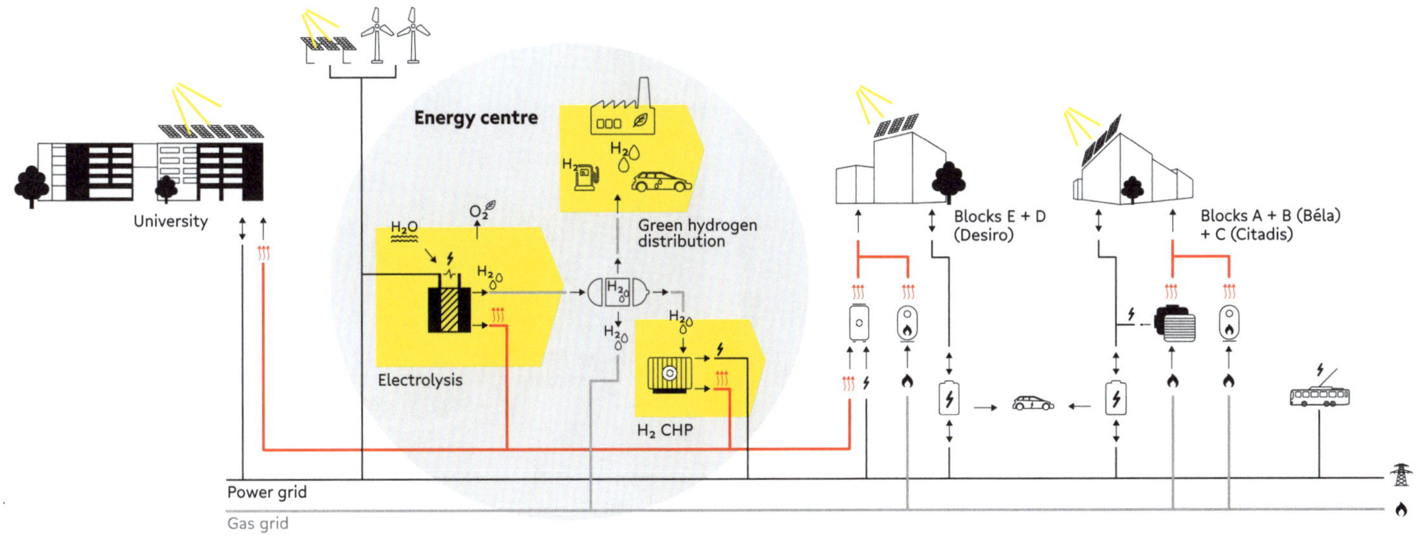

tial and 30 % commercial uses (Fig. 3). To the west of the new district square, a new building for Esslingen University of Applied Sciences was constructed with lecture halls, seminar rooms, offices, refectory, computer centre and a library (approx. 18,500 m² of usable space). The new university campus thus directly adjoins the residential and commercial blocks of the quarter and is close to both the city centre and railway station. At the edge of the district square, a 12-storey tower with offices and shops (approx. 7,500 m²) is planned, the so-called Crystal Rock (Block E), that will serve as a landmark for the site.

Designs for each of the individual urban blocks were determined through separate architecture competitions organized by the City of Esslingen and the developer RVI GmbH from Saarbrücken. The overall goals of the climate-neutral district were outlined in the competition briefs, stipulating, among other things, maximal use of roof surfaces for solar energy generation. The strong support and commitment of the city – represented by the mayor and the city administration – and the developer have been crucial to the success of the project.

ENERGY CONCEPT

The energy concept takes a holistic approach to cost effectiveness by reducing demand for heating and electricity and using energy generated from renewable sources. Ensuring the buildings are well insulated (almost to KfW efficiency house level EH 55) reduces the heating energy demand and results in a comfortable indoor climate.

Residential blocks A, B and C are supplied with bio-methane via the municipal gas mains (not actually but indirectly through the natural gas mix sourced by the Stadtwerke Esslingen, the municipal utility company). Cogeneration CHP plants and gas boilers in the respective buildings convert this into heat and electricity. The remaining residential block D, office tower E and the university campus building are connected to a local district heating network powered by the energy centre. This separation into two energy supply concepts came about as a result of delayed funding notices for the research project while the neighbourhood development advanced rapidly. Alongside the 1000 kW_{el} electrolyzer, the energy centre beneath the district square also contains a gas CHP plant (biomethane and H_2) and an electric heat pump to recover waste heat from the transformers and inverters, as well as a gas boiler. Its inner-city location also makes it possible to recover waste heat from the stack cooling (220 kW_{th}), greatly improving the efficiency of the system – an increase from approx. 55 % to over 85 % for the electrolysis. The waste heat from electrolysis (60–65 °C) covers about half of the overall annual heat demand (~1200 MWh/a) for the units it is connected to. To utilize the heat supplied by the district heating net-

4

Energy concept – waste heat utilization from green hydrogen production.

DIOR
HEAVY LIFT
www.diorheavylift.com

work, the relevant apartments are equipped with low-temperature heating systems (surface heating) and fresh water stations for domestic hot water.

The innovative heart of the energy centre is an alkaline electrolyzer (30 % caustic potash), divided into two skid-mounted 500 kW_{el} capacity units, which together convert around 5,000 MWh of renewable electricity into 85 t of hydrogen per year. To produce 1 kg of H_2 requires about 60 kWh of green electricity and 18 l of drinking water. To accommodate the start-up process of the electrolyzer, a horizontally mounted stainless steel cylindrical hydrogen tank is installed next to the electrolyzer unit.

The original plan for marketing the green hydrogen envisaged the construction of a hydrogen refueling station on the nearby premises of Esslingen's municipal utility, to complement the existing natural gas filling station for cars. As the project progressed, the decision was made to concentrate solely on charging stations for electric vehicles, with hydrogen use planned instead primarily for fuel cells used in heavy goods vehicles. The original plan to build a hydrogen refuelling station was therefore not implemented.

Another option investigated but ultimately not pursued was to supply hydrogen by truck for use in industry or vehicle refuelling stations. However, the low capacity of trailer tanks, which can hold around 15 MWh (equivalent to ~1,500 l of heating oil), the 40 tonnes vehicle weight and high investment costs for a 500-800 bar compressor mean that the cost of green hydrogen is unfavourably high compared to conventional hydrogen.

To supply large quantities of hydrogen, a suitable distribution network is required. As part of the H2 GeNeSiS project funded by the State of Baden-Württemberg and the EU, a hydrogen pipeline is planned to run between Stuttgart and Esslingen. Once built, the district's energy centre will then supply it with green hydrogen.

As an interim solution, the green hydrogen produced at 11.5 bar will initially be fed via a 180-m-long DN 40 stainless steel pipeline laid in sand to a gas pressure regulating and metering station, where it will then either be added to the mix in the existing medium- and low-pressure gas supply where it contributes to decarbonizing the gas network or, in research operation, converted back into electricity in a bivalent CHP cogeneration plant (biomethane: 200 kW_{el}, H_2: 150 kW_{el}).

The individual supply components are integrated into a cross-sector digital information network (smart grid). The energy flow can then be regulated according to the electricity market and demand in the supply area using a central energy management system.

The flat roofs of the district have been utilized for solar generation by installing photovoltaic panels in an east-west orientation for maximum gain. The total output of ~1400 kW is used in the first instance to supply the electricity needs of the residents and for e-mobility, with any surplus used for H_2 generation or fed back into the power grid.

A separate management and operating company was founded by the research consortium partners for the new climate-neutral district. The Green Hydrogen Esslingen GmbH (GHE) acts both as the investor for the plant and the main applicant for approvals. The company can draw on the expertise of its partners in dealing with gas supply (Stadtwerke Esslingen) and electricity market trading (Polarstern GmbH), as well detailed systematic knowledge of the operation of electrolysis plants. The fact that the partners already hold licenses for the local distribution of gas and electricity simplifies the subsequent application procedures.

In 2022, the Climate-neutral Urban District Neue Weststadt was awarded first prize in the sustainability category as part of the BMWK Federal Ministry for Economic Affairs and Climate Action's "Real-world Lab" programme.

TRIAL OPERATION AND INITIAL EXPERIENCES

After installation of the components in the energy centre, the plant modules were verified for compliance with industrial health and safety regulations by the inspection and certification body TÜV SÜD. Alongside an explosion safety audit, all safety mechanisms were subject to a Hazard and Safety Operability Study (HAZOP). All installations for producing hydrogen using electrolytic

5 ←

Installation of the two container skids in the energy centre. Each contains a 500 kW_{el} electrolysis stack.

6 ↙

Underground energy centre beneath the district square – two electrolysis units, each with a capacity of 500 kW_{el}.

7 ↑

Hydrogen storage tank (vol. ~34 m^3, max. 29 kg H_2, 11.5 bar) installed next to the electrolysis units.

8

The climate protection effects of different hydrogen utilization scenarios on the GHG balance of the district.

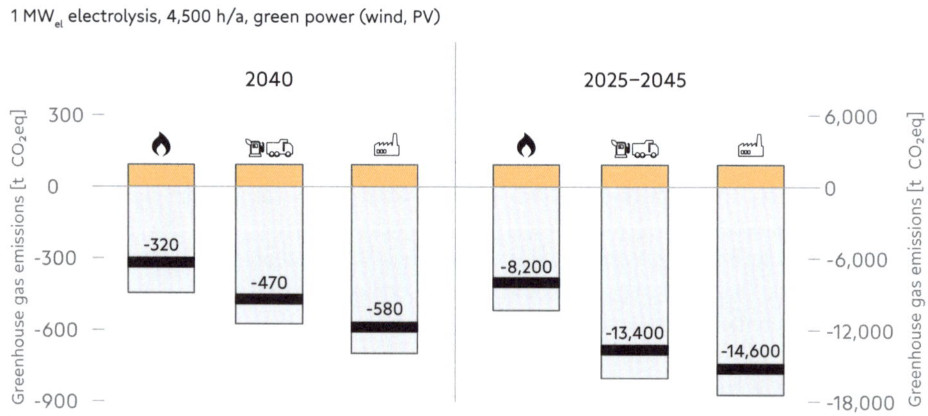

Road closure and trench excavation

Pipeline on sand bed

Backfilling of sand

Underground warning tape

Road surface closure

Gas pressure regulating and metering station

9 ↑

Construction of the H_2 pipeline to the natural gas grid and connection via a gas pressure regulating and metering station.

10 →

Levels of control: Building Management System (BMS), Energy Management System (EMS) and optimizers.

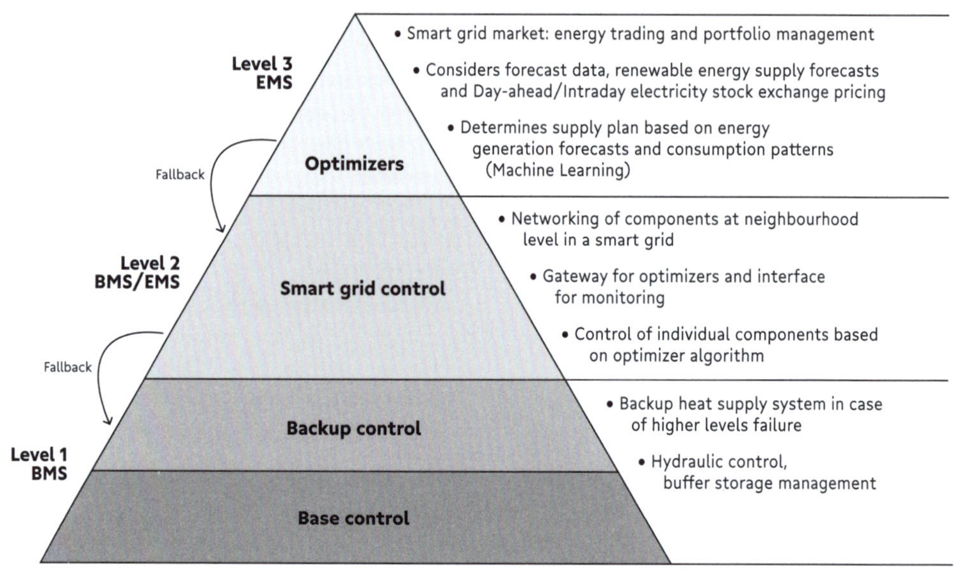

11

Maximum solar utilization of flat roofs – east-west oriented PV modules.

processes are subject to approval as set out in the Fourth Ordinance for the Implementation of the Federal Immission Control Act (BImSchV). The operator is additionally required to submit annual reports on the plant's operation including values for water consumption, wastewater discharge and noise emissions to the relevant authority. In Baden-Württemberg, responsibility for enforcing the Federal Immission Control Act lies with the regional councils.

The operation hours of the electrolyzer are dependent on the availability of electricity from renewable energy sources. As power generated on site through the roof-mounted photovoltaic panels is used primarily by the residents, the P2G system draws a large proportion of its power from outside the district via the power grid. Alongside electricity purchased directly from a wind park in the vicinity, green electricity is drawn via the grid using an algorithm that forecasts prices on the electricity stock exchange as an indicator of the share of renewable energy in the electricity mix (Fig. 12). The hydrogen produced by the plant is fed back into the gas supply. To this end a gas connection contract and corresponding feed-in tariff agreement was set up with the municipal utility company (Stadtwerke Esslingen).

Trial operation of the electrolysis plant started in March 2022. In the first few months, extensive defects in hardware and software were identified and rectified in cooperation with the manufacturers. The volatile pattern of operation also resulted in considerable teething problems in the industrial electrolyser used. Adjustments to the BImSchG permit and the retrofitting of a silencer in the oxygen blow-off pipe caused further delays to regular operation. The goal for 2023 was regular operation as envisaged in the original plan – optimized for "day-ahead" electricity purchases on the Leipzig electricity stock exchange and based on capacity forecasts for the company's own photovoltaic and wind power plants.

The exceptional rise in electricity prices in 2022 has impacted the economic viability of regular hydrogen production, even despite national subsidies, because the cost price of green hydrogen is largely determined by the price of the electricity used and only partially by the investment costs (Fig. 13). In Esslingen, the H_2 production price lies at around 6–8 EUR/kg or 20–27 ct/kWh while electricity purchase prices are approx. 8 ct/kWh (including subsidies for investment costs).

8 *Neues Strommarktdesign*, study commissioned by BEE e.V., 2021, https://www.klimaneutrales-stromsystem.de/pdf/Strommarktdesign-studie_BEE_final_Stand_14_12_2021.pdf. *New Electricity Market Design Study*. Abbreviated English-language synopsis: https://klimaneutrales-stromsystem.de/pdf/english/20211213_BEE_New%20Electricity_Market_Design_Study_Short_version_ENG.pdf.

CONCLUSION – OUTLOOK

Green hydrogen is a key component in the transition to clean energy and plays an essential part in decarbonizing the industrial and mobility sectors. Central to the P2G&H concept is that green hydrogen is produced close to the point of consumption (industry, heavy goods transport) so that when situated in an urban context it can also supply heat to local districts. By utilizing waste heat and reducing transport distances to end users, this system approach is highly efficient. For direct waste heat utilization, consumers should ideally have heating systems that can operate with temperatures below 65 °C and have consistent year-round demand for heat. Heating systems in existing neighbourhoods with requirements for higher temperature levels can employ additional high-temperature heat pumps to boost waste heat temperature levels.

To achieve the climate policy goals of net-zero greenhouse gas emissions, we need a highly efficient means of providing emission-free energy so that we can in the first instance meet the expansion targets for electricity supply and in turn gain corresponding social acceptance. The decentralized approach of the P2G&H concept, as trialled here for the first time in the real-world research project for the Climate-neutral Urban District Neue Weststadt, demonstrates the feasibility and potential added value of this regional energy cycle economy.

The real-world laboratory paves the way for the adoption of electrolysis as an essential part of our future energy infrastructure, and it is imperative that this not be put back any further. Among other things, the BEE study (2021) calls for an accelerated expansion of electrolysis in Germany: "This not only promotes stronger market growth and provides a basis for higher annual rates of electrolysis expansion over the coming decades. This would bring about the necessary sector coupling and also stabilize the market for renewable energy sources."[8] The greatest beneficial effect of the P2G&H concept for the climate is that it can directly replace fossil fuel sources. In recognition of this, the state of Baden-Württemberg is funding the construction of an H_2 pipeline between Esslingen and Stuttgart as part of the H2 GeNeSiS project. This new marketplace for emission-free energy aims to connect generation plants, such as the electrolysis plant in Esslingen's Neue Weststadt, with large-scale consumers of conventional grey hydrogen in industry and of diesel in the mobility sector such as public transport providers, and heavy goods transport suppliers.

Further Reading

▶ Neighbourhood planning, "Circular Construction Over Again", p. 142
▶ Heterogeneity, "Sustainability – Strategies for Action", p. 10
▶ Renewable energy, "The Clean Energy Transition in the Context of Sustainability", p. 20

12 ↗↗

Electrolysis operation times as influenced by power exchange prices and wind power supply forecasts, Saturday and Sunday, 18–19 June 2022.

— Market price forecast [ct/kW]
— Wind energy forecast [kW]
— Target plan electrolysis [kW]
— Actual electrolysis [kW]
— Target plan CHP [kW]
— Actual CHP [kW]

13 ↗

Production costs for green hydrogen by means of electrolysis.

Investment scenarios

------ 1,000 €/kW
– – – 2,000 €/kW
—— 3,000 €/kW

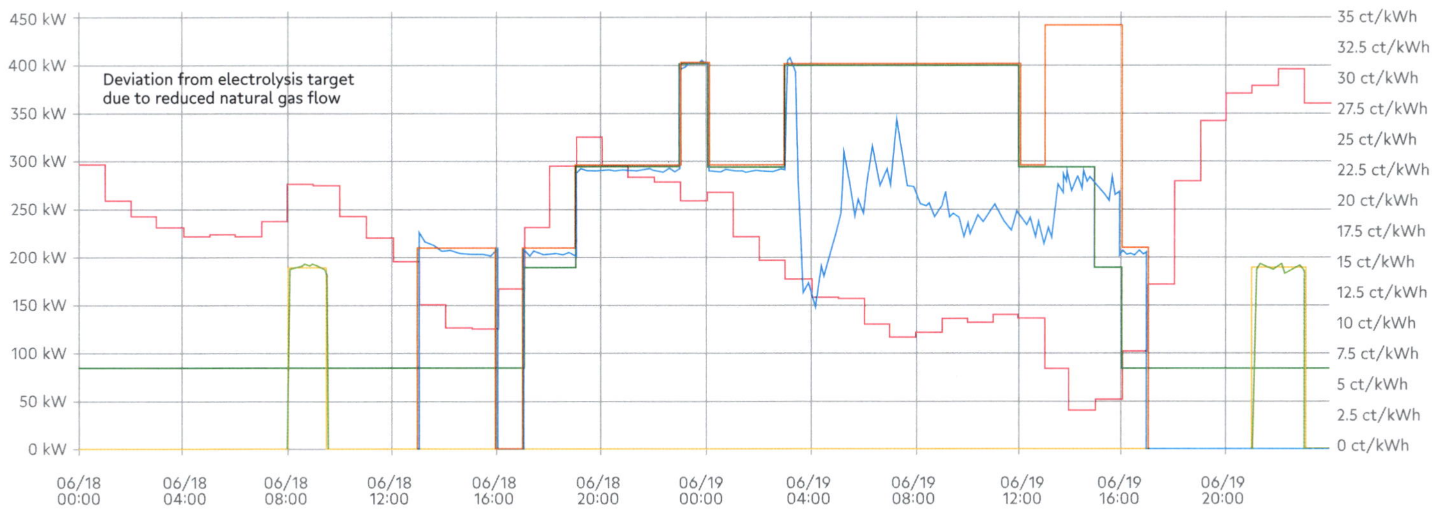
450 kW
400 kW
350 kW
300 kW
250 kW
200 kW
150 kW
100 kW
50 kW
0 kW
35 ct/kWh
32.5 ct/kWh
30 ct/kWh
27.5 ct/kWh
25 ct/kWh
22.5 ct/kWh
20 ct/kWh
17.5 ct/kWh
15 ct/kWh
12.5 ct/kWh
10 ct/kWh
7.5 ct/kWh
5 ct/kWh
2.5 ct/kWh
0 ct/kWh
Deviation from electrolysis target
due to reduced natural gas flow
06/18 00:00
06/18 04:00
06/18 08:00
06/18 12:00
06/18 16:00
06/18 20:00
06/19 00:00
06/19 04:00
06/19 08:00
06/19 12:00
06/19 16:00
06/19 20:00

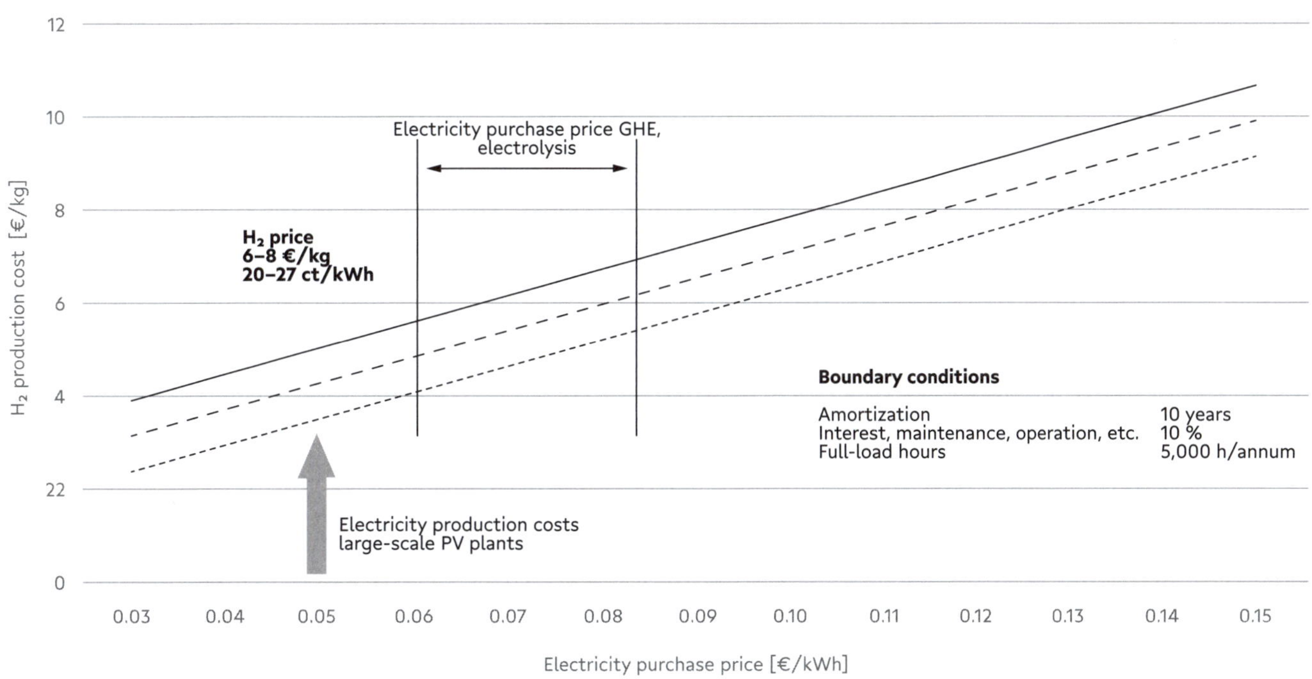
12
10
8
6
4
22
0
H_2 production cost [€/kg]
Electricity purchase price GHE,
electrolysis
H_2 price
6–8 €/kg
20–27 ct/kWh
Boundary conditions
Amortization 10 years
Interest, maintenance, operation, etc. 10 %
Full-load hours 5,000 h/annum
Electricity production costs
large-scale PV plants
0.03
0.04
0.05
0.06
0.07
0.08
0.09
0.10
0.11
0.12
0.13
0.14
0.15
Electricity purchase price [€/kWh]

ADVANCED SUPER-COOL MATERIALS TO MITIGATE URBAN OVER-HEATING

Article by Mattheos Santamouris and Konstantina Vasilakopoulou

Urban overheating is among the most serious and well-documented environmental problems. It deals with the increase of the ambient temperature in cities compared to the surrounding rural environment due to the positive urban heat balance. Anthropogenic heat released in cities, storage of solar radiation by buildings and other urban structures, lack of vegetation and water as well as limited urban ventilation are among the main causes of urban warming. The magnitude of urban overheating depends on the characteristics of a city and in particular of the land use, topography, urban size and density as well as the magnitude of the urban heat sources and sinks. It may vary from 1 to 10 °C, with an average value close to 5 °C.

According to the literature, there are more than 13,000 cities in the world facing serious overheating problems and more than 1.7 billion people living under severe overheating.[1] Higher urban temperatures cause very serious energy, environmental, health and social problems: the cooling energy consumption of urban buildings increases, peak electricity demand rises, and the efficiency of thermal and nuclear power plants decreases (Fig. 1). In particular, analysis of a large number of studies has found that the cooling penalty induced by the urban overheating varies between 0.1 and 20 $kWh/m^2/y$ with an average close to 2.4 $kWh/m^2/y$, corresponding to 2.7 $kWh/m^2/y$ per degree of temperature increase.[2] Furthermore, high temperatures raise the concentration of harmful urban pollutants such as ground level ozone, intensify health problems like heat-related mortality and morbidity, affect the survivability levels of vulnerable populations, and lower the productivity of urban workers.

To counterbalance the impact of urban overheating, efficient mitigation technologies have been developed and implemented in numerous international projects. More traditional strategies include the intensive use of urban greenery, the increase of evapotranspiration in cities, the use of low-temperature heat sinks as well as other solar control technologies.[3] One path of advanced mitigation technologies deals with the development and use of reflective and fluorescent materials for buildings and other urban structures.

THREE GENERATIONS OF SUPER-COOL MATERIALS

The first generation of reflecting materials, white cool materials, was developed 20 years ago. They were used for the urban building envelope and other city structures and have very high reflectance across the entire solar spectrum, combined with a high thermal emittance. Such materials have been extensively implemented in roofs and pavements in cities and have contributed to a decrease in the peak temperature in cities of up to 1.5 °C.[4] A second generation of coloured cool materials with high reflectance in the IR solar spectrum were developed and brought to market in a later phase and offer high mitigation potential in cities.[5]

The third generation of advanced mitigation materials, known as super-cool or radiative cooling materials, consist of photonic structures that exhibit very high reflectance of the solar spectrum, combined with high emittance at wavelengths corresponding to the atmospheric window.[6] Because of their specific radiative characteristics, super-cool materials can achieve up to 10 °C subambient surface temperatures during the peak summer period under the sun.[7] Parallel to the development of these photonic super-cool materials, additional mitigation opportunities such as fluorescence techniques for building materials are being investigated.[8, 9]

The following sections give a short overview of the state of the art of super-cool materials for urban heat mitigation, including qualitative and quantitative information on their cooling potential in cities.

CHARACTERISTICS OF PHOTONIC RADIATIVE COOLING MATERIALS

Daytime radiative cooling materials and structures are the most promising technology for mitigating urban overheating. Radiative cooling materials exhibit a very high solar reflectance of above 95 %, combined with a very high emittance in the atmospheric window

1 C. Tuholske et al., "Global urban population exposure to extreme heat", *Proc. Natl. Acad. Sci. U. S. A.*, 118, 41, 2021, pp. 1–9, https://doi.org/10.1073/pnas.2024792118.

2 M. Santamouris, "Recent progress on urban overheating and heat island research. Integrated assessment of the energy, environmental, vulnerability and health impact. Synergies with the global climate change," *Energy Build.*, 207, 2020, https://doi.org/10.1016/j.enbuild.2019.109482.

3 H. Akbari et al., "Local climate change and urban heat island mitigation techniques – the state of the art", *J. Civ. Eng. Manag.*, 22, 1, 2016, pp. 1–16.

4 M. Santamouris and Y. Geun Young, "Recent development and research priorities on cool and super cool materials to mitigate urban heat island", *Renewable Energy*, 2020, pp. 792–807.

5 A. Synnefa, M. Santamouris and K. Apostolakis, "On the development, optical properties and thermal performance of cool colored coatings for the urban environment", *Solar Energy*, 81, 2007, pp. 488–497.

6 M. Santamouris and Jie Feng, "Recent Progress in Daytime Radiative Cooling: Is It the Air Conditioner of the Future?", *Buildings*, 8, 12, 2018, https://doi.org/10.3390/buildings8120168.

7 J. Feng, M. Santamouris and K. Gao, "The Radiative Cooling Efficiency of Silica Sphere Embedded Polymethylpentene (TPX) Systems", *Solar Energy Materials and Solar Cells*, 215, 15 September 2020, Article 110671.

8 S. Garshasbi, Shujuan Huang, Jan Valenta and Mattheos Santamouris, "Can quantum dots help to mitigate urban overheating? An experimental and modelling study", *Solar Energy*, 206, August 2020, pp. 308–316.

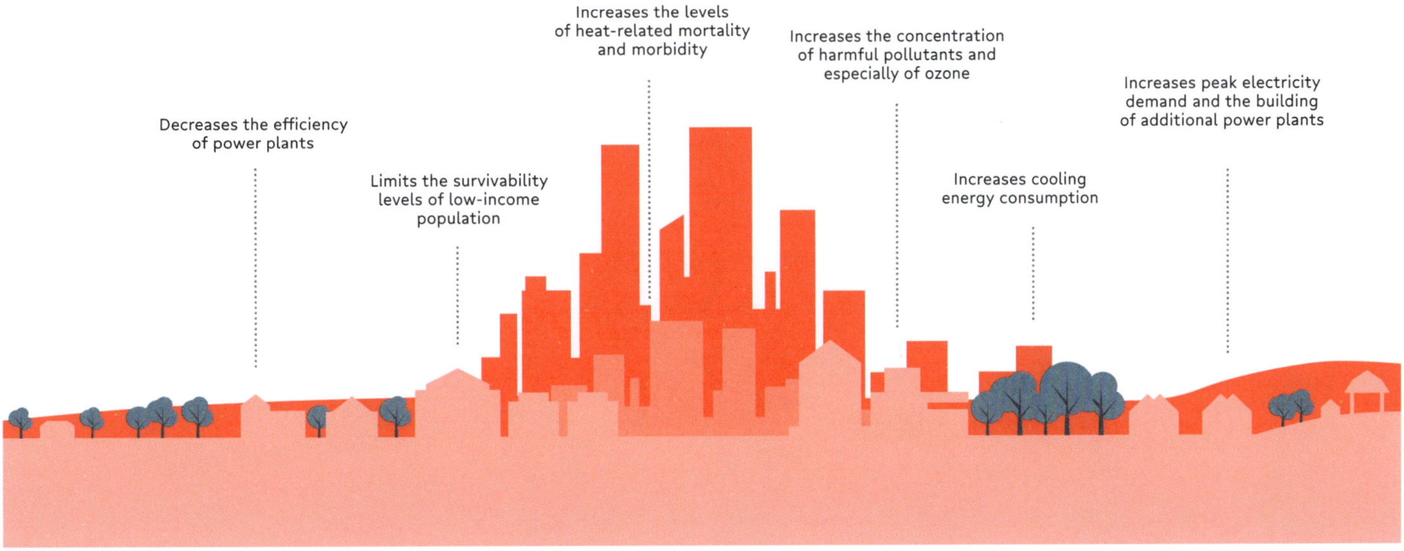

1

Global impact of urban overheating.

(8-13 μm), and can operate under negative thermal balance conditions. This means that the materials absorb very little of solar radiation while emitting most of their internal energy, contributing to a lower surface temperature.

Daytime radiative cooling materials can be classified in four main technological groups (Fig. 2):

PHOTONIC SURFACES WITH A MULTILAYER PLANAR STRUCTURE

Multilayer planar photonic composite materials involve two main components to maximize the solar reflectance (between 0.3 to 2.5 μm) and also emittance in the atmospheric window (between 8–13 μm). Metallic mirrors of aluminium or silver, or a sequence of a metal mirror with a thin film composed of several layers of variable refractive indices, are usually used to increase the reflectance. To increase emittance in the atmospheric window, highly emitting materials are usually placed on top of the reflectors. In most of the existing materials SiO_2, HfO_2, MgF_2, Al_2O_3, PDMS or PMMA are used. According to experimental measurements, these types of photonic surfaces achieve surface temperatures between 5 and 9 °C below the ambient temperature.

PHOTONIC METAMATERIALS CONSISTING OF TWO- OR THREE-DIMENSIONAL DEVICES

Two- and three-dimensional metamaterial structures as a second type provide a net cooling capacity of up to 120 W/m². Experimental data show that such materials could reach up to 11 °C subambient temperatures under the summer sun. However, metamaterials require a very complicated and sophisticated manufacturing process and also their scalability potential is quite limited.

RADIATIVE COOLING PAINTS

Photonic paints can be fabricated quite easily using low-cost materials and can be easily implemented on the surface of buildings and other urban structures. Photonic paints usually include SiO_2 microspheres. Experiments have shown that such paints may reach up to 12 C° subambient surface temperatures.

Photonic paints have superb thermal and optical properties and offer an excellent option to promote heat mitigation in cities. However, problems associated with the deposition of pollutants on the surface of paints as well as optical ageing may significantly affect the cooling capacity of photonic paints.

9 S. Garshasbi and M. Santamouris, "Using Advanced Thermochromic Technologies in the Built Environment. Recent Development and Potential to Decrease the Energy Consumption and Fight Urban Overheating", *Solar Energy Materials and Solar Cells*, 191, 2019, pp. 21–32.

2

Schemes of four photonic structures.

A

A double-layer coating with TiO_2 embedded on top and carbon black at the bottom.

B

A double-layer coating with TiO_2 embedded on top and SiC or SiO_2 at the bottom.

C

Vikuiti Enhanced Specular Reflector (ESR) coated with silver at the back.

D

A metamaterial composed of a transparent polymer with randomly distributed SiO_2 microspheres.

Based on: M. Santamouris and Jie Feng, "Recent Progress in Daytime Radiative Cooling: Is It the Air Conditioner of the Future?", *Buildings*, 8, 12, 2018, https://www.mdpi.com/2075-5309/8/12/168.

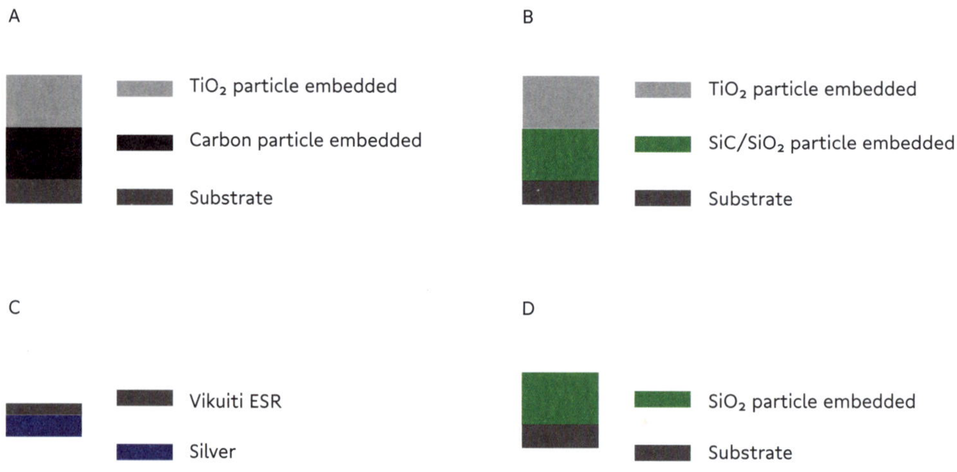

3

Violin plots of the ambient, surface, roof and canopy temperatures for non-modulated super-cool materials, materials with modulated reflectance, modulated emittance and both reflectance and emittance modulated.

Based on: Ansar Khan, Laura Carlosena, Samiran Khorat, Rupali Khatun, Quang-Van Doan, Jie Feng and Mattheos Santamouris, "On the Winter Overcooling Penalty of Super Cool Photonic Materials in Cities", *Advances Solar Energy*, Vol. 1, 2021.

$T_{ambient}$

$T_{surface}$

T_{roof}

T_{canopy}

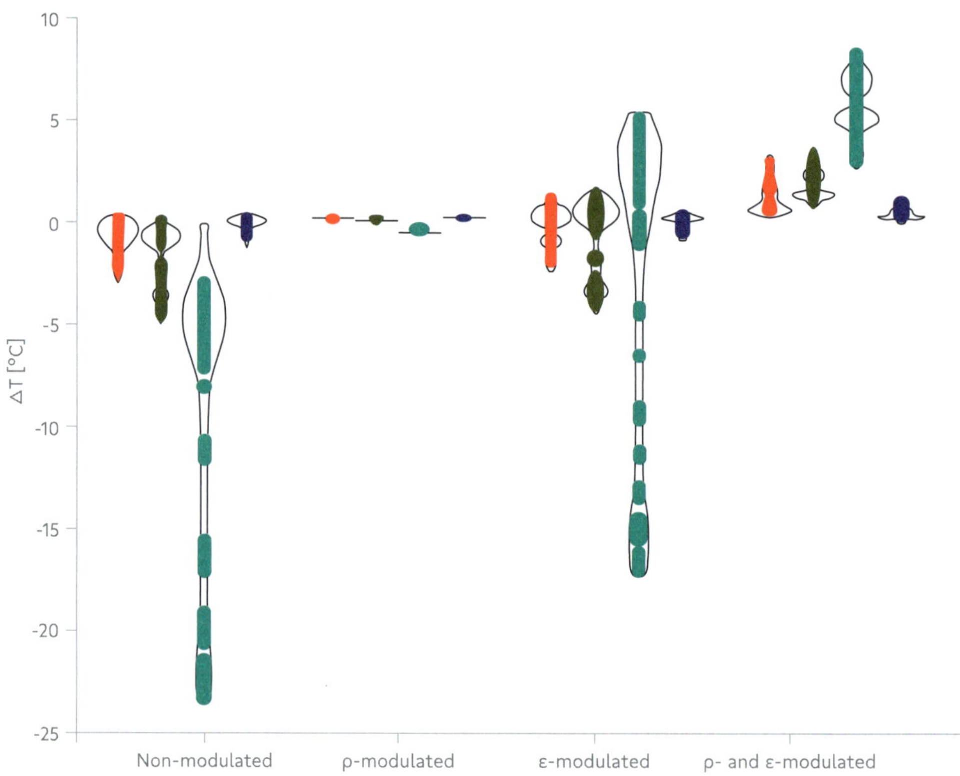

POLYMERS

Polymeric photonic materials employ electromagnetic resonators that are excited collectively in a polymer. They exhibit high emittance in the atmospheric window and can achieve subambient surface temperatures under the summer sun.

The main problems associated with the use of photonic super-cool materials are the limited scalability of some of the proposed technologies, potential overcooling during the winter period and also glare caused by the extreme reflectance. To overcome these problems, technologies to modulate the optical properties of the materials have been developed and proposed.[10] Modulation technologies permit the modification of both the reflectance and the emittance of the materials throughout the year. During the summer period, the modulated materials should exhibit high reflectance and emittance contributing to cooling, while during the winter period, both the reflectance and the emittance should be low to absorb solar radiation and decrease radiative losses, thereby contributing to the reduction of heat losses. Mesoscale simulations of the potential mitigation impact of modulated super-cool materials for the city of Kolkata, India, have shown that it is possible to reduce the peak summer temperature by up to 5 °C and increase the winter temperature by up to 2 °C (Fig. 3).[11]

FLUORESCENT MATERIALS FOR HEAT MITIGATION

Fluorescence is a phenomenon associated with the emission of non-thermal radiation by electrons excited by absorbed light during the relaxation to their ground state. The emission occurs at longer wavelengths than the light absorption and is associated with the energy difference between the absorption peak and the fluorescent peak wavelength, known as Stokes shift. The efficiency of the fluorescent materials is measured using the so-called "quantum yield", which is the ratio between the emitted and the absorbed photons.

Fluorescent materials are usually clustered in two types: bulk fluorescent materials such as ruby and nano fluorescent materials, mainly quantum dots.

Quantum dots exhibit unique optical characteristics and a significant potential to modulate these using surface chemistry and modifications of their size.[12] In the latter, the potential increase of the particle size of quantum dots shifts both the emission and absorption wavelengths to longer wavelengths.

The use of quantum dots as a material to mitigate urban heat has been experimentally investigated. CIS/ZnS quantum dots were found to reject almost 54 W/m², corresponding to 8.5 % of the absorbed radiation.[13] It has been demonstrated that quantum dots can be up to 2 °C cooler than a non-fluorescent material of the same colour. Current research on the potential development of fluorescent materials for mitigation purposes aims to increase their quantum yield by using over-coating quantum dots semiconductors with a wider bandgap.

COOLING POTENTIAL OF SUPER-COOL MATERIALS IN CITIES

The cooling potential of super-cool materials has been fully assessed for the city of Riyadh, Saudi Arabia. The study analysed the implementation of modified very high albedo materials in the whole city of Riyadh, involving citywide implementation of super-cool material in roofs with an albedo of 0.95 and an emissivity of 0.95. Using advanced mesoscale climatic modelling, it was found that the implementation of super-cool material in roofs helps to achieve a maximum temperature reduction of 2.3 °C at 2 pm and 3.7 °C at 6 am compared to the existing situation (Fig. 4). The average reduction of ambient temperature at peak hour (2 pm) is 1.3 °C compared to the current condition's scenario, while the maximum decrease of the average 24-hour temperature is 3.1 °C. The ambient temperature decrease caused by the super-cool materials reduces the cooling demand of buildings up to 20 %.[14]

10 G. Ulpiani, Gianluca Ranzi, Kwok Wei Shah, Jie Feng and Mattheos Santamouris, "On the energy modulation of daytime radiative coolers: A review on infrared emissivity dynamic switch against overcooling", *Solar Energy*, 209, October 2020, pp. 278–301.

11 A. Khan, Laura Carlosena, Samiran Khorat, Rupali Khatun, Quang-Van Doan, Jie Feng and Mattheos Santamouris, "On the Winter Overcooling Penalty of Super Cool Photonic Materials in Cities", *Solar Energy Advances*, 1, 2021.

12 G. E. LeCroy, F. Messina, A. Sciortino, C. E. Bunker, P. Wang, K. A. S. Fernando and Y. Sun, "Characteristic excitation wavelength dependence of fluorescence emissions in carbon 'quantum' dots", *J. Phys. Chem.*, 121, 50, 2017, Article 28180e28186.

13 Ibid.

14 M. Santamouris et al., "Urban Heat and Mitigation Potential in Riyadh, KSA", 2022.

FUTURE DEVELOPMENTS AND CONCLUSIONS

Technologies based on the use of photonic structures, nano-fluorescent materials, quantum dots and other materials above dyes, have recently been developed and used in large-scale mitigation projects all around the world. Experimental results obtained for numerous large-scale mitigation projects have revealed that the use of super-cool materials can reduce the peak summer temperature in cities by up to 4 °C, reduce the cooling energy consumption by up to 40 %, reduce heat mortality and morbidity by up to 30 % and contribute to alleviating energy poverty and protecting the vulnerable population in cities. The developed super-cool materials are environmentally friendly and exhibit very low optical aging. Development costs are low and the materials can be easily fabricated on an industrial scale.

Further Reading

▶ Ecology, "Ecology must have Priority!", *Circular Construction and Circular Economy,* p. 102
▶ Heat mitigation, "Evaluating and Improving the Thermal Resilience of Residential Buildings", p. 36
▶ Scalability, "Architecture in Large Quantities", p. 132

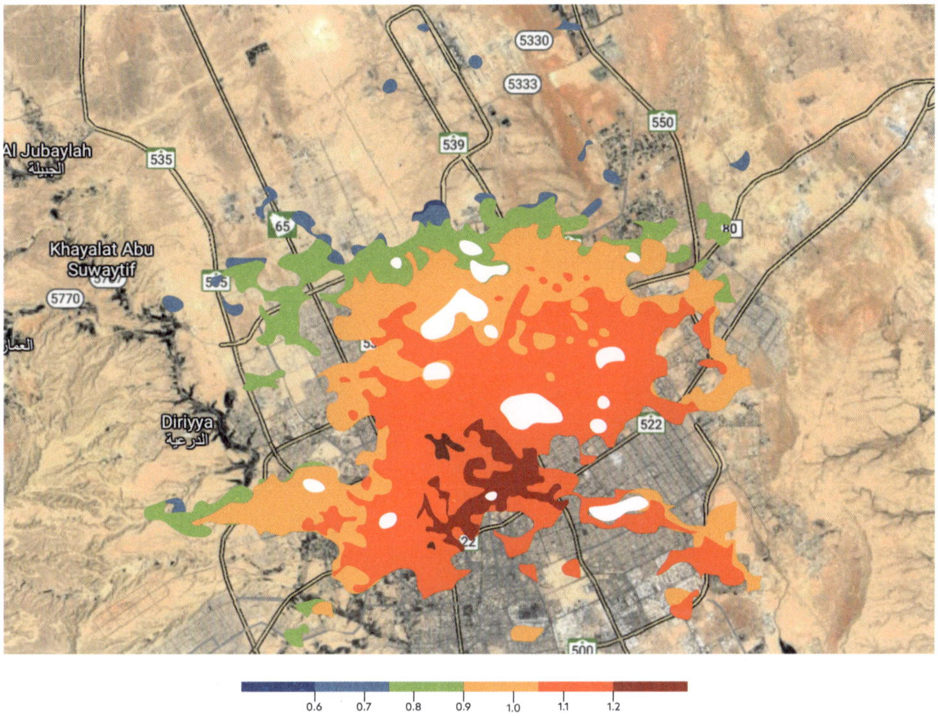

4

Average ambient temperature reduction in Riyadh, Saudi Arabia, by urban zone when super-cool materials are implemented.

DIFFERENT

Innovation Fast Forward

Introduction to Digital Transformation by Moritz Dörstelmann and Erik Zanetti

The architecture, engineering and construction (AEC) sector has traditionally been characterized by a cautious approach towards digitalization and innovative practices, primarily due to a combination of factors such as low demand for change and the stringent requirements imposed by building codes. This has resulted in a relatively slower adoption of cutting-edge technologies and forward-thinking methodologies compared to other industries.

Creating stronger connections between practice, industry and research is crucial for fostering innovation. On the one hand, there is a need for increased collaboration and interaction between practitioners and researchers to bridge the gap between theory and real-world applications. On the other, educational institutions should nurture innovative thinking among students beyond traditional teaching methods. While fundamental research is a long-term pillar of our scientific system, the current urgency of change in the construction industry needs novel yet application-oriented and rapidly transferable research. At the intersection of teaching and research, computational design and digital fabrication have demonstrated their potential in the implementation of Research through Design. Bridging academia and industry, knowledge and insights acquired through practical design work can be translated and materialized in a structured and scientific manner. By employing initial explorative prototypes and leveraging digital processes, researchers and students gain unique insights into materials, construction systems, fabrication processes and structures that go beyond what is typically found in textbooks or codified knowledge. Through rapid iterations, this approach can be used to test key assumptions, strengths and weaknesses of a concept. They facilitate research-based decision-making that can disrupt the conventional way we interpret architecture and construction.

Another crucial element embraced by computational design and digital fabrication in academic environments is the assessment of concepts through 1:1 prototypes or full-scale research demonstrators. These play a vital role in bringing the concepts closer to real-world application and practice, demonstrating how each part of the design and construction processes converges into a unified workflow.

The final convergence of research and practice occurs through the transfer of innovative ideas to the industry. This transfer has given rise to a multitude of start-ups operating in the realm of digital design and fabrication. Advancing either the evolution or disruption of the industry, they pave the way for the implementation of new materials and technologies as well as novel models of interdisciplinary collaboration.

The innovation pipeline enabled by computational design and digital fabrication, from teaching and research to practice, presents a remarkable opportunity to redefine the architect's role as an instigator of innovation, extending beyond traditional design practices.

Adopting digital design and fabrication techniques in construction opens up the possibility of envisioning construction cycles as being dynamic and adaptable to specific conditions, characterized by constant change. In this paradigm, construction materials and elements become transient, subject to flux and availability. Digital fabrication techniques would cater to case-specific scenarios with a diverse range of technologies, including on-site robotics, distributed processes and augmented craftsmanship.

Taking a fresh perspective starting from the materials, this part critically examines how digital design and fabrication can be harnessed to develop innovative construction systems with a strong emphasis on circularity and digital techniques. The articles showcase how digital material passports can enable circular supply chains; how custom digital design and fabrication technologies enable us to reconsider the fundamental resources utilized in construction; and how heterogeneous materials can be reused. We discuss how ressource-efficient modular wood construction can encourage the exploration of unique architectural expressions; speculate on future constructions to be digitally designed for robotic reconfiguration; and explore an ephemeral understanding of buildings in constant change through biological construction paradigms. The articles showcase how a digital transformation of the building sector enables radically *different* paradigms of design and construction.

A DIFFERENT ARCHITEC-TURAL PRACTICE

Circular Design, Fabrication and Living with Biogenic and Reclaimed Materials

Commentary by Martin Tamke and Mette Ramsgaard Thomsen

The building industry's transformative process towards a truly circular practice disrupts the guiding concepts of materials in architecture, engineering and construction: availability, predictability and longevity. The current ideal material is everlasting, maintenance-free, homogeneous and readily available. Engraved in industrial and regulatory frameworks, this thinking results in extremely wasteful and energy-intensive processes of material selection and homogenization. Reclaimed and bio-based materials follow a different logic because they are inherently heterogeneous and their maintenance, harvesting and processing requires foresight and long-term planning.

These complexities can become opportunities for a different, more holistic and sustainable *modus operandi* in the building industry if we shift our linear approaches in the design and fabrication of buildings to circular ones, which include data from supply and reclamation. What is necessary though is to leave behind the industrial logics of global uniformity, expressed in industry-wide norms and standards.

Today we can understand material properties and behaviours on the level of individual pieces and utilize this information in adaptive digital design and fabrication processes. Non-destructive techniques like CT scanning provide means to gain a deep view into the geometry and composition of any piece of virgin or reclaimed biomaterial. Subsequent analysis allows to predict the objects' material properties and behaviours. We can take advantage of these insights in tailored digital design and fabrication processes and compose the individual elements into larger assemblies, so that their combined performances match the overall structural and other requirements. These processes demand that data follows, and is enriched along, the materials' journey from harvest to production use and reuse. Such concepts promise a way out of the current crisis. The question is whether we can leave behind the comfort of silos and regulations and move to a more holistic and complex understanding.

An awareness of temporal aspects is key to understanding and working with circular biomaterials. Being part of the biological cycle of life and death, they are poised to decay and become part of new life the moment they are harvested. So far efforts have concentrated on extending their lifetime – often through the application of harmful chemicals – and we see materials as static objects under conservation. A different approach takes the temporality of materials into account in concepts for design, making and living with materials in buildings. Design for disassembly, smart monitoring, repair and replacement allows buildings to adapt and renew and become better over time. This should go hand in hand with social considerations and a shift from considering aware and capable humans solely as occupants to engaging with them as empathic caretakers.

Further Reading

- ▶ Biological metabolism, "Principles of Circular Construction", *Circular Construction and Circular Economy*, p. 22
- ▶ Reuse, "Designing with Matter as Met", p. 124
- ▶ Design for disassembly, "Deconstruction Policy in Portland, Oregon", *Circular Construction and Circular Economy*, p. 62

DIGITAL CRAFT AND CIRCULAR CONSTRUCTION

Article by Daniel Fischer, Erik Zanetti and Moritz Dörstelmann

The building sector's staggering consumption of global resources underscores the critical need for a paradigm shift towards circular construction. With digital technology becoming increasingly accessible and integrated into our daily lives, the potential for its application in construction is more apparent than ever before. In their pioneering role of conceptualizing and planning future constructions, architects assume a pivotal position in seeking ecological solutions and capitalizing on technological opportunities while reflecting upon their practices' cultural implications. This article focuses on digital craft in architecture and illustrates how integrating digital technologies, circular systems and interdisciplinary collaboration can revolutionize how we design, construct and operate buildings.

DIGITAL CRAFT

Behind artificial structures lies a team of creators, each contributing their expertise to bring them into existence. In historic buildings and construction, these creators encompass a range of skilled professionals including architects, engineers and craftspeople. During the mediaeval ages, these creators, often referred to as master builders, were predominantly skilled craftspeople. They possessed a profound understanding of both the principles and practical techniques within their discipline, with a strong focus on construction. However, various degrees of integration or separation between execution (*fabrica*) and design (*ratiocinatio*) became predominant in the construction sector over the centuries, with a significant shift, during the Industrial Revolution and era of Fordism, from design and artisan to prioritization of cost-efficient production and mass standardization. Consequently, there was a diminished emphasis on intricate detailing and individual artistry in the common building practice. It is important to recognize that historical construction methods are closely intertwined with their social and economic context. The availability of technology and construction materials greatly influenced the practices and capabilities of local craftspeople, leaving a distinctive mark on the architectural heritage of different regions.

Due to global challenges, we are witnessing a digital renaissance combined with an interest in locally available materials and traditional artisanship. The *Oxford Dictionary* defines craftsmanship as "the level of skill shown by someone in making something beautiful with their hands" or "the quality of design and work shown by something that has been made by hand". This definition suggests the possibility of a digital craftsmanship where the traditional means of making – the craftsperson's hands – are replaced by digital tools, such as industrial robots or bespoke machines. What used to be specialized, individual tools for manual use can now be seen as robots and individually designed or custom-made machines. Based on available digital technologies and materials, they mimic, improve or re-interpret a historical construction and design repertoire. Within this interpretation, digital craftsmanship replicates human labour, making it more efficient and less reliant on personal knowledge. Moreover, it can also lead to a higher level of complexity and resolution. This development shifts the focus towards mass customization, where digital fabrication is implemented to produce infinite but similar variants of solutions, generated with the same computational or fabrication methods. One of the earliest examples of this shift towards the digital reinterpretation of craftsmanship explored using robotic arms to lay bricks (Fig. 1), while recent examples abandoned the paradigms of full automation and are exploring human-machine collaboration (Fig. 2).

Recently, new inspiring directions have emerged. Thanks to the growing importance placed on sustainability and circularity in the construction industry, there has been a renewed interest in historically sustainable materials and their industrialization, which has presented the opportunity to find new meanings for their architectural applications. The first material to reappear was wood, which is today the most industrialized among them. Simultaneously, other materials such as bamboo, earth and willow are likewise being revisited.

The transfer from analogue to digital craftsmanship represents a step towards industrializing a material and opens the opportunity for its reinterpretation and reengineering. Thus the design, structural articulation, detailing and fabrication processes take a transformative shift, paving the way for a digital approach that distinguishes the final result from its historical origins. With an eye to the future, the rise of new technologies, such as artificial intelligence and machine learning, and the refinement of 3D scanning techniques, now create opportunities to deal with process deviations and inhomogeneous material. This has allowed shifting the perspective from using standardized materials to developing tailored processes and novel strategies that emerge from the complexity and irregularity of bio-based, waste or reclaimed materials. This can be seen as an opportunity to reintroduce a specific skill of artisanship that was left behind: the flexibility and adaptability of the craftsperson. As the underlying techniques and knowledges are still present, the craftsperson can apply them to the specific characteristics of the material in their hands. In terms of circularity, this potential is particularly great for bio-based materials and their waste, whose structural properties depend greatly on fibre orientation and geometry.

1 ↑↑

Robotic brick laying.

2 ↑

Human-robot collaboration.

DIGITAL WICKER

Bio-based materials have become a central focus in developing circular construction systems due to their ability to regenerate and be composted at the end of their life cycle. Wood is currently the only significant renewable building material. However, forestry cycles are long (40–100 years), making it difficult to match supply and demand. Indeed, wood supply chain disruptions and price volatility are already starting to emerge in some European countries. Future increasing demand for construction wood, paired with the requirements of sustainable and climate-adapted forestry, showcase the dependence on a single renewable resource as a risk to slow down the urgently required circular transformation of the construction industry. By diversifying the sources of materials and the production methods, the construction industry can become more resilient and sustainable by, for example, complementing classical timber construction with fast-regrowing or rapidly renewable materials with growth cycles shorter than ten years.

Bamboo is the best-known example, extensively used in traditional Asian construction. In the European context, where bamboo does not grow easily, willow, hazel, reeds and poplar are promising alternative options. The energy sector has already established forestry practices that enable these plants to grow up to 2 m in height per year. It is important to consider that this fast growth happens in the form of thin woody branches with widely varying cross-sections. Thus, working with these materials brings about new challenges, including non-standard behaviour to changes in the load-bearing capacity due to internal factors.

Research at the Professorship for Digital Design and Fabrication (DDF) at the Karlsruhe Institute for Technology (KIT) explores tailored digital fabrication processes that deal with these irregularities. The reinterpretation of analogue processing techniques provides these materials with structural rigidity through complex three-dimensional arrangements (Fig. 4). Starting from extensive research into traditional crafting techniques, a process-based understanding of material behaviour provides a crucial foundation for advancing the digital transformation and reinterpretation of traditional craft-based construction systems. The particular research focuses on digital fabrication techniques for various spatial arrangements of willow.

Traditionally, long, thin branches of willow are used in wicker weaving, a technique in which they are woven together to make works such as baskets and furniture. This technique exploits geometry and textile techniques to provide structural stiffness not inherently present in the material. Research aims to enhance the structural rigidity of inherently flexible and relatively weak branches, measuring only a few millimetres in thickness, as load-bearing structures. The resulting willow structures can be seen as proto building components to be subsequently further developed into a willow-based construction system.

This approach opens fresh avenues for material cycles that complement the traditional forestry industry through the ecological and economic use of wetlands as carbon sinks, valuable ecosystems and for the agricultural production of reed, hazel and willow as construction materials. The combination of fast growth cycles, regional availability, forestry practices for commercial exploitation and untapped structural potential can make fast-regrowing materials a significant factor in implementing digital circular construction.

NATURAL COMPOSITE BUILDING COMPONENTS

Natural composites offer the opportunity for a load-adaptive tailored combination of tension-bearing fast-regrowing materials, such as the above-described willow structures, with abundant and infinitely recyclable compression-bearing materials such as earth. The resulting natural hybrid material system can fulfil structural design requirements which exceed the structural performance of each individual constituent (Fig. 6). The utilized materials can be locally sourced and require limited energy and processing intensity. A multi-scalar approach towards a hybrid material system tailored from natural short fibres, long fibres and lumber sections, in combination with insulative straw and reed embedded within an earth mixture, further extends the large solution space for spatial geometric variation and high-resolution performative differentiation. Navigating this vast design space and enabling the fabrication of such a hybrid construction system requires further research. Integrative digital design and fabrication methods are suitable for negotiating reciprocal relations between material behaviour, structural design, fabrication constraints and architectural design.

DIGITAL WILLOW-EARTH CONSTRUCTION SYSTEMS

The emerging architectural design and construction potentials of digitally prefabricated willow-earth composite building components have been explored at KIT through the prototyping of custom digital fabrication workflows and testing of 1:1-scale building components at the intersection of research-driven teaching and third-party funded research projects. Imperative for the transferability of this research-based construction system into the building sector is the consideration of production speed and scalability. Traditional willow-weaving, predominantly a manual craft, proves inadequate for manufacturing due to its inherent limitations in speed, cost-effectiveness and skilled labour requirements. Custom digital fabrication processes are able to facilitate the viability of the proposed construction system.

A simple machine with two axes was the first approach to developing a digital fabrication system for willow. It featured an end-effector that allowed for the manual feeding of individual willow branches, like a craftsperson would manually do, through a bed of wooden positioning poles (Fig. 5). The resulting spatial structures exemplified the potential of spatial willow structures to be developed into building components. At this stage, however, they were only moderately resilient to compression.

A hybrid system of willow and earth-based materials was subsequently tested to improve these initial prototypes. A 1:1 scale demonstrator (Fig. 8) emerged as a further collaborative effort between students and researchers in pursuit of a building system that combines the tensile strength of willow with the compression-bearing capacities of earth, in a material system analogous to steel-reinforced concrete. These proto components were conceptualized as fully functional building elements with integrated connection details and further developed as a modular willow-earth construction system.

To address the time-consuming issue of individually placing single willow branches, the digital willow-weaving concept was extended towards the continuous extrusion of a spliced willow macro fibre. Drawing inspiration from textile technology, this machine extension enabled the splicing of individual branches into an endless willow bundle. This development signified the fusion of two traditional crafting techniques by integrating digital tools as an enhancement of the existing processes. The effectiveness of this technique was demonstrated through a first application in a willow-earth hybrid construction system within the ReGrow research project (Fig. 10). The resulting structure was showcased at the Federal Garden Show 2023 in Mannheim, successfully integrating the innovative digital 3D willow-weaving approach.

The relevance of this hybrid construction system as a scalable and sustainable construction method is currently being evaluated in another collaborative research project (Fig. 9). It focusses on the development of an application-ready 1:1-scale vaulted ceiling building component which combines wood, willow and earth into a digital reinterpretation of historic Prussian vaulted ceiling systems. This approach showcases the ability of reinforced earth

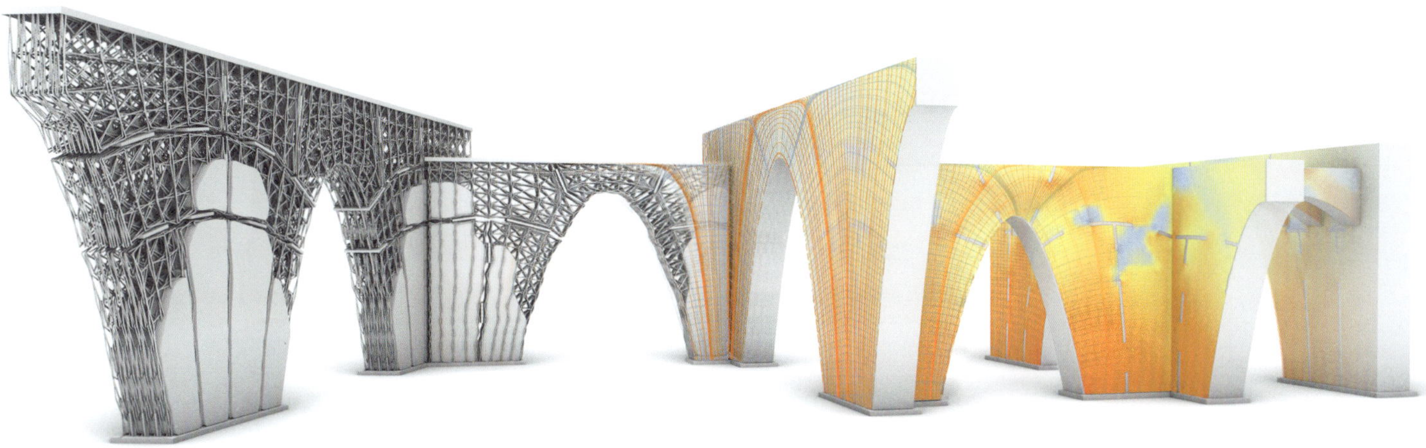

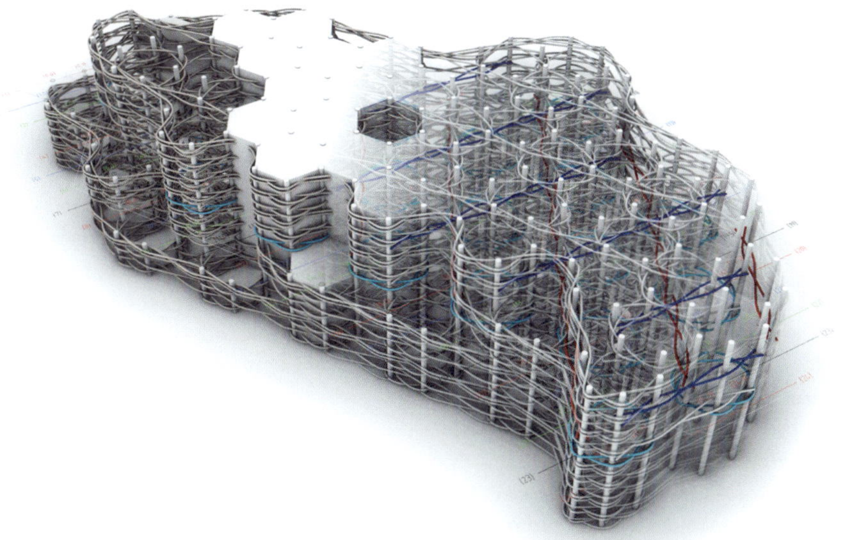

3, 4, 5

Digital design (top and middle) **and fabrication** (bottom) **of spatial willow structures.**

6

Natural hybrid material system: willow-reinforced earth.

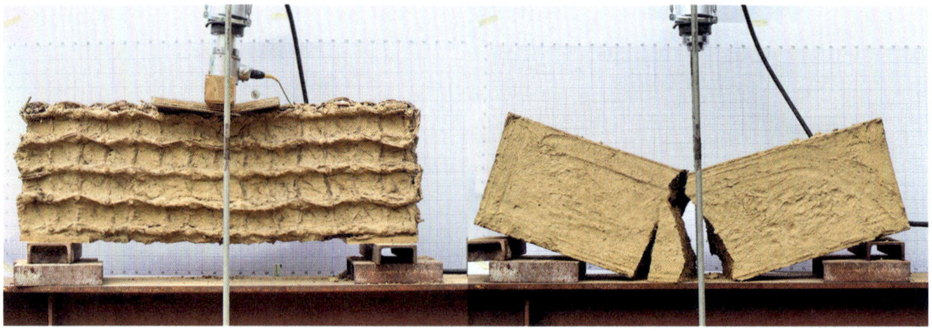

components to be used in horizontal building components. The willow-earth-wood hybrid construction enables a very selective use of construction lumber in the ceiling's tension zone, while the willow-earth composite transfers shear and compression load and provides fire and sound protection.

Such digitally reinterpreted natural composite structures can contribute to energy-efficient buildings by providing thermal insulation and thermal mass. They reduce heating and cooling requirements and moderate interior air quality and climate. As such, the advanced digital utilization of basic natural materials can reduce the need for additional technical building services.

While the resulting building components are spatially complex in their makeup and require advanced design and fabrication technology, their materiality and circular usage are extremely simple in terms of energy intensity and recycling. The digitally prefabricated components are designed for reusability through simple reversible screw connections. At their end-of-life the earth can be simply washed out and reused. The lumber sections can be reused as well. Willow and the other fibre materials can be composted and brought back into the biological cycle, thus closing local material cycles as a waste-free and fully circular digital construction method.

SHAPING CHANGE

The example of willow-earth hybrid structures shown here highlights the importance of gaining hands-on experience with analogue material processing and digital design and fabrication methods to enable process-based thinking for novel circular construction concepts in research and education. The underlying innovation pipeline exemplifies a research strategy at the interdisciplinary interface of research and education that rapidly translates speculative and forward-looking explorations into application-oriented full scale prototypes. The relevance and ultimate goal of contributing to the digital transformation of the construction industry has yet to be proven through its transfer potential and practical implementation. At this point, the research results yield the promise that digital construction technology can address global challenges through a digitally enabled local reinterpretation of vernacular construction processes.

Architecture can address the necessary adaptation and transformation of our built environment in a variety of domains, such as discussions on societal sufficiency, novel spatial living and working concepts, and the fundamental reevaluation of our current material cycles and building processes. At the intersection of design and technology, it is a culturally highly relevant responsibility for architecture to shape change and drive digital transformation, not only from a building technological perspective but as a nexus of cultural, economic and technical implications.

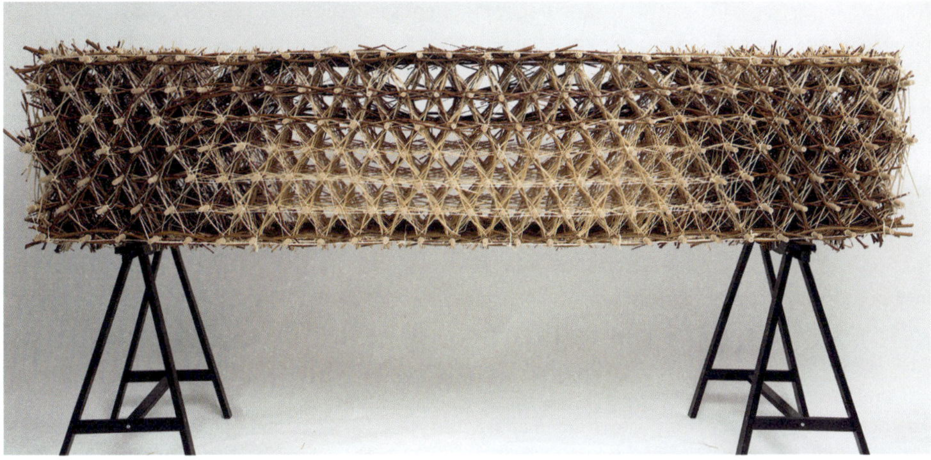

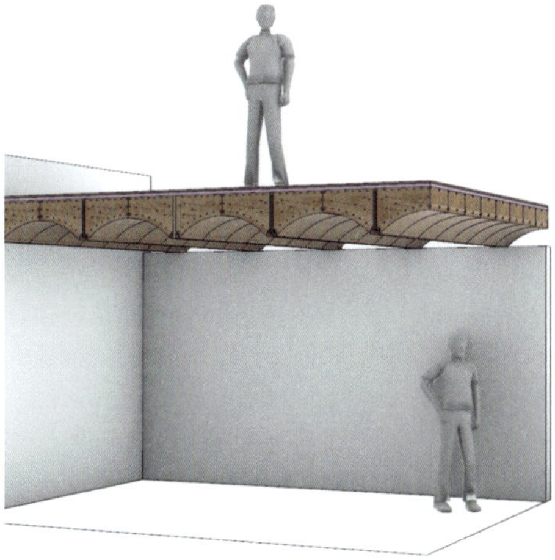

7 ↖

Explorative prototyping: DigitalWicker

8 ↑

1:1 research demonstrator: InterTwig.

9 ←←

Application-oriented development of ceiling components: WillowWeave.

10 ←

Hybrid construction system: ReGrow.

Further Reading

- ▶ Material loop, "Sustainability – The Importance of a Holistic Approach", *Circular Construction and Circular Economy*, p. 10
- ▶ Digital transformation, "Digital Transformation – A Techno-optimistic Outlook", p. 24
- ▶ Earth construction, "A Different Architectural Practice", p. 109

THE REUSE POTENTIAL OF STEEL PROFILES FOR HYBRID MULTI-STOREY CONSTRUCTION

Article by Hilke Manot and Julian Lienhard

A large proportion of the structural steel components in buildings in Germany are rolled open sections typically found in industrial buildings and factory halls or in composite steel structures such as multi-storey parking decks.

The potential these have for reuse is enormous but as yet largely untapped. Given the relevant quantities available and the specific properties of the material – its durability, the predominance of standardized components and their capacity for disassembly – these kinds of steel profiles are in principle well suited for reusing. Currently, however, their reuse has been hampered by various challenges, especially with respect to localization, testing and recertification. This looks set to change with the advent of materials passports and building component databases, as well as the forthcoming harmonization of standards, which will pave the way for numerous possibilities for reusing steel components in new contexts.

In Europe, steel is not widely used for housing or other multi-storey structures due to its comparatively poor fire performance characteristics. Hybrid steel construction methods, for example in combination with natural building materials such as wood or earth, may offer a possible solution to employing reclaimed steel elements in these contexts.

In 2020, the production of crude steel reached an all-time high of 1.878 million tonnes per year (Fig. 1).[1] Global steel production has thus increased almost fivefold since 1960 and, according to forecasts,[2] will continue to rise to nearly 1.7 times current levels by 2050.[3] About half of the steel produced worldwide is used in the construction industry.[4]

The industrial production of steel remains extremely energy- and emissions-intensive. In 2019, global steel production consumed a total of 845 million tonnes of oil equivalent (toe), representing 20 % of industrial and 8 % of total global energy consumption. In the same year, iron and steel production accounted for 2.6 Gt of direct CO_2 emissions, equivalent to a quarter of all industrial emissions and almost 7 % of total global process and energy-related emissions (Fig. 2). A primary reason for this is the sector's dependency on fossil fuels such as coal or natural gas for smelting iron ore, which is many times more energy- and emissions-intensive than scrap steel processing, which is mostly powered by electricity.[5]

Although in Germany, some 93–94 % of structural steel is recycled, only about 5–6 % is reused within the value chain (Fig. 3). And while recycling steel represents a positive contribution to conserving resources and avoiding waste, it also entails high levels of energy input and associated emissions.[6]

STEEL IN CIRCULAR CONSTRUCTION

The possibility of reusing construction elements made of steel is preferable to recycling not just in terms of the waste hierarchy but also because it avoids the need for melting and refabrication, which would otherwise incur significant greenhouse gas emissions.[7] Reusing steel components extends their overall useful life, continuing the value chain in the circular economy.[8] In addition, the rising cost of producing new steel products – as a result of carbon pricing[9] or future hydrogen-powered production processes[10] – when compared to the potential savings from reuse in the procurement, dismantling, material testing and reprocessing of reclaimed elements could lead to a reappraisal of how costs are assessed.[11]

As cities grow to accommodate an ever greater number of inhabitants, multi-storey housing and other buildings offer a way of limiting sprawl by enabling more dense urban construction. In 2022, most new buildings were still constructed using reinforced concrete and masonry bricks, despite their comparatively poor ecological balance,[12] but new technical innovations are bringing about a shift towards timber in multi-storey buildings. Alongside ever more sophisticated timber-only constructions, hybrid material and construction methods are also being explored. An example of the latter is the SKAIO building in Heilbronn by Kaden + Lager architects which, at a height of 34 m, is billed by the designers as the first timber high-rise structure in Germany.[13] The reinforced structural steel components of such buildings could in future be mined from existing urban resources such as disassembled parking decks.

1 World Steel Association, *Energy use in the steel industry*. Fact sheet, 2021, p. 1, https://worldsteel.org/wp-content/uploads/Fact-sheet-Energy-use-in-the-steel-industry.pdf (accessed September 2021).

2 World Steel Association, *Steel Facts*, 2021, https://www.worldsteel.org/about-steel/steel-facts.html (accessed 12 September 2021).

3 Julian Allwood and Jonathan Cullen, *Sustainable Materials. Without the Hot Air. Making Buildings, Vehicles and Products Efficiently and with Less New Material*. UIT Cambridge, 2015, p. 66.

4 World Steel Association, *Steel Facts*.

5 International Energy Agency, *Iron and Steel. Technology Roadmap. Towards more sustainable steelmaking*. 2020, pp. 35–37, https://www.iea.org/reports/iron-and-steel-technology-roadmap (accessed 9 September 2021).

6 Danielle Densley Tingley and Julian Allwood, *Reuse of structural steel. The opportunities and challenges*. European Steel Environment & Energy Congress, Cambridge, 2014, p. 1, https://www.researchgate.net/publication/279441808_Reuse_of_structural_steel_the_opportunities_and_challenges (accessed 25 July 2021).

7 Ibid., p. 3.

8 Bergische Universität Wuppental, *Entwicklung und Validierung einer Methode zur Erfassung der Sammelraten von Bauprodukten aus Metall*. 2019, p. 23, https://www.dbu.de/OPAC/ab/DBU-Abschlussbericht-AZ-32396_01-Hauptbericht.pdf (accessed 15 May 2023).

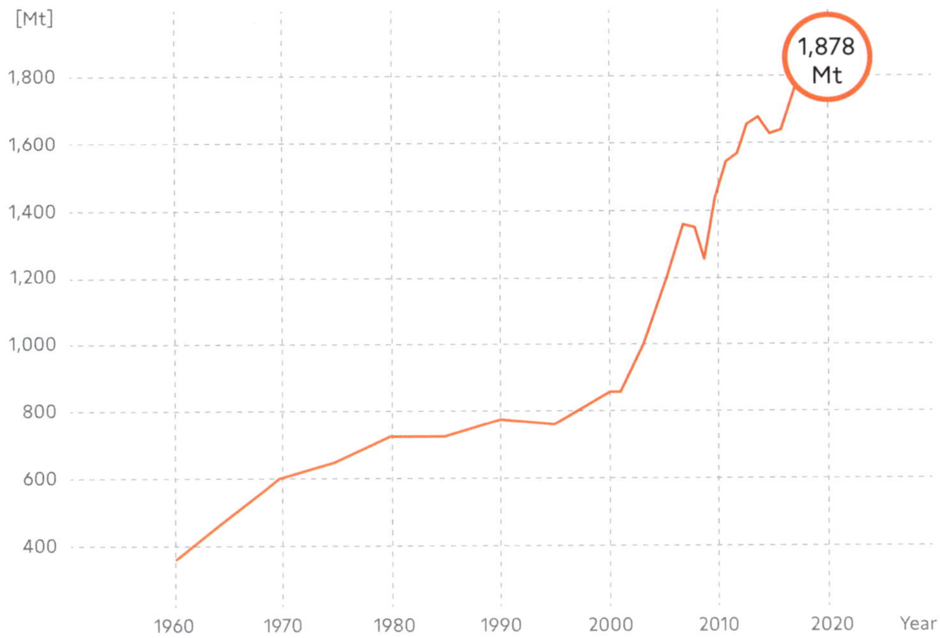

1

Development of global crude steel production.

Based on: World Steel Association, *2021 World Steel in Figures*, p. 7, https://worldsteel.org/wp-content/uploads/2021-World-Steel-in-Figures.pdf (accessed 6 September 2021).

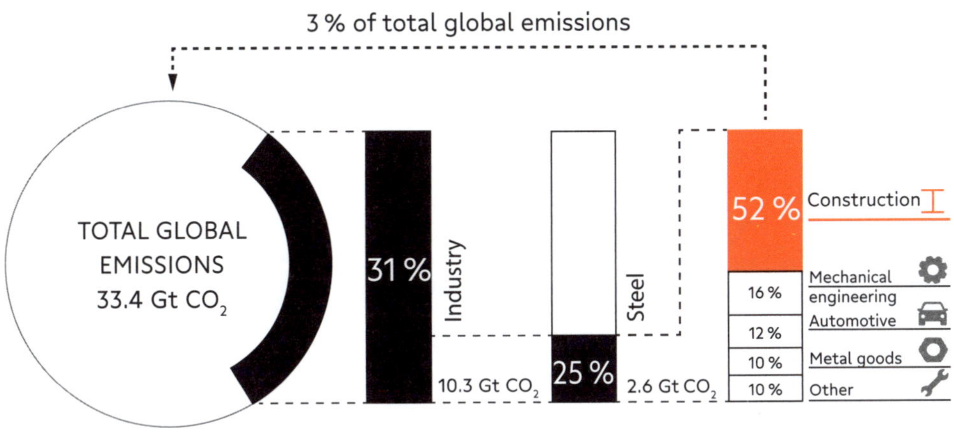

2

Global steel production – related emissions by sector.

Based on: International Energy Agency, *Iron and Steel. Technology Roadmap. Towards more sustainable steelmaking*, 2020, pp. 35–37, https://iea.blob.core.windows.net/assets/eb0c8ec1-3665-4959-97d0-187ceca189a8/Iron_and_Steel_Technology_Roadmap.pdf (accessed 9 September 2021).

9 Anse Smeets, Ke Wang and Michael P. Drewniok, "Wiederverwendung von Baustahl. Wie Materialpässe finanzielle Barrieren der Wiederverwendung im Bausektor senken – ein Beispiel aus Großbritannien", in Felix Heisel and Dirk E. Hebel (eds.), *Urban Mining und kreislaufgerechtes Bauen. Die Stadt als Rohstofflager*. Stuttgart: Fraunhofer IRB, 2021, pp. 168–176, and specifically p. 173.

10 Bundesministerium für Wirtschaft und Energie, *Für eine starke Stahlindustrie in Deutschland und Europa. Handlungskonzept Stahl*. 2020, p. 16, https://www.bmwi.de/Redaktion/DE/Publikationen/Wirtschaft/handlungskonzept-stahl.pdf (accessed 6 December 2021).

11 Anse Smeets, Ke Wang and Michael P. Drewniok, "Wiederverwendung von Baustahl", pp. 170–175.

12 United Nations Environment Programme, *Global Status Report for Buildings and Construction. Towards a zero-emissions, efficient and resilient buildings and construction sector*. Nairobi, 2022, p. 25 ff., https://www.unep.org/resources/publication/2022-global-status-report-buildings-and-construction (accessed 28 February 2023).

13 Stefan Krötsch and Lutz Müller, "Entwicklung des mehrgeschossigen Holzbaus", in Hermann Kaufmann, Stefan Krötsch and Stefan Winter, *Atlas Mehrgeschossiger Holzbau*. Munich: Detail, 2021, pp. 8–13, specifically p. 10 ff., https://www.degruyter.com/document/doi/10.11129/9783955535575/html (accessed 28 February 2023).

3

The value chain of structural steel in Germany.

Based on: Bergische Universität Wuppertal, *Entwicklung und Validierung einer Methode zur Erfassung der Sammelraten von Bauprodukten aus Metall*, 2019, p. 17, https://www.dbu.de/OPAC/ab/DBU-Abschlussbericht-AZ-32396_01-Hauptbericht.pdf (accessed 23 September 2021). BDSV Bundesvereinigung Deutscher Stahlrecycling- und Entsorgungsunternehmen e. V., *Zukunft Stahlschrott. Technische, ökonomische, ökologische und gesellschaftliche Faktoren von Stahlschrott. Ergebnisse der Fraunhofer Umsicht-Studie zur Zukunft des Stahlschrotts, Stand 10/2018*, p. 4, https://www.bdsv.org/fileadmin/user_upload/030-Bro-ZuSt-RZ-20.1.pdf (accessed 25 July 2021). Wirtschaftsvereinigung Stahl, *Circular Economy mit Stahl. Beitrag zum Klimaschutz in Europa*, 2020, p. 6/7, https://www.stahl-online.de//wp-content/uploads/Circular-Economy_2020-rz_WEB.pdf (accessed 6 September 2021). Wirtschaftsvereinigung Stahl, *Fakten zur Stahlindustrie in Deutschland. 2020*, p. 8, https://www.stahl-online.de/wp-content/uploads/WV-Stahl_Fakten-2020_rz_neu_Web1.pdf (accessed 6 September 2021).

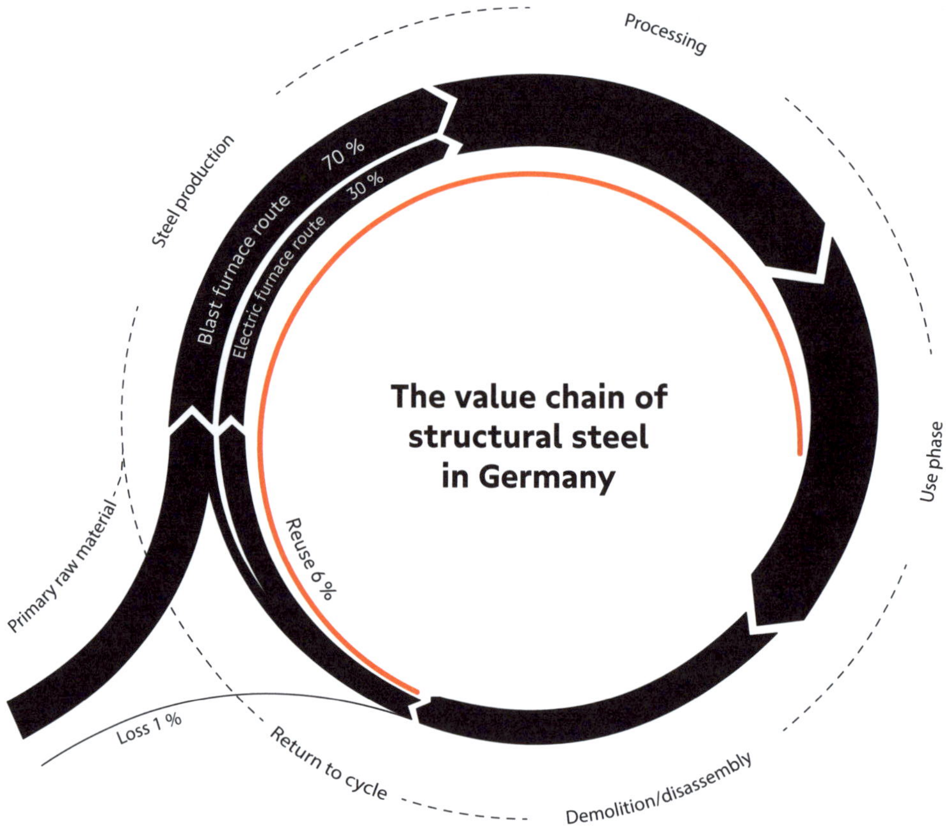

REUSING STEEL

The material characteristics of structural steel – its durability, standardized production and potential for disassembly – make it well suited for reusing in new contexts. Standards and strength classes have applied to structural steel production for many decades, and material degeneration with age is negligible.[14] Its chemical, physical and mechanical material properties have remained virtually unchanged since the early 20th century,[15] and significant material deterioration only occurs when subject to extreme influences such as a high heat stress, corrosion and decomposition due to environmental influences or excess fatigue loads.[16] In addition, the high degree of prefabrication and simple connection methods make both assembly as well as disassembly comparatively straightforward.[17]

THE POTENTIAL OF STEEL FROM URBAN MINING

Steel components from existing buildings generally only become available when a building is decommissioned or converted, i.e., during demolition or dismantling. In terms of both gross volume[18] and total tonnage, steel components are primarily found in Germany in warehouses, business parks and industrial construction.[19] In 2019, these accounted for approx. 23 % by volume of all implemented new building in Germany, or some 42 million m^3 of enclosed volume built using steel construction. Warehouses accounted for the largest share (approx. 39 %), followed by factory and workshop buildings (approx. 25 %) and agricultural buildings (approx. 17.5 %) (see Fig. 4).[20]

Multi-storey open parking garages are a further important potential source for mining structural steel, as some 80 % of all open parking decks are composite steel constructions.[21] This construction method affords good bending-load-bearing performance at low construction heights and is thus considered the standard approach to designing open parking deck structures.[22]

14 Julian Allwood and Jonathan Cullen, *Sustainable Materials. Without the Hot Air. Making Buildings, Vehicles and Products Efficiently and with Less New Material*. UIT Cambridge, 2015, p. 223.

15 Terri Meyer Boake, *Stahl verstehen. Entwerfen und Konstruieren mit Stahl*. Basel: Birkhäuser, 2012, p. 220.

16 David Brown, Ricardo Pimentel and Michael Sansom, *SCI P427. Structural Steel Reuse. Assessment, testing and design principles*. Berkshire: SCI – The Steel Construction Institute, 2019, p. III, https://www.researchgate.net/publication/339713300_SCI_P427_-_Structural_Steel_Reuse_assessment_testing_and_design_principles (accessed 27 July 2021).

17 Ute Dechantsreiter, Peter Horst, Angelika Mettke, Stefan Asmus, Stefanie Schmidt, Florian Knappe, Joachim Reinhardt, Stefanie Theis and Jens Jürgen Lau, *Instrumente zur Wiederverwendung von Bauteilen und hochwertigen Verwertung von Baustoffen*. Umweltbundesamt, 2015, p. 101, https://www.umweltbundesamt.de/publikationen/instrumente-zur-wiederverwendung-von-bauteilen (accessed 25 September 2021).

18 Statistisches Bundesamt, *Bauen und Wohnen. Baufertigstellungen von Wohn- und Nichtwohngebäuden (Neubau) nach überwiegend verwendetem Baustoff. Lange Reihen ab 2000*. Wiesbaden, 2020, pp. 8–84, specifically pp. 21–26, https://www.destatis.de/DE/Themen/Branchen-Unternehmen/Bauen/Publikationen/Downloads-Bautaetigkeit/baufertigstellungen-baustoff-pdf-5311202.pdf?__blob=publicationFile (accessed 21 September 2021).

19 Deutscher Stahlbauverband, *Statistisches Jahrbuch Deutscher Stahlbau 2019*, Münster: Stahlbau Verlags- und Service-GmbH, 2020, p. 15.

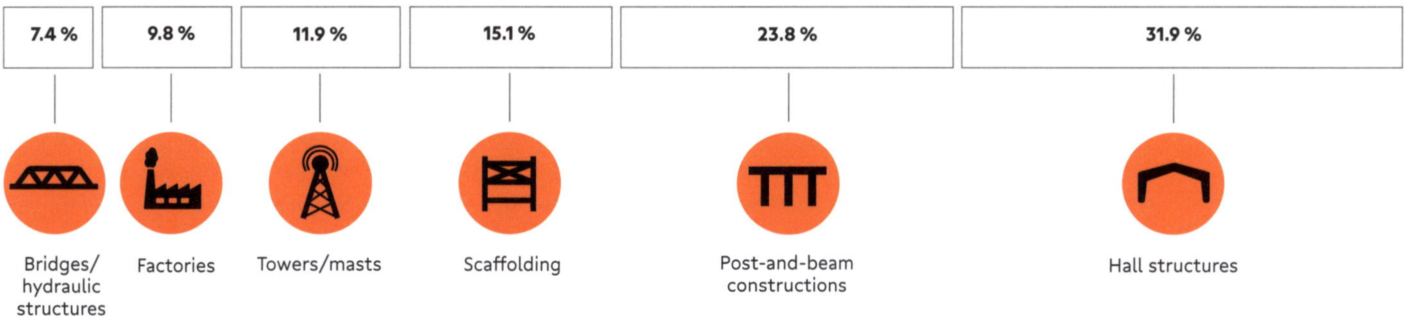

4

Total tonnage of steel component use by construction types in Germany.

Based on: Deutscher Stahlbauverband, *Statistisches Jahrbuch Deutscher Stahlbau 2019*, Stahlbau Verlags- und Service GmbH, 2020, p. 15.

In all of the above construction types, significant quantities of steel are present in the form of standardized components such as the variety of rolled open sections typically used in column-beam construction.[23] As such, these components are also inherently well suited for reuse in future multi-storey buildings.[24]

CURRENT CHALLENGES IN REUSE

The ability to reuse structural steel profiles currently still faces diverse complex challenges, especially with regard to localization and dismantling, inventorization and processing, as well as testing and recertification, since such processes require considerable time and effort and thus incur high costs. Above all, testing and recertification pose a significant hurdle to reuse due to insufficient knowledge of the component-specific properties.[25] The requirements that steel profiles must fulfil are in general no different for reused components than they are for new components. It is therefore necessary to assess how a potential components' material properties may have changed through its previous use, loadbearing situation, means of construction or installation method and to assess these with respect to the new usage scenario and applicable standards. Only in specific cases is it possible to avoid the need for often complex testing, for example by assuming the lowest steel grade for structural calculations or deliberately using larger than required components.[26]

However, two developments look set to transform our ability to reuse structural steel components: the introduction of material passports and building component databases on the one hand, and the harmonization of construction standards on the other will reduce the time, labour and cost entailed for reuse while at the same time making optimum and efficient use of materials.

THE PATH TO LARGE-SCALE CIRCULAR CONSTRUCTION

These approaches are already the focus of research in the construction sector and related research fields, but as yet only few projects have managed to achieve a larger scale of component and material reuse. The main challenges are time and warranty issues as well as planning fees and contract awarding procedures, which do not currently foresee the need for such up-front detailed research at early planning and product-specific tendering stages. Current research focusses on how digitalization strategies can support this process.

Material passes and construction methods that are designed for disassembly will simplify the reuse of building components in 20, 30 or 50 years' time. Assigning materials and products an identity via a digital materials passport makes it possible to ensure they retain value beyond their immediate period of use.[27] Companies such as Concular have started to build databases of products, building elements and entire structures, in this case titled Life-Cycle Passport, as a means of inventorizing the urban mining stock available today.[28] In February 2023, the German Sustainable Building Council (DGNB) presented the Building Material Passport, an assessment and documentation tool compatible with the Life-Cycle Passport that aims to facilitate the systematic adoption of circular construction practices in the building sector.[29] It documents all relevant information on resource use,

20 Statistisches Bundesamt, *Bauen und Wohnen. Baufertigstellungen von Wohn- und Nichtwohngebäuden (Neubau) nach überwiegend verwendetem Baustoff. Lange Reihen ab 2000*.

21 Burkhard Büscher, "Deutscher Stahlbautag. Stahlbau ist bedeutender Wirtschaftsfaktor in Deutschland", *Allgemeine Bauzeitung*, 2014.

22 Wolfgang Kurz, "Parkhaussysteme in Stahlverbundbauweise", *Stahlbau 76* (11), 2007, p. 786–793, specifically p. 786–788. https://www.researchgate.net/publication/230400771_Parkhaussysteme_in_Stahlverbundbauweise (accessed 13 December 2021).

23 Ibid.

24 Julian Lienhard and Patrick Teufel, "Circular structures – Ressourcenerhaltende Tragwerksplanung in Neubau und Bestand", in Bundesingenieurkammer (eds.), *Ingenieurbaukunst 2022*, Berlin: Ernst & Sohn, 2022.

25 Anse Smeets, Ke Wang and Michael P. Drewniok, "Wiederverwendung von Baustahl", pp. 168–173.

26 European Commission – Research Fund for Coal and Steel, *PROGRESS. Provisions for a Greater Reuse of Steel Structures. Final Report. 2017-2020. 2020*, pp. 46–47, https://www.steelconstruct.com/wp-content/uploads/PROGRESS-final-report-for-web.pdf (accessed 16 January 2021).

27 https://concular.de/life-cycle-passport/.

28 Concular 2 2023: https://shop.concular.de/.

29 DGNB, 14 February 2023, https://www.dgnb.de/de/aktuell/pressemitteilungen/2023/gebaeuderessourcenpass.

climate impact and circularity potential for each individual building as a basis for expanding the availability of data for urban mining and supporting circular approaches to the construction, refurbishment and demolition of building structures.

To make use of steel building components from the last century without time-consuming and costly testing procedures, we also need a corresponding normative basis for straightforward structural verification. After the Second World War, when building materials were scarce but a large amount of scrap steel was available, *DIN 1050-2 1947-06 Altstahl im Hochbau* (Scrap Steel in Building Construction) was published in 1947, which designated scrap steel according to different classes – I and II for post-1900, SI and SII for pre-1900 steel. DIN 1050 set out permissible stress loads for class I and II scrap steel, while the older SI and SII designations were limited to loading cases not exceeding 100 N/mm², along with 80 % reductions in the corresponding moments of resistance and inertia for SII and II. Along with approval criteria for companies and cold forming tolerances, this 1.5-page document paved the way for reusing structural steel components. A set of simple and clear rules of this kind can therefore create the conditions for large-scale application.

New normative bases for reusing steel building components are currently being developed at both European and national levels. *EN 1090 Execution of steel structures and aluminium structures – Steel structures – Part xxx: Reuse of structural steel* draws a distinction between steel components reclaimed from buildings constructed before and after 1970, and limits the use of reclaimed steel to quasi-static load situations, such as buildings (i.e., not for the dynamic load situations seen in bridges and similar structures).

NEW HYBRID CONSTRUCTION METHODS FOR HOUSING AND MULTI-STOREY BUILDINGS

STEEL AND WOOD HYBRID STRUCTURES

Timber and steel are often combined for structures with wide spans and high point loads. Contemporary examples of hybrid timber and steel housing and multi-storey constructions include the SKAIO in Heilbronn by Kaden + Lager architects,[30] the OR6 Workspace in London by Waugh Thistleton Architects[31] or the Building D(emountable) office building in Delft by architectenbureau cepezed, which was also designed to be completely deconstructable (Fig. 5).[32] In such constructions, steel profiles reclaimed, for example, from open parking decks or industrial buildings are ideally suited for reuse as secondary raw materials for connecting elements, beams and columns. Depending on the respective installation scenario, timber can act as a fire retarder, encasing the steel elements to achieve a sufficient fire resistance class without the need for additional fire-protective steel coatings.[33]

STEEL AND EARTH HYBRID STRUCTURES

Unlike wood, earth is an abundant local resource around the world, and is also ecologically non-hazardous with excellent thermal and environmental properties. Its heat-retention and moisture-regulating properties create pleasant indoor climates, and air-dried earth bricks are practically infinitely recyclable.[34] Hybrid construction methods in combination with reclaimed steel profiles sourced through urban mining can potentially achieve high savings in energy and raw material use, CO_2 emissions and waste generation compared with conventional construction methods.[35]

The specific material properties of earth and steel building materials also complement one another in terms of both loading mechanisms and building physics. While steel girders, especially slender I-profiles, are designed to absorb bending and tensile forces, earth as a monolithic building material is more well suited to absorbing compressive loads. As earth is classified as non-combustible (fire safety class A1, DIN 4102), earth building materials can potentially be used to improve the fire resistance of reused steel components to prolong their structural integrity in the event of a fire.[36]

30 Thomas Geuder, "Wohnen im Holz-Hybrid. SKAIO, Heilbronn", *DBZ*, 06, 2019, https://www.dbz.de/artikel/dbz_SKAIO_Heilbronn-3371361.html (accessed 1 March 2023).

31 Binderholz, Reference. *Office Building Orsman Road 6*, 2019, https://www.binderholz.com/en-us/mass-timber-solutions/office-building-orsman-road-6-hackney-greatbritain/ (accessed 1 March 2023).

32 Baunetz, "Demontierbar in Delft. Bürogebäude von cepezed", 2020, https://www.baunetz.de/meldungen/Meldungen-Buerogebaeude_von_cepezed_7201633.html (accessed 1 March 2023).

33 Hermann Kaufmann, Wolfgang Huß, Stefan Krötsch and Stefan Winter, "Struktur und Tragwerk", in Hermann Kaufmann, Stefan Krötsch and Stefan Winter, *Atlas Mehrgeschossiger Holzbau*, Munich: Detail, 2021, pp. 42–55, specifically p. 48, https://www.degruter.com/document/doi/10.11129/9783955535575/html (accessed 28 February 2023).

34 Gernot Minke, *Building with Earth. Design and Technology of a Sustainable Architecture*, Basel: Birkhäuser, 4th edition. 2021, pp. 11–16.

35 Sabrina Madeleine Machanek, *Konstruktionsgeschichte mit Zukunft. Analyse und Optimierung historischer, gemauerter Deckensysteme und Ermittlung von möglichen Ökobilanz-Einsparpotentialen unter heutigen Fertigungsmöglichkeiten*. Unpublished Master's dissertation, Bauingenieurwesen, Universität Stuttgart, 2022, pp. 159 ff.

36 Gernot Minke, *Building with Earth*, p. 30.

37 Michael Baumann, Walter Haase, Christina Eisenbarth, Clemens Freitag, Roberta Graf, Rafael Horn, Daniel Schmeer and Paula Lie Sternberg, *Leichtbau im Bauwesen. Ein Praxis-Leitfaden zur Entwicklung und Anwendung ressourcen- und emissionsreduzierter Bauprodukte*. Published by Ministerium für Wirtschaft, Arbeit und Wohnungsbau Baden-Württemberg, Stuttgart, 2018, pp. 4 ff., https://www.baufachinformation.de/leichtbau-im-bauwesen/bu/2018059007813 (accessed 30 September 2022).

38 Anton Pech, Andreas Kolbitsch and Franz Zach, *Decken*. Basel: Birkhäuser, 2nd ed., 2021, pp. 21–22.

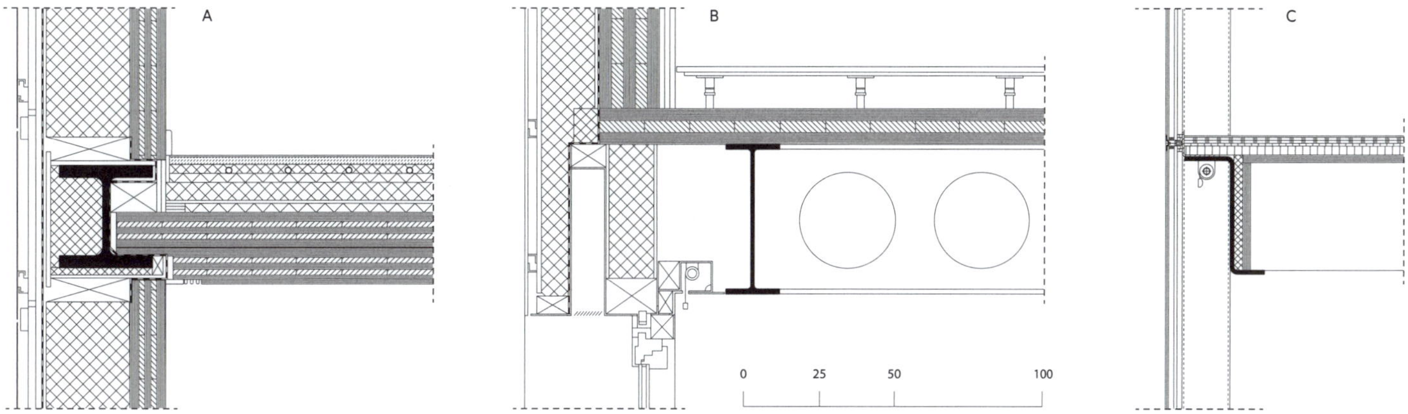

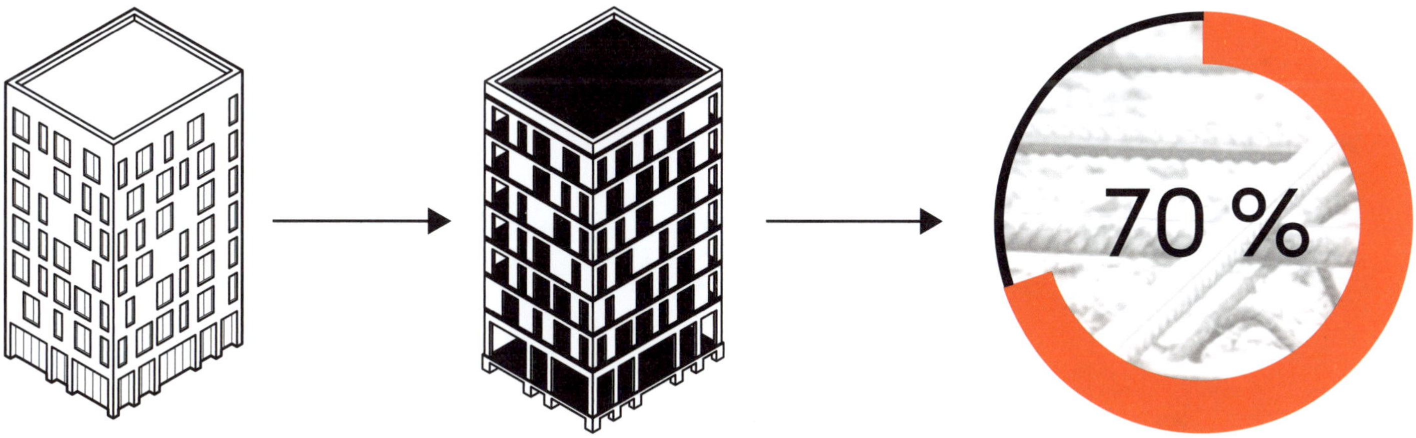

LEARNING FROM HISTORY FOR A CIRCULAR FUTURE

As part of the primary loadbearing structure of buildings, ceiling elements account for around 70 % of the total mass of multi-storey buildings. Optimizing their construction therefore offers high potential for making material savings.[37]

Ceilings are typically realized as flat floor slabs, which from a structural perspective are subject to bending stresses. Earth is not a suitable choice here due to its compression-loading characteristics. However, historical construction techniques from early industrial times prior to the introduction of reinforced concrete can offer possible inspiration. At that time in Germany, shallow-vaulted Prussian cap ceilings were widespread, in which the load borne by the ceiling is transferred into purely compressive stresses in the vaulting. Such constructions can achieve high loadbearing capacities under uniform loads while also making efficient use of materials. Historical capped ceilings usually comprise a series of steel girders spaced at regular intervals between which span shallow masonry arches made of fired brick, lightweight concrete or pumice brick.[38] A contemporary reinterpretation of this technique could employ reclaimed steel girders for the structural components subject to bending and tensile loads (beams and columns) in combination with earthen construction for the two-dimensional and compression-loaded sections (walls and vaults). Here, the adaptation of a historical example serves as an interesting model that can respond to modern noise reduction and fire protection requirements while also providing thermal mass. Moreover, this has potential for use in multi-storey construction in many parts of the world (Fig. 7).

5 ↑↑

Sectional details of example projects.

A

SKAIO Heilbronn, Kaden + Lager, Berlin.

B

6 Orsman Road Workspace London, Waugh Thistleton Architects + Storey, London.

C

Building D(emountable), Architectenbureau Cepezed, Delft.

6 ↑

The proportional building mass of ceilings in multi-storey buildings.

Based on: Michael Baumann, Walter Haase, Christina Eisenbarth, Clemens Freitag, Roberta Graf, Rafael Horn, Daniel Schmeer and Paula Lie Sternberg, *Leichtbau im Bauwesen. Ein Praxis-Leitfaden zur Entwicklung und Anwendung ressourcen- und emissionsreduzierter Bauprodukte*, Ministerium für Wirtschaft, Arbeit und Wohnungsbau Baden-Württemberg (ed.), Stuttgart, 2018, p. 13, https://wm.baden-wuerttemberg.de/fileadmin/redaktion/m-wm/intern/Publikationen/Innovation/Praxis-Leitfaden_Leichtbau_im_Bauwesen_2018_Web.pdf (accessed 30 September 2022).

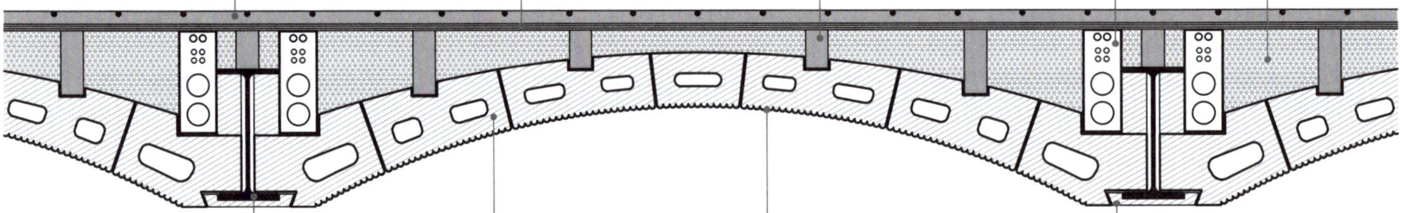

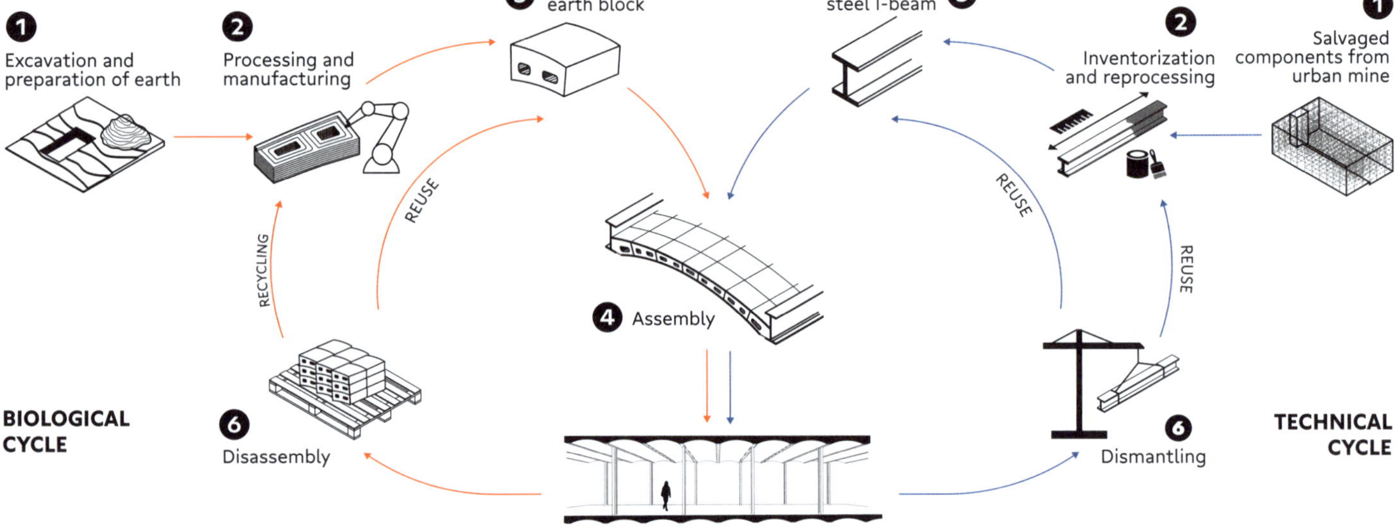

7 ↑↑

Contemporary reinterpretation of the construction principle of a historical cap ceiling. Ferrum Lutum research project, Institute for Structural Design, University of Kassel.

8 ↑

Closed-loop circularity potential of clay and steel.

OUTLOOK

To exploit the potential of reusing steel components for hybrid multi-storey construction at a large scale, it will be necessary to digitally link the many and diverse processes and techniques. Along with the provision of suitable standards regulating the reuse of reclaimed loadbearing components, this includes linking material passports with databases that can provide information on the technical properties and availability of building components. It will also require that we develop construction techniques and design solutions that enable non-destructive and separable disassembly of distinct building materials and components. In this respect two building materials offer particular promise: earth as a locally abundant resource in the biological cycle, and steel as a particularly durable and resistant material in the technical cycle (Fig. 8).

Further Reading

▶ Materials passports, "Materials Passports", *Circular Construction and Circular Economy*, p. 118

▶ Carbon fees and dividends, "Carbon Fees and Dividends, and a Circular Construction Industry", *Circular Construction and Circular Economy*, p. 92

▶ Life cycle analysis, "Concular", *Circular Construction and Circular Economy*, p. 114

DESIGNING WITH MATTER AS MET

Article by Oliver Tessmann, Max Benjamin Eschenbach, Christoph Kuhn and Anne-Kristin Wagner

Circular economy in architecture requires us to fundamentally reassess the meaning of permanence in architecture. The conventional notion of permanence of buildings prevents an integration of circular strategies within the design, use and reuse of buildings and their components. While precedents from architectural history lasted hundreds of years, current real estate investments are commonly based on a life cycle of 50 years, which the market often does not even exhaust. Such a take-make-waste-approach destroys building components as well as design intelligence and energy that architects, engineers, designers and builders have invested in them. This highlights one of the current core issues in the struggle for circular construction: the short duration of the use phase of an architecture not designed for disassembly leads to its destructive end-of-life. This issue receives increasing public and political attention.[1, 2]

Our work aims to fundamentally rethink the notion of permanence in architecture by proposing a process of continuous transformation of the built environment. Here, permanence is not established within a single building but through building elements that endure as reused components in potentially numerous buildings, sites and functions. Design then does not start with a blank piece of paper but with *matter as met*[3] – existing material that needs to be mined and upcycled for future constructions.

CAPTURING AND INTEGRATING MATTER AS MET

In order to design with *matter as met* we conceive algorithmic strategies that capture the existing, assemble it into novel constructions and complement it with newly added parts. Those strategies allow for more differentiated recycling and reuse processes that push matter, gathered through urban mining, into a circular economy.

Capturing *matter as met* requires digitalization through processes like laser scanning, structured light 3D scanning as well as photography and photogrammetry. Thorough analysis of the acquired geometry and data-driven modelling are the first steps to revealing the potential of the objects to be upcycled and reused as future building components. Once the *matter as met* is precisely digitized it can be complemented with digitally fabricated elements that serve as adapters, extensions or precious seams that resemble the Japanese art of Kintsugi. The core feature of digital fabrication – its ability to yield customized objects – can thus contribute to increasing reuse in architecture.

Within the project Digital Rubble we developed a process of scanning natural rocks, printing adapters and assembling old and new elements into a coherent structure. The dry-joining of old and new extends the service life of the elements and maintains their flexibility for future reuse by avoiding weakening through bolts, screws or adhesives during assembly. We used graphic statics and conceived an optimization algorithm to design structures from dry-stacked, unprocessed rocks along a thrust line. To find the optimal position and orientation of the stones, they were algorithmically rotated three-dimensionally around their centre of mass and along the thrust line in order to maximize the load transfer between the elements through normal forces. Subsequently, the adapter components' geometry was automatically generated, ready for 3D printing (Fig. 1). Different rock arrangements and 3D-printed connectors were tested and evaluated with regard to printing time, amount of material used, assembly and structural performance.[4] The Digital Rubble project demonstrates that a digital workflow from object digitization to 3D-printing and assembly can help to bring reused elements into novel constructions.

In order to maximize the amount of reused parts and minimize the 3D-printed additions we took inspiration from Kintsugi, a Japanese philosophy and form of art that emphasizes the beauty of imperfection and brokenness by repairing cracks and fractures in pottery using lacquer and gold or silver. We sought to apply this concept in architecture by using 3D printing to fill in the cracks and gaps and create new building components from scrap parts. The technological process allows us to incorporate these pieces into the design. This not only provides a creative solution for reducing waste and reusing materials, but also creates a unique aesthetic that celebrates the past and present of the building. The combination of Kintsugi and 3D printing in architecture offers a way to not only reduce waste, but also

1 European Commission, *The European Green Deal*, COM(2019)640 (2019), https://eur-lex.europa.eu/legal-content/EN/TXT/?uri=COM:2019:640:FIN (accessed 9 May 2023).

2 European Commission, *A New Circular Economy Action Plan for a Cleaner and More Competitive Europe*, COM(2020)98 (2020), https://eur-lex.europa.eu/legal-content/EN/TXT/?uri=COM:2020:98:FIN (accessed 9 May 2023).

3 Y. Bréchet, *The Science of Materials: from Materials Discovered by Chance to Customized Materials*. Inaugural Lecture delivered on Thursday 17 January 2013, Collège de France, 2015, https://doi.org/10.4000/books.cdf.3641.

4 B. Wibranek and O. Tessmann, "Digital Rubble – Compression-Only Structures with Irregular Rock and 3D Printed Connectors", in *Proceedings of the IASS Annual Symposium 2019 – Structural Membranes*, Barcelona, 2019.

5 M. Yang, K. Kpalma and J. Ronsin, "Shape-Based Invariant Feature Extraction for Object Recognition", in R. Kountchev and K. Nakamatsu (eds.), *Advances in Reasoning-Based Image Processing Intelligent Systems*, Intelligent Systems Reference Library. Berlin, Heidelberg: Springer, 2012, pp. 255–314, https://doi.org/10.1007/978-3-642-24693-7_9.

6 C. Mueller, D. Marshall, Y. Huang and D. White, *Architectural Design Workshop: Kintsugi, Upcycling and Machine Learning*, 2020, https://web.archive.org/web/20211127232045/https://architecture.mit.edu/subject/summer-2020-4181 (accessed 9 May 2023).

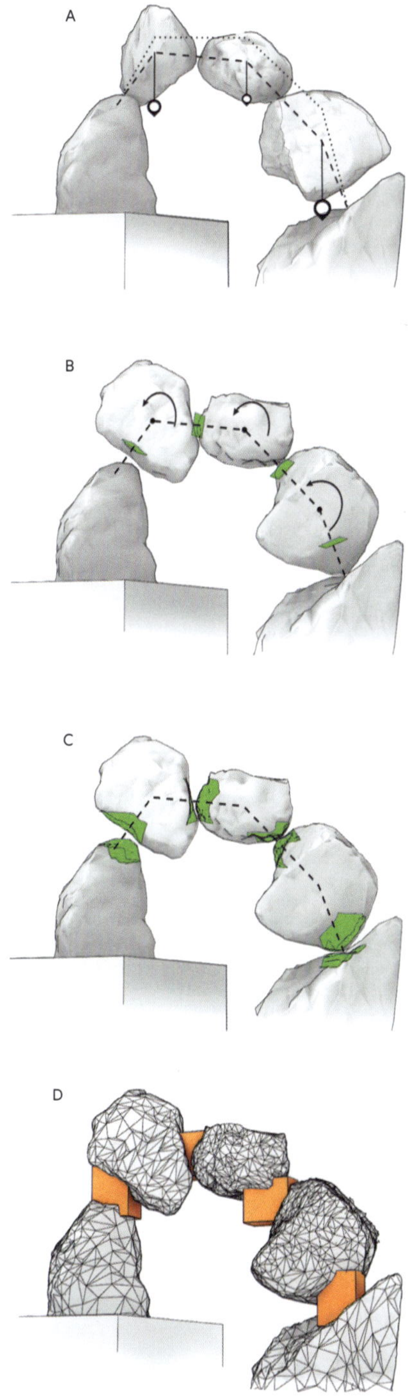

create a sublime architecture, paying tribute to the heritage of our built environment and highlighting its history through design.

Contrary to standardized building components, elements stemming from demolition are highly diverse. This heterogeneity has to be handled to correctly classify *matter as met* according to its geometry, material as well as functional and structural performance. The first step consists of cataloging the harvested components in a database of material stock (Fig. 2). Using a suitable feature extraction technique, numerical features can be computed for every object within the material stock database, based on the geometry of the components.[5, 6, 7, 8]

The same feature extraction process is applied to the components of an architectural design, enabling a standardized and numerical description of supply and demand. Computational means help to navigate the repository and conduct a matchmaking process by synchronizing a given demand (architectural design) with the available material stock (*matter as met*). This matchmaking process can be expressed as an optimization problem, which is solved using combinatorial optimization algorithms. Such an approach can also be adapted and applied to increase the human agency in the selection process: the component repository may be browsed through filtering for component types, manually choosing or pre-selecting components that fit the design idea. Selected components are then manually inserted into the digital design model.[9]

In the Circular Production design studio we tested this approach with students on the task of building a square pyramid from scrap material. In a first step, small-scale debris pieces were digitized using photogrammetry. A feature extraction procedure was performed for each piece. Tessellation patterns were designed individually for each of the four sides of the pyramid, using a combination of pattern generation techniques and manually defined target cells. The designs were matched with the material database, providing direct visual feedback (Fig. 3). Form-fit connections were designed on the basis of the digitized debris and fabricated using 3D printing. The assembly of the four-sided pyramid demonstrator was the final step.

Computation plays a major role as an aid in the design process. However, navigating a certain stock of components and transforming them into an architecture is first and foremost a question of novel design strategies that the discipline has to develop and refine. How do designers and architects envision the aspect of reuse: do we establish a new aesthetic language that employs the reused components' patina and imperfections or do we dissolve it within established aesthetic expressions?

1

Left: **Digital Rubble demonstrator.**

Above: **Recalculated thrust line based on the weights of stones** (A)**, rotating stones to match stone interfaces and thrust planes** (B)**, interfaces of stones** (C) **and connectors generated based on the interfaces** (D)**.**

2

Concrete debris is digitized, cataloged in a database and can subsequently be reused using computational discrete and combinatorial design tools.

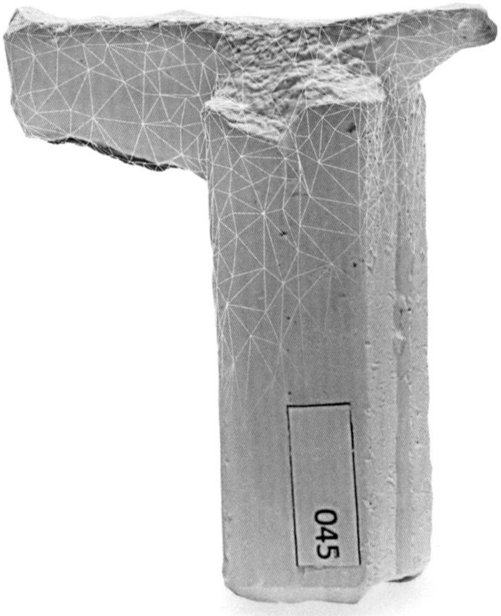

REFRAMING DIGITAL-REAL PROJECT CHAINS

In the project Precast Concrete Components 2.0 (Fertigteil 2.0) our interdisciplinary team of researchers and industry experts in architecture, engineering, surveying and building digitization develops novel circular economy processes to reuse concrete components of obsolete buildings. The project aims to overcome linear material flows and flips the order of conventional digital-real process chains. While typically a building design starts with digital planning and goes on to materialization, we start from an existing, obsolete building and transform it into a repository of precast concrete components (PCC). PCCs are building components decoupled from the lifespan of an individual building; their durability and permanence enable them to endure as reused components in potentially numerous buildings, sites and functions.

In a real-digital process chain, concrete components harvested from disassembled buildings are digitized, refurbished and robotically transformed into PCCs. Computational tools similar to those described above help to aggregate the discrete elements into dry-joint structures that serve as buildings for today and component repositories for future constructions. Today smartphones and tablets equipped with Lidar distance sensors as well as powerful camera systems enable us to perform 3D scanning and photogrammetry even without specialized equipment. Software to analyse the captured data and recompose the scanned components is also readily available, allowing us to capture data at a scale as large as the available anthropogenic building stock.[10] To prototype industrial processes, we partnered with FARO Europe GmbH for 3D scanning the concrete components. These scans provide highly accurate information on the geometry, which is complemented with on-site observations for quality and material inspection.

The components are harvested by sawing at key points to disassemble the obsolete structure into individual components for reuse (Fig. 4). Harvested components are categorized according to the time of their initial production, allowing certain assumptions to be made regarding their performance when reused. Additionally, the elements must be tested to assess their potential for reuse. Angelika Mettke's research work provides useful guidance on how the inspection of concrete components can be carried out,[11] as well as on the energy

7 R. L. Johns, M. Wermelinger, R. Mascaro, D. Jud, F. Gramazio, M. Kohler, M. Chli and M. Hutter, "Autonomous dry stone: On-site planning and assembly of stone walls with a robotic excavator", *Construction Robotics*, 4, 2020, pp. 127–140, https://doi.org/10.1007/s41693-020-00037-6.

8 J. J. Park, P. Florence, J. Straub, R. Newcombe and S. Lovegrove, "DeepSDF: Learning Continuous Signed Distance Functions for Shape Representation", *arXiv*, Cornell University, 2019, https://doi.org/10.48550/ARXIV.1901.05103.

9 J. Runberger, V. Ondejcik and H. Elbrrashi, "Design from Finite Material Libraries: Enabling Project-Confined Re-use in Architectural Design and Construction Through Computational Design Systems", in C. Gengnagel, O. Baverel, G. Betti, M. Popescu, M. R. Thomsen and J. Wurm (eds.), *Towards Radical Regeneration*. Design Modelling Symposium Berlin 2022, Springer, Cham, 2022, pp. 343–359, https://doi.org/10.1007/978-3-031-13249-0_29.

10 Felix Heisel and Dirk E. Hebel (eds.), *Urban Mining und kreislaufgerechtes Bauen: Die Stadt als Rohstofflager*. Stuttgart: Fraunhofer IRB Verlag, 2021, https://doi.org/10.51202/9783738805642.

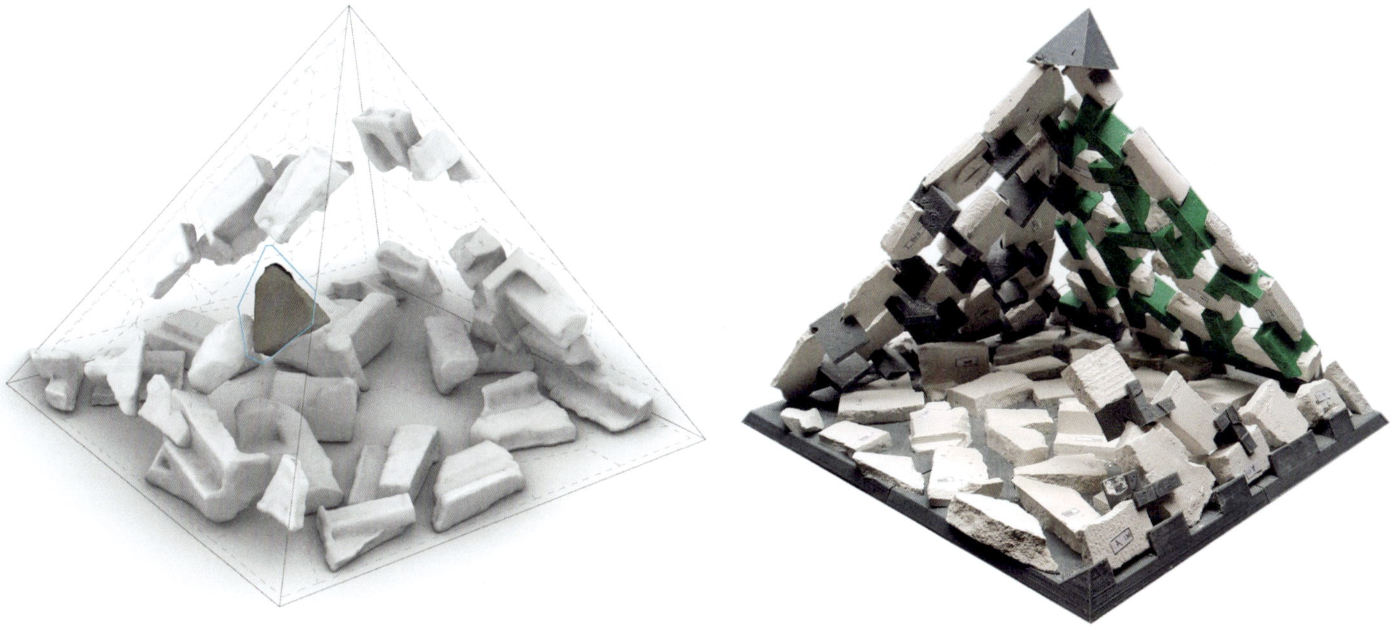

3

Visualization of a feature extraction and arrangement method. The feature extraction is done using a centroid function. The arrangement is computed using a predefined tessellation and subsequent assignment of fitting debris.

Based on: C. Mueller, D. Marshall, Y. Huang and D. White, *Architectural Design Workshop: Kintsugi, Upcycling and Machine Learning*, 2020, https://web.archive.org/web/20211127232045/https://architecture.mit.edu/subject/summer-2020-4181 (accessed 9 May 2023).

consumption involved in producing concrete raw materials for newly produced concrete as well as recycling concrete.[12]

All relevant processes are tracked for their environmental impacts and resource consumption: the sawing of the stock, the processing and preparation of the reused components, their installation with dry-jointed connections as well as the associated transport. Combining this data with data from literature[13] and research databases,[14] impact coefficients can be computed and used to inform a combinatorial optimization process in the next step. While in the Circular Production case study a well-known Hungarian method[15] was sufficient for the combinatorial optimization step, a more sophisticated approach is applied in the Precast Concrete Components 2.0 project, exploring the relation of multiple variables and fulfillment of multiple constraints for a much more complex objective. We conceived an optimization model based on mixed-integer programming (MIP), allowing a more sophisticated recombination of the PCCs into new skeleton structures while utilizing the gathered data from our component repository and integrating the environmental impact coefficients into the objective function.[16, 17]

The next step is the reconditioning of the harvested concrete components using dry-joint connection details. The Digital Building Fabrication Laboratory (DBFL) at the TU Braunschweig's Institute for Structural Design (ITE) provides a fabrication centre including a freely movable robot as well as a CNC sawing and milling unit. Here, the team around Harald Kloft uses subtractive machining of reclaimed concrete components at full scale to produce high-precision dry joints that can be integrated directly during the subtractive processing. The joints also simplify the future dismantling of segmental structures, a key aspect in keeping costs of reuse processes low enough to be competitive. The entire process chain is evaluated by building a demonstrator structure (Fig. 5). Furthermore, to gain insights on how such a process chain can be used within the industry at scale, our partner Thing Technologies GmbH is evaluating ways in which their BIM and business process management tools can be employed to track and coordinate all involved processes, from uploading a BIM model through a web interface to the final delivery of the PCCs on site.

4 ↑

Selective and controlled deconstruction using diamond-fitted concrete saws as a proof of concept of harvesting concrete components for reconditioning and reuse.

Sawing and dismantling by Bierfreund Beton-Bearbeitung.

5 ↗

Digital design of a demonstrator structure made from reused concrete components with dry-jointed connections.

The result of the comparative life cycle assessment by the Department of Design and Sustainable Building (ENB) shows that reuse can save about 70 % of the greenhouse gas emissions and about 50 % of the energy input (Fig. 6). These savings are due in particular to the conditions of virgin cement production, which requires a high energy input and causes about 90 % of the greenhouse gas emissions both in conventional concrete production and production of recycling concrete. Reusing whole concrete components means that no new cement is needed, thereby significantly reducing the environmental impact.

DESIGN FOR FUTURE REUSE

The urban mining of parts and their refurbishment for future reuse can only be an intermediary step on a path towards full circularity in architecture. Unlike parametric design with its over-individualization of parts that only fit one specific project, we focus on a discrete design approach in which repetitive parts are combined in various ways. Computation is used to explore vast combinatorial solution spaces instead of individualizing elements for digital fabrication. The discrete design embraces a *Design for Reuse* practice: given their modularity and standardization, the components may be disassembled, recombined and reassembled into alternative structures.

Discrete design requires novel digital design tools. At the Digital Design Unit (DDU) at TU Darmstadt we developed Wasp,[18] a Grasshopper[19] plug-in offering combinatorial tools to design with discrete elements. Wasp is intended to contribute to circular design approaches in architecture. The description of each part includes all information necessary for the aggregation process (part geometry, connection locations and orientation). Wasp offers a series of aggregation procedures, allowing geometry- and data-driven generation of structures, as well as utilities to visualize and process them.

When constructing without adhesives or mortar, elements need to interlock and transfer loads through contact surface and friction. In 2016 the Taiwanese researcher Shen-Guan Shih designed a specific type of polycube, called SL-Block.[20] It is formed by S-and L-shaped tetracubes. Two SL-Blocks can be joined in six different ways, which leads to different forms of aggregations (Fig. 7). This formal versatility in combination with its interlocking capacities makes the SL-Block system interesting for discrete design approaches. While other topological interlocking assemblies form sheet-like aggregations and require rigid boundaries that are able to absorb the shear forces of the system, SL-Blocks interlock

11 A. Mettke et al., *Schlussbericht zum Forschungsvorhaben Rückbau industrieller Bausubstanz – Großformatige Betonelemente im ökologischen Kreislauf*. Cottbus: Brandenburgische Technische Universität, 2008, https://www-docs.b-tu.de/ag-baurecycling/public/Forschungsberichte/0__Einfuehrung.pdf (accessed 9 May 2023).

12 S. Heyn and A. Mettke, *Ökologische Prozessbetrachtungen-RC-Beton (Stofffluss, Energieaufwand, Emissionen)*. Cottbus: Brandenburgische Technische Universität, 2010, http://www.rc-beton.de/vortraege_pdfs/Stofffluss-Energie aufwand-RC-Beton101102.pdf (accessed 9 May 2023).

13 Ibid.

14 Bundesministerium für Wohnen, Stadtentwicklung und Bauwesen (BMWSB), ÖKOBAUDAT-Release 2021-II Internet Database, 2021, https://www.oekobaudat.de (accessed 9 May 2023).

into linear, volumetric, diagonal and spiraling configurations – a perfect prerequisite for aggregations forming a wide range of shapes.

As all aggregations are reversible, SL-Blocks can be easily disassembled and reused in other constructions. We consider SL-Blocks as small-scale and function-agnostic elements that can be aggregated into functional building components such as walls, columns or beams of conventional constructions and reused after a building is disassembled. We furthermore envision constructions made entirely of reversible elements that allow for a permanent transformation of the building (Fig. 7 and 9).

Assembly, disassembly and reassembly would ideally be conducted by autonomous robots. We collaborate with the Intelligent Autonomous Systems Group (IAS) at TU Darmstadt, headed by Jan Peters, to experiment with Machine Learning (ML) strategies for robot control. The sequential assembly of structures, including all assembly steps, is based on an architectural 3D model. Robots then determine their Task and Motion Planning (TAMP) and "understand" the weight, dimensions and surface properties of components using visuo-tactile sensors. The robot learns to assemble parts by being rewarded for producing sound constructions (Fig. 8). ML and sensor technology help to autonomously perform construction tasks that currently cannot be programmed in advance due to the need for permanent adaptability.[21] The combination of autonomous robots and reversible constructions could allow for a different notion of permanence in architecture, represented through durable building elements that are subject to constant transformation and reuse.

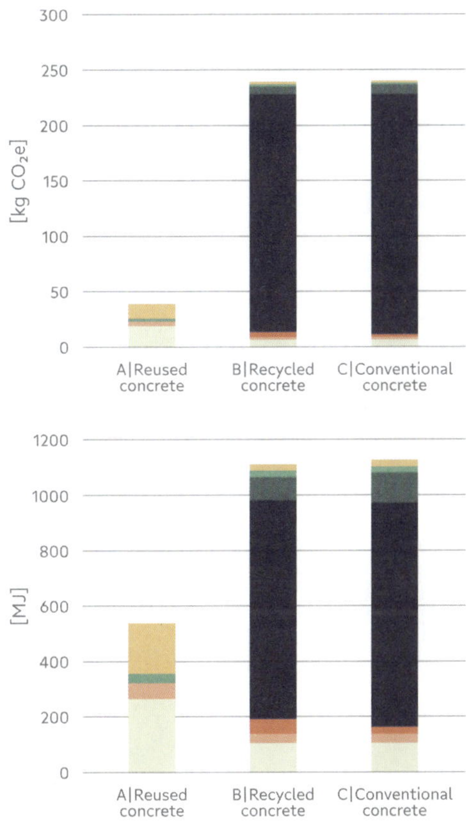

6

Global warming potential (GWP, top**) and primary energy non-renewable total (PENRT,** bottom**) for the processes and scenarios considered.**

- Installation/construction
- Production/reconditioning concrete
- Production of concrete raw materials
- Recycling of materials
- Demolition/deconstruction
- Transport (to construction site)
- Transport (of concrete raw materials)
- Transport (of recycled materials)
- Transport (to recycling/ reconditioning site)

7

Demonstrator made from SL-Blocks of different materials.

8 ↑

Autonomous robotic assembly of SL-Blocks.

9 ↗

Visualization and speculation about a concrete beam made from SL-Blocks.

CONCLUSION

Circular Economy in architecture and construction is an enormous challenge. Digital technologies and robotics can contribute to such a paradigm shift as they offer novel approaches for all aspects of the design to production process chain. Designing with *matter as met* is fostered by algorithmic feature extraction and computational resources invested in turning scrap into a puzzle of valuable pieces. Robotics helps to upcycle reused parts through precise subtractive and additive manipulations of elements. Giving robots autonomy in assembling, disassembling and reassembling unlocks novel discrete constructions using elements currently impossible or non-imageable to use because they are too labor intensive. Implementing these technologies in construction processes needs to go along with the exploration of novel spatial and architectural concepts that emerge when the notion of permanence is transferred from the building to its components.

Further Reading

▶ Prefabricated concrete elements, "New Buildings from Old", *Circular Construction and Circular Economy*, p. 44

▶ Urban mining, "The Case for Deconstruction", *Circular Construction and Circular Economy*, p. 32

▶ Hybrid systems, "The Reuse Potential of Steel Profiles for Hybrid Multi-storey Construction", p. 116

15 H. W. Kuhn, "The Hungarian method for the assignment problem", *Naval Research Logistics*, 2, 1955, pp. 83–97, https://doi.org/10.1002/nav.3800020109.

16 J. Brütting, C. Vandervaeren, G. Senatore, N. De Temmerman and C. Fivet, "Environmental impact minimization of reticular structures made of reused and new elements through Life Cycle Assessment and Mixed-Integer Linear Programming", *Energy and Buildings*, 215, 2020, https://doi.org/10.1016/j.enbuild.2020.109827.

17 E. B. Eschenbach, A. K. Wagner, L. Ledderose, T. Böhret, D. Wohlfeld, M. Gille-Sepehri, C. Kuhn, H. Kloft and O. Tessmann, "Matter as Met: Towards a Computational Workflow for Architectural Design with Reused Concrete Components", in C. Gengnagel, O. Baverel, G. Betti, M. Popescu, M. R. Thomsen and J. Wurm (eds.), *Towards Radical Regeneration*. Design Modelling Symposium Berlin 2022, Springer, Cham, 2022, pp. 343–359, https://doi.org/10.1007/978-3-031-13249-0_29.

18 A. Rossi, *Wasp – Discrete Design for Grasshopper*, 2021, https://github.com/ar0551/Wasp/ (accessed 9 May 2023).

19 Robert McNeel & Associates, *Rhinoceros® 7 & Grasshopper®*, 2021. https://www.rhino3d.com/ (accessed 9 May 2023).

20 Shen-Guan Shih, "On the Hierarchical Construction of SL Blocks: A Generative System that Builds Self-Interlocking Structures", in *Advances in Architectural Geometry 2016*, Zürich: vdf Hochschulverlag AG an der ETH Zürich, 2016, https://doi.org/10.3218/3778-4_10.

21 B. Belousov, B. Wibranek, J. Schneider, T. Schneider, G. Chalvatzaki, J. Peters and O. Tessmann, "Robotic architectural assembly with tactile skills: Simulation and optimization", *Automation in Construction*, 133, 2022.

ACKNOWLEDGEMENTS

The research on reuse of concrete components was developed within the research project *Precast Concrete Components 2.0 (Fertigteil 2.0)*, funded by the Federal Ministry of Education and Research Germany (Bundesministerium für Bildung und Forschung, BMBF) through the funding measure *Resource-efficient circular economy – Building and mineral cycles* (ReMin). The project is a collaboration between the Digital Design Unit (DDU) at TU Darmstadt (Prof. Dr.-Ing. Oliver Tessmann, Dipl. Des. Max Benjamin Eschenbach), Design and Sustainable Construction (ENB) at TU Darmstadt (Prof. Christoph Kuhn, Dipl.-Ing. Anne-Kristin Wagner), the Institute of Structural Design (ITE) at TU Braunschweig (Prof. Dr.-Ing. Harald Kloft, Dipl.-Ing. Lukas Ledderose), Thing Technologies GmbH (Dr. Marc Gille-Sepehri) and FARO Europe GmbH (Dr. Denis Wohlfeld, Tobias Böhret).

The four-sided pyramid demonstrator was built in the design studio *Circular Production*. Teaching and scientific development by Prof. Dr.-Ing. Oliver Tessmann, Dr. Nadja Gaudillière-Jami and Dipl. Des. Max Benjamin Eschenbach. Demonstrator design and fabrication by Zahra Babadi, Dominik Binzel, Mirko Dutschke and Aysenur Gültekin.

The research on robotic assembly was developed within the project *Tactile Robotic Assembly* funded by the Federal Institute for Research on Building, Urban Affairs and Spatial Development (Bundesinstitut für Bau-, Stadt- und Raumforschung, BBSR) on behalf of the The Federal Office for Building and Regional Planning (Bundesamt für Bauwesen und Raumordnung, BBR) with funds from the Zukunft Bau research grant programme. The project is a collaboration between the Digital Design Unit, DDU (Oliver Tessmann, Yuxi Liu, Mehrzad Esmaeili) and the Intelligent Autonomous System Group, IAS (Jan Peters, Boris Belousov, Tim Schneider) at TU Darmstadt.

ARCHITECTURE IN LARGE QUANTITIES

Article by Gilles Retsin

There has probably never been as much "good architecture" as today. Each new issue of magazines such as *El Croquis*, *2G* or *Arquitectura Viva* reveals another fantastic architecture practice, with a unique and interesting body of work, beautiful homes with thoughtful plans and sophisticated details. When leafing through these magazines, it is easy to forget about the wider state of architecture. The houses presented in these magazines are rare exceptions to the rule, unique instances of beauty, built for a very limited subset of the population.

Outside of this niche, we have an endless accumulation of "bad architecture", a carbon-intensive amalgamation of cladding, commodified parts and industrially produced elements sourced from all over the world. Supported by a global late-capitalist system of production, "bad architecture" has proven to be scalable and has relentlessly proliferated across the world.

In contrast, "good architecture" attempts to get rid of commodified parts and repeatable solutions. "Good architecture" reinvents itself for every single project. In an attempt to bypass the industry and its products and processes, "good architecture" relies heavily on craft, excellence and endless architectural labour. "Good architecture" is therefore non-scalable, not repeatable, expensive and not accessible for the many. Beauty is expensive.

Behind "good architecture" also lies an increasing crisis of the profession itself. Architects are slowly being banished from the built environment, with a large part of their job outsourced to other disciplines. Young architects attempt to form unions, to protest against long working hours and low pay – or generally, to express disillusionment with the reality of the profession. Architecture has never been as good as today, but it has also never been as isolated and irrelevant. Architecture today is niche.

Outside of architecture bookshops, the world challenges us to think beyond our niche. Our times are defined by extreme challenges in which architecture has a stake. We are faced with an unprecedented housing crisis, both in the Global North and South. Estimates on how much housing we need vary, but the numbers are in the range of hundreds of millions. How can we build millions of homes without further damaging the planet? And could these millions of homes be "good architecture"? One thing is for sure, architecture is due for a fundamental reset, a rewiring of its core and its systems of production.

Architecture has rewired itself before, when it attempted to come to terms with mechanized mass production in the early 20th century. Some of the first attempts by architects at grappling with industrial construction were focused on architecture's parts, its elementary building blocks. Frank Lloyd Wright's development of the Usonian Automatic in the 1920s was an attempt to make his earlier Textile Block houses available to the many, to industrially produce them. Wright developed a limited set of typical concrete building blocks, which could be assembled into a wide variety of quite exuberant houses – while remaining economical. Ultimately, only a few were built. In 1947, Walter Gropius and Konrad Wachsmann's General Panel Corporation built a factory for 10,000 homes, based on modular timber panels which could be assembled into an endless variety of homes. The panels formed the basis for a democratic architecture, on a large scale. Again, only a few were built – mainly for employees of the General Panel Corporation itself.

Instead, modular architecture took a different turn. It became known for uncompromising repetition rather than combinatorial difference. Large, wall-sized elements could be assembled in exactly one way, leading to repetitive types of cookie-cutter housing. This effort, while architecturally debatable, contributed greatly to society, creating thousands of homes. Housing was a project, architecture was societally relevant. This project of industrially produced modular parts as a means for a democratic and shared architecture was gradually put on hold with the emergence of early neo-liberalism and the end of the social-democratic welfare state from the late 1970s onwards. The images of the 1972 destruction of the Pruitt-Igoe social housing apartment blocks came to symbolize both the end of modernism and of mass-housing as a project. It would ultimately also mark the end of architecture's central importance to society. After this, architecture was gradually evacuated from the forefront, to end up in the lifestyle sections of weekend magazines.

1

AUAR Garden Studio, Bristol. The garden studio is built from AUAR's building blocks, windows and cladding. The assembly is customized to the specific conditions of the site and wishes of the client. These types of small projects were used as 1:1 prototypes for the development of the building system and robotic assembly.

Architecture's attempt to industrialize itself, to reinvestigate its parts, was put on hold. All attempts after modernism to innovate architecture were no longer connected to systems of production or in relation to scale. Late capitalism optimized modernist building elements, commodified them into brands and trained architects and consultants to manage their assembly. The world became a thin and ugly assembly, unequal, extractivist and bad for the planet.

To rewire architecture today means that we pick up our attempt to industrialize construction again: this time around, not through the idea of mechanized, cookie-cutter repetition, but through automation. Doing this means redefining the very material we build with, the elementary parts and their systems of production that define architecture.

MODULARITY AND DIGITAL MANUFACTURING

A particularly interesting approach to rethinking architectural parts for increased automation is Programmable Matter, a field of mechanical engineering, which develops materials that can be programmed to assume any desired form or function, similar to a computer program which performs different tasks. Programmable Matter blurs the notions of materials, robotics, digital programs and parts into one operation. This approach is useful in manufacturing, medicine and robotics to create customizable and adaptable materials and machines. While it is still largely hypothetical in those fields, some of its ideas have the potential to find a more immediate application in architecture and construction, which is fundamentally a "simpler profession" than medicine or mechanical engineering.

A subset of Programmable Matter is focused on so-called Digital Materials, developed by Neil Gerschenfelt at the Center for Bits and Atoms at MIT. These digital materials can be understood as versatile, repeating, voxel-like parts which can be programmed or compiled by robots, or through self-organization, into a variety of machines and structures. Digital Materials and Programmable Matter introduce a radically different approach to modularity, even to the very notion of digital design and fabrication. Applying this thinking to architecture rewires some of the most fundamental concepts of how we design. It collapses the notion of the "part" with the notion of "material", and it closes the gap between design and fabrication, between the digital and physical, between function and form.

The experiments of the early digital architects, such as Greg Lynn or Bernard Cache in the 1990s and 2000s, form an important precedent for the effort to automate architecture. As the architectural historian Mario Carpo argues, the early digital developed a radical innovation: the idea that we could use digital machines for mass customization. However, through its focus on formal complexity it missed the opportunity to turn this idea into an industrial paradigm at scale. The missing link between the industrialized production of buildings and digital design is the notion that we can mass-customize buildings through their assembly, rather than through crafting thousands of different components.

This implies developing a new form of parts that bridge the gap between the digital and the physical and enable us to automatically compile endless variations of buildings, at no extra cost. Rather than relying on large, centralized factories typically associated with industrialized construction, we can imagine a future of local micro-factories which could operate by sharing collectively manufactured parts. The micro-factory concept is related to another seminal idea from the Center for Bits and Atoms: the Fab Lab. Fab Labs are a network of small-scale workshops with digital fabrication tools, which give individuals open access to technologies such as 3D printers or CNC machines.

In architecture, a precedent for the Fab Lab approach can be found in WikiHouse, an open-sourced housing project where individual families can build their own housing using CNC-cut timber elements. While WikiHouse initially used mass-customized parts, it has now shifted to producing modular, repeating parts. WikiHouse recognized that the FabLab ideology fell short in its focus on individual craft, which was inhibitive to scale and impact.

Ultimately, automation in architecture can be understood as calibrating mass customization to operate at scale. It is a balancing act between what we all share and what we do not share. We can share the base building blocks, inherited from modular and industrialized construction, but these we assemble into continuously differentiated and mass-customized buildings as inherited from the early digital and the FabLab. It is precisely in this tension between what we share and what we do not share that a new form of architecture emerges.

AUTOMATED ARCHITECTURE

In 2020, Mollie Claypool and myself founded a technology company called AUAR (Automated Architecture), which puts these ideas into practice. AUAR proposes a discrete form of digital design and fabrication, where architectural parts are understood as repeating, versatile building blocks that can be robotically assembled into endless varieties of housing. The basic building block is composed of standard cross-laminated timber sheets, which can be assembled by a single off-the-shelf industrial robot in under 45 seconds. These building blocks have a limited set of precut connections and a custom steel joint which creates structural connectivity. Industrial robots are used to assemble building blocks into larger fragments or chunks of buildings. These can take the form of panels, volumes or compartments, such as for example a bathroom or kitchen.

This process can be understood as a form of additive assembly, not through extruding and layering concrete, but through compiling pixel-like building blocks. Every panel or volume can be mass-customized through the differentiated placement of building blocks by the robot – without adding cost. This process integrates design and fabrication, as every digital building block corresponds to a physical building block. Any design can be generated by compiling blocks into a whole, which can then be evaluated on its properties and qualities. Cost, but also CO_2 emissions or lead time are made transparent during the design process. For example, the decision to place a larger or smaller window can be evaluated on its cost, but also its impact on the energy performance of the house, besides its qualitative effect on the overall architecture and living quality.

Each building block is understood as an array of voxels, measuring 30 × 30 × 30 cm. These dimensions result in an ideal wall depth in terms of insulation but also correspond to the standard dimensions used in the industry for wall panels and finishes, thereby reducing waste. Building blocks can be defined by their properties: structural, dividing, insulating, operable, transparent, finished. A transparent block is, for example, materialized as a window. These window blocks share the same connections as the structural blocks and are also made from standard sections of timber. The system does not differentiate between blocks used as floors, walls or roofs.

The building system is developed according to the principles of circular design. All connections are dry and reversible, and all blocks can be reused for other buildings, or broken back down to their component parts. This also implies that buildings can be easily adapted without having to craft custom solutions. For example, building an extension to a house would merely imply removing the cladding, attaching a series of new blocks and reusing the cladding to finish the extension.

AUAR operates through an approach where it is the building block that forms its product, rather than the house itself – as every house can be different. The building blocks establish a shared base quality, which can be instantiated across different iterations and versions of buildings. Each AUAR building is recognizably an AUAR building, but at the same time can be fundamentally different. In this way the design remains open and can be defined by architects and other stakeholders outside of AUAR. A generative software allows architects to develop and evaluate the implications of design options. By contrast, a typical configurator for modular housing would present a limited design space, where architects can accumulate different panels or volumes into designs. The freedom in such configurators is rather limited, and the design space is often so constrained that the configurator becomes redundant: the only solution is an array of container-like volumes of a specific number of levels. In AUAR's approach, design can occur at a more granular level, that of the building block. In principle, the resolution of the design space is 30 × 30 × 30 cm, the size of the voxel underlying the building blocks. This resolution creates a vast design space, in which a multiplicity of architectural positions can be explored. For example, an architect could

2

AUAR Robot Cell, Milton Keynes. AUAR's systems are based on timber building blocks, which are assembled by an industrial robot. This allows to build distributed micro-factories which can be set up in existing estates or in a container on site.

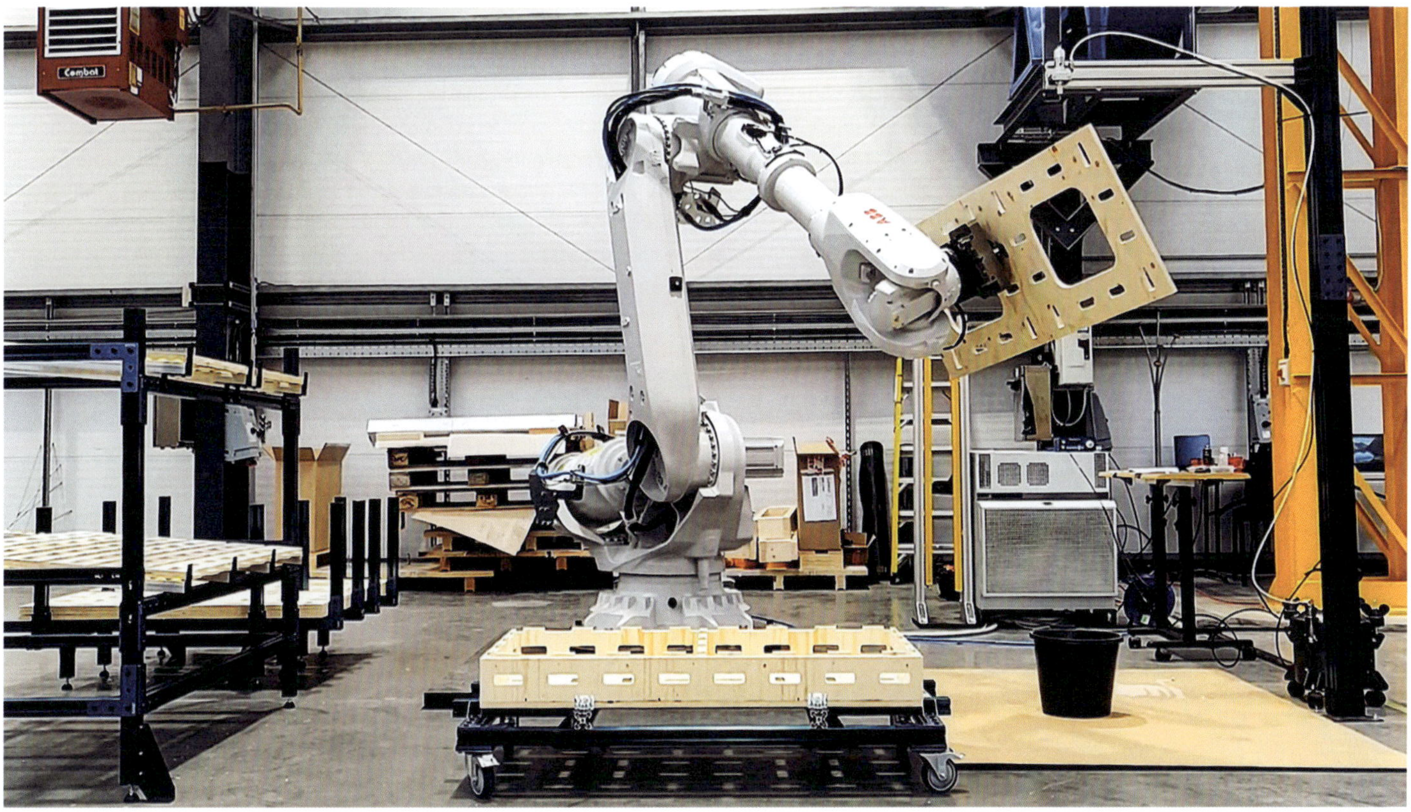

develop a Miesean-style fluid space, a more classical gridded space based on a Palladian 9 × 9 grid, or an organic cave-like space.

Conceptually, this approach radically differentiates AUAR from modular housing builders. The AUAR building system is universal and generic, but its instantiations are always subjective and unique. This is, at its heart, an architectural innovation and solves the key problem of modular prefabricators, stuck between adaptation and standardization. In theory, this approach can be traced back to the early 1990s ideas of "digital design", where buildings were amorphous blobs, adapting to a field of forces – just, in this case, set within a voxel space and built with repeating parts.

The implications for architectural practice are vast. Architects would be enabled to operate through a product-based model, and rather than being siloed into small, competing practices, they could share what they learn across a network. AUAR could update its systems in conversation with its network of architects, contractors and clients, so that its building system can gradually improve and remain open. Projects are no longer one-off prototypes. An idea is no longer confined to a single instance but could benefit the many.

GOOD ARCHITECTURE

Automated architecture is about distributing default qualities on a large scale and across variations, resulting in the mass production of houses which are always "good". The project of researching and understanding what exactly constitutes default "good" in large quantities is what I identify as an architectural mission. Many of the startups operating in the space of housing are agnostic to this question, and go with the market average of the white plasterboard one-, two- or three-bedroom apartment layout. There is a clear scope for architecture in this context to forefront that some of the fantastic qualities we see in the work of the boutique architects and learn in architecture school can in fact be distributed on a large scale, at no extra cost. This repetition does not make these qualities less valuable or culturally irrelevant. We need to unlearn the instinct to couple cultural relevance with scarcity. Excellence is not unexpected, never-seen-before and visually arousing – tropes inherited from the visual arts – but the ability to establish a base quality that can be instantiated thousands of times, in thousands of variations.

Beyond architectural and spatial qualities there are other values that make an automated architecture "good". These are, or should be, no-brainers: in order to be good, the mass replication of houses should be regenerative for the planet. Of course, housing should be low-energy, net-zero, non-extractive in terms of both natural resources and human labour. These should be thought of in the first place with the end user in mind, and involve end users as much as possible. They should be affordable, as otherwise they would defeat their purpose. Much of the current architectural discourse seems focused on sustainable, carbon-negative materials and processes, and seems to have little to say about architecture beyond this. In this sense, the sustainability- and material-obsessed architectural activists, commercial developers and new construction platforms seem to all agree that architectural ideas are a dangerous distraction, to be avoided. Ultimately, AUAR proposes an optimistic claim for architecture itself in the age of automation, for the possibility of beauty in large quantities. If we cannot even consider this possibility, what then is the relevance of our discipline?

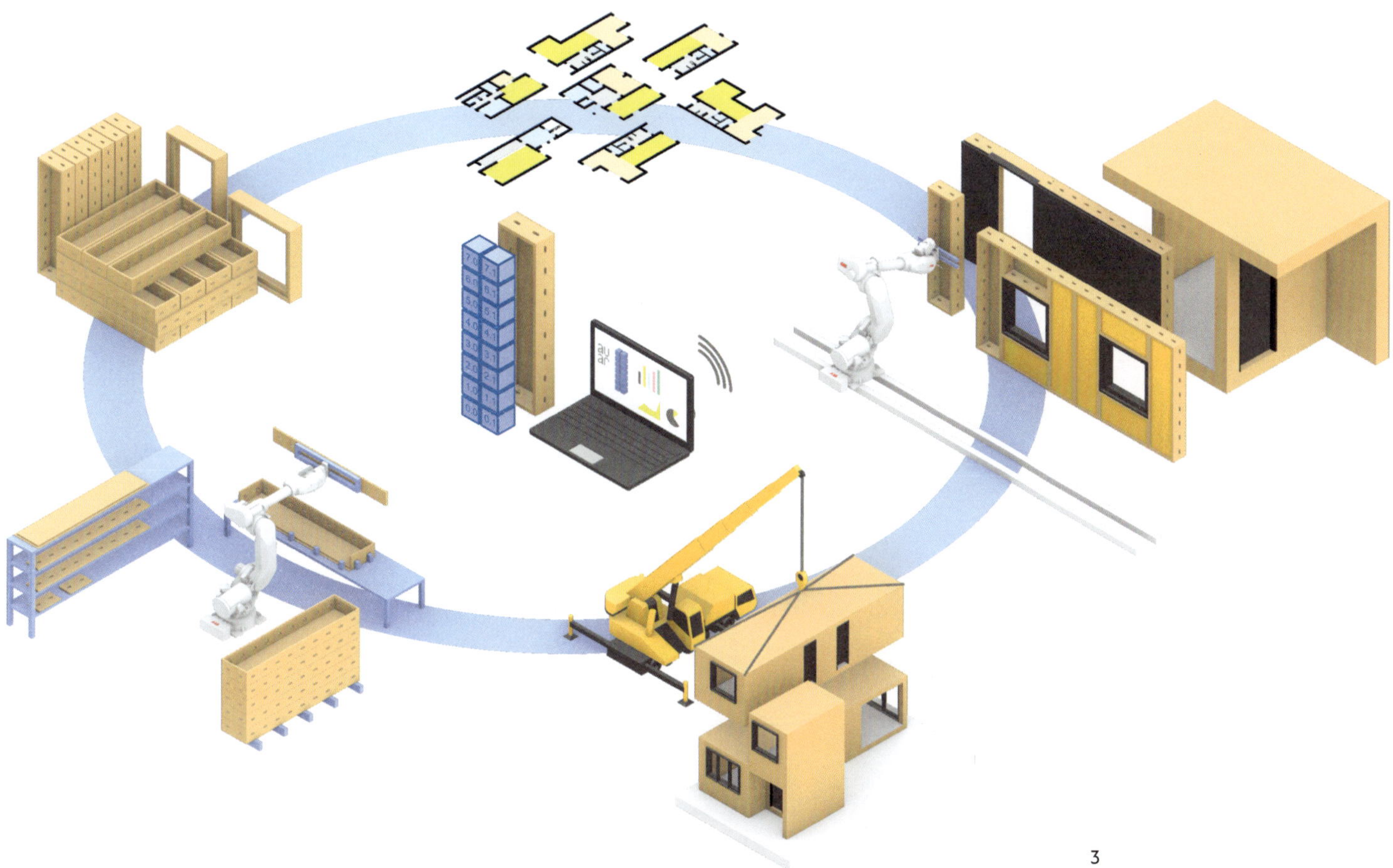

3

AUAR Tech Stack.
AUAR's tech stack is based around a building block, which forms the core of both the building system and the software platform.

4

House Block (2021) is a prototype for a two-storey affordable house, built using just one type of modular building block. The project was developed in collaboration with Hackney City Council and engaged the local community in conversations around robotic automation and affordable housing.

Further Reading

- ▶ Prefabrication, "The Urban Village Project", *Circular Construction and Circular Economy,* p. 122
- ▶ Parametric design, "Parametric Design-to-Fabrication Platforms for Scaled Industrial Implementation", p. 50
- ▶ Sustainability, "Sustainability – The Importance of a Holistic Approach", *Circular Construction and Circular Economy,* p. 10

Better

Less

Different

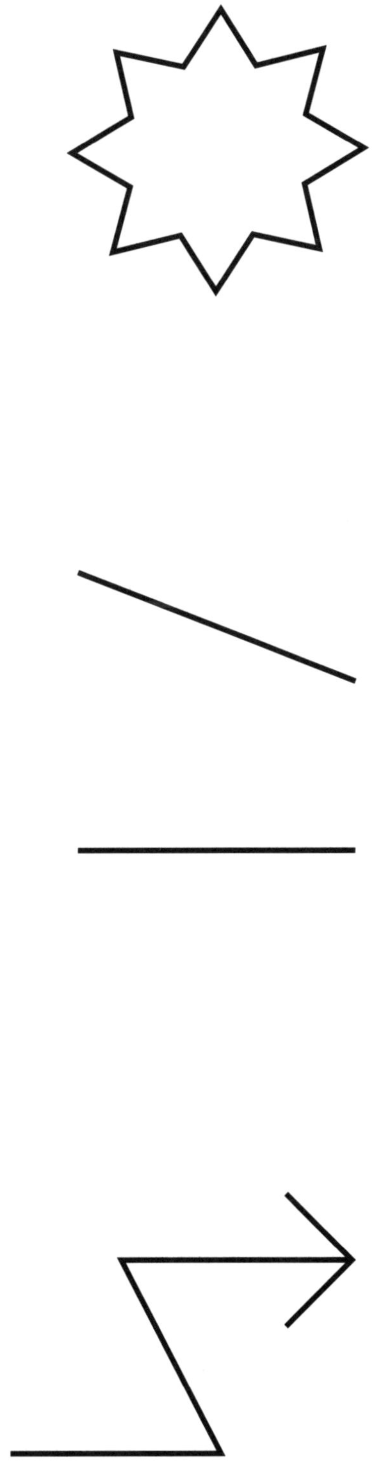

CIRCULAR CONSTRUCTION OVER AGAIN

The RoofKIT Project at Solar Decathlon Europe 21/22 – An Example of a Holistic Approach to Sustainability

Case Study by Elena Boerman, Dirk E. Hebel, Felix Heisel and Andreas Wagner

Since the publication of the first volume of *Building Better – Less – Different* in October 2022, public and political awareness of its focal topics of circular construction and the circular economy has grown considerably. Hardly a day goes by without a newspaper feature or journal article discussing closed material cycles or the need to rethink how we deal with existing buildings. In May 2023, the 18th International Architecture Exhibition titled "The Laboratory of the Future" opened at *La Biennale di Venezia* under the curation of Lesley Lokko. At the Arsenale and in many of the national pavilions in the Giardini this was taken as an opportunity to address the issue of resource consumption. The Turkish pavilion, for example, asked how we can prevent the demolition of buildings, the US pavilion examined the role of plastics in the natural and built environment, and the Finnish pavilion highlighted water wastage in wastewater management. The German pavilion, titled "Open for Maintenance – Wegen Umbau geöffnet", unpacks the topic of reuse and circular construction: addressing the question of wastage caused by the exhibitions themselves, the curatorial team from Arch+, Summacumfemmer and Büro Juliane Greb opted to reuse exhibition installations by Maria Eichhorn from the preceding Art Biennale and make its materials available for reprocessing in an on-site laboratory workshop. The national pavilion was in effect a (well documented) materials depot.

Public awareness of the topics of this second book – the clean energy transition and digital transformation – is similarly high, not least because energy aspects have been the subject of public discourse for some time now and because technological innovations in general exert a certain social fascination. Unfortunately, the building sector has been slow to incorporate any of these topics into general practice. It is, however, our opinion that the combination of these various approaches and their positive reciprocal effects have huge potential to accelerate a change towards holistic sustainability. To demonstrate these possibilities, the Faculty of Architecture at the Karlsruhe Institute of Technology (KIT) developed RoofKIT as its entry to the Solar Decathlon 21/22 in Wuppertal.

SOLAR DECATHLON EUROPE 21/22 IN WUPPERTAL

The Solar Decathlon is the largest and most important architecture and building competition for universities in the world. Organized by the US Department of Energy, the competition was first held in 2002. Its declared goal is to "prepare the next generation of building professionals to design and build high-performance, low-carbon buildings powered by renewables". The international biennial event has since been held 15 times, attracting the participation of more than 25,000 students from over 90 teams around the world, in the process promoting innovation in education and the construction industry.[1] A common feature of all Solar Decathlons is that, after an initial planning phase, the student teams must realize a fully functional building, typically a section of their overall design proposal. The university teams then compete against one another with their demonstration units and accompanying design concepts in ten different disciplines.

Since 2010, the competition is organized in global regions, though the field of participants is not restricted to these boundaries. The 2022 Solar Decathlon Europe (SDE 21/22 edition) was the first to be held in Germany and was organized by the University of Wuppertal. SDE 21/22 expands on the traditional themes of the competition – energy generation, energy efficiency, technical implementation, climate resilience and quality of living – to include further issues such as the identity of European cities, increasing urban density and a mix of uses, associated socio-economic contexts, urban mobility and, above all, a more comprehensive understanding of the issue of resources: circular construction methods, urban mining principles and the use of renewable, reused or recycled building materials. In addition, for the first time, the organizers outlined three concrete urban situations to work on, all located in Wuppertal's late 19th century Mirke district: an infill project to close a gap in the urban grain, the renovation and horizontal extension of a mid-20th-century building, and a roof top-up of an existing two-storey structure which is currently used as a cultural event location. Entrants were asked to consider the prevailing characteristics of the

1 Solar Decathlon, U. S. Department of Energy, USA, https://www.solardecathlon.gov/about.html (accessed 18 May 2023).

1

Three different options and locations in Wuppertal were available for the participants' interventions.

neighbourhood and its social and economic realities. Alternatively, the teams could choose a comparable building task from their respective country of origin.

After almost two years of design, planning and construction, 16 teams presented their design concepts for the urban context and their respective demonstration units on the Solar Campus, a site on the disused railway lines of the former Mirke Railway Station in the north of Wuppertal. A welcome effect of the expanded brief is that all the participating teams gave greater attention to systemic issues. It would seem that increased awareness in the academic realm is leading to an approach that no longer focuses solely on the design of individual buildings but sees buildings as part of a wider communicative network.

How fixed structures and mobile infrastructures interact is becoming an increasingly important topic, fuelled by questions of energy distribution. It has implications for one of the central questions we are facing for the future: how should we deal with our existing buildings? Should we upgrade the energy performance of individual buildings according to "one size fits all" regulations, or should we broaden our perspective to consider a building's neighbours and district and try to decarbonize the system as a whole? The entries for the Solar Decathlon Europe 21/22 took the latter systemic approach, as described below through the example of the RoofKIT project.

2 ↑

The RoofKIT project – a rooftop addition to an existing two-storey building in Wuppertal.

3 →

The RoofKIT project encompasses both the renovation and conversion of the existing building as well as a three-storey modular timber rooftop extension.

THE ROOFKIT PROJECT

In 2019, the Faculty of Architecture at the Karlsruhe Institute of Technology (KIT) decided to take part in the Solar Decathlon 21/22. What motivated the team headed by the Professorship of Building Science and Technology and the Professorship of Sustainable Construction was the broader thematic remit of the competition brief. In the end, more than 100 students from KIT as well as the Offenburg University of Applied Sciences and the Heinrich Meidinger School for Technical Systems in Karlsruhe worked together on the project. From the three available options, the team chose the rooftop extension to an existing building from the turn of the century, which currently houses a café and a dance hall and therefore plays a prominent public and social role in the neighbourhood. The project name RoofKIT derives from the task of adding a new roof coupled with KIT – which stands for both the institute name and the conceptual principle of a modular "kit of parts".

In times of climate change and depleting resources, architecture has an increasing responsibility – beyond the traditional categories of beauty, solidity and utility – to society as a whole. RoofKIT therefore aims to be a lighthouse project that addresses both the traditional and the contemporary objectives of the discipline in the current context of climate change, social alienation and resource scarcity and uses them as the design parameters of responsible architecture. If we as architects, engineers, scientists, designers and planners are to take responsibility for our planet as a place for future generations, we need to design in harmony with our existing natural cycles and energy transformation systems and must understand the act of building from an integrative social perspective: away from linear, short-term solutions towards circular metabolism approaches that unite durability, regeneration and circularity with functionality, flexibility and design. Buildings themselves then serve as producers of renewable forms of energy and act as material depots for the future.

The overall design concept for RoofKIT envisages retaining the café on the ground floor, repurposing the first floor as a small boarding house and extending the building with three additional upper floors offering important functions for the neighbourhood. The two uppermost floors will contain new, socially responsible and affordable forms of housing in a modular timber construction while the recessed floor between the existing building and the new flats – which has been dubbed the "Urban Gap" – will give space for possibilities in the urban realm. It can serve as a performance area and venue for events, a meeting place for clubs and groups, and space for family celebrations, play and leisure – in short a location that is socially just, democratic and diverse reflecting today's modern society. Various ancillary facilities such as storage, kitchens, a bar area and outdoor terrace around the perimeter are included to facilitate these flexible patterns of use.

The principle of adding new storeys to an existing building increases urban density without sealing any new outdoor surfaces. At the same time, by making functionally open interventions, it is possible to tap unused potential within the existing building. By sensitively refurbishing the existing building fabric and increasing its energy efficiency, the character of the former industrial building and its recognizable visual presence within the neighbourhood is preserved. The new rooftop addition picks up the characteristic form of the building's former shed roof and also creates south-facing surfaces that can be used for generating solar energy.

THE ENERGY CONCEPT

The challenge when adding new storeys to an existing building is to meet the total energy demand for both the new extension – in this case residential units – and the existing building. In inner-city urban situations, surface areas for generating solar energy are generally limited, and multi-storey buildings have smaller roof surfaces proportional to their total floor area. The densely built character of European cities also means that other environmental sources cannot be easily exploited: accessible ground for harvesting geothermal energy is often lacking and air source heat pump systems may cause noise problems. The RoofKIT project aims to cover as much of the total energy demand for building services, appliances and e-mobility as possible using solar systems installed on the building envelope and surrounding surfaces.

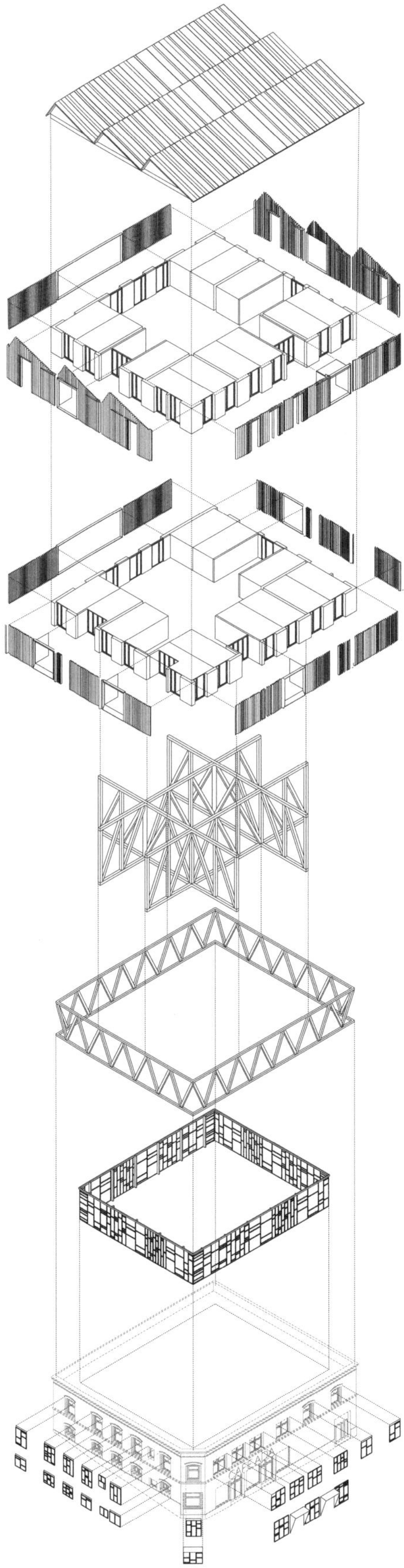

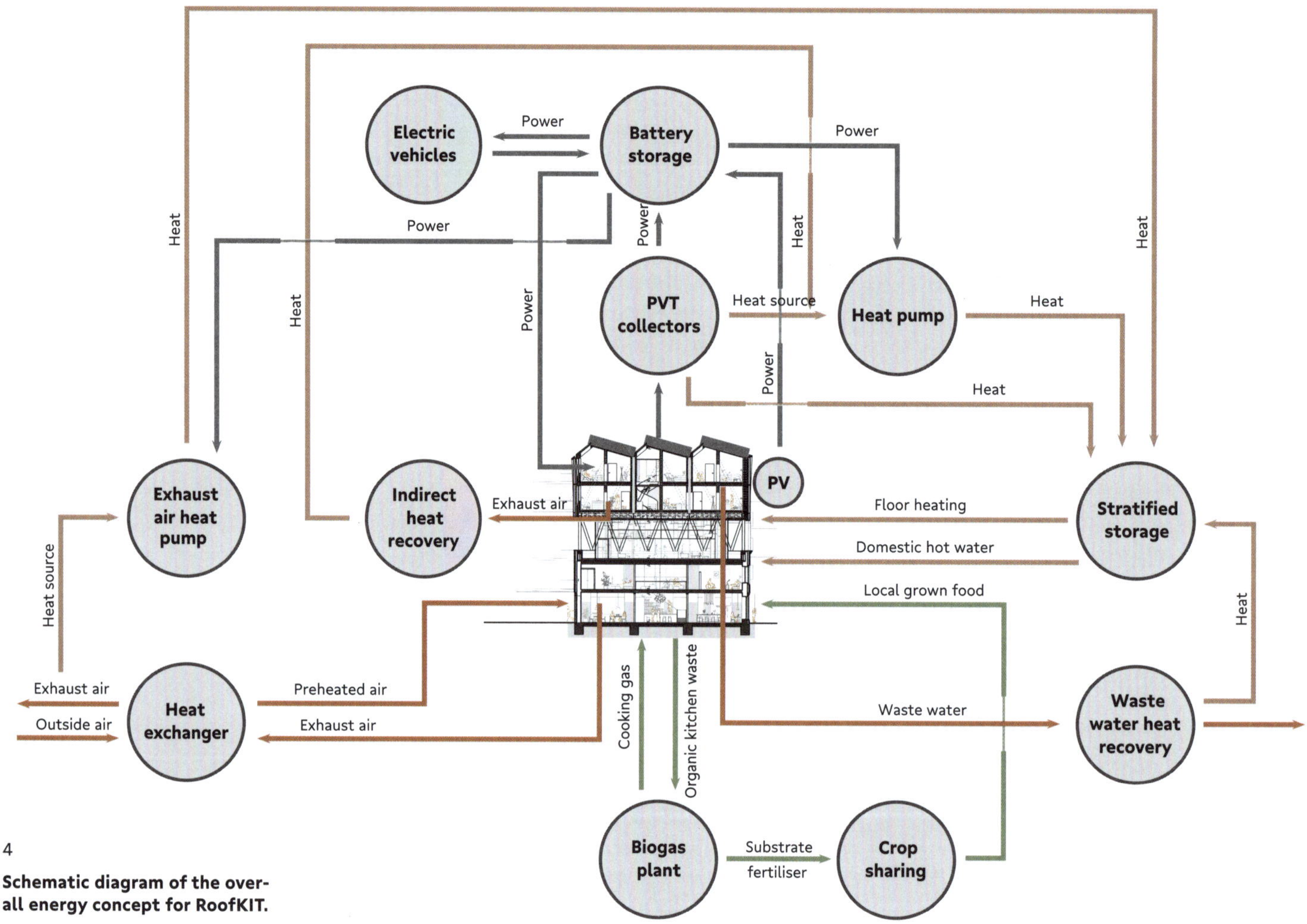

4

Schematic diagram of the overall energy concept for RoofKIT.

5

Schematic diagram of the energy concept for the RoofKIT House Demonstration Unit (HDU).

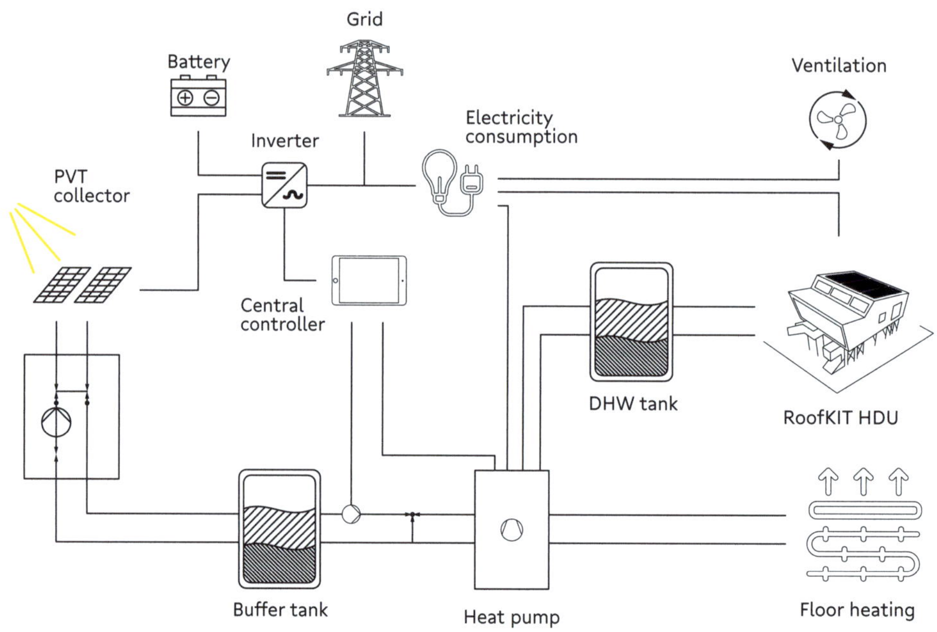

To achieve the desired high degree of self-sufficiency, the new addition needed to meet very high energy efficiency standards. Significant improvements were also planned for the existing building. Hybrid photovoltaic thermal solar collectors (PVT collectors) were incorporated into the roof surface: these generate not only electricity but also heat by serving as the source for a heat pump for the underfloor heating and hot water tank. The PV modules are coloured using an innovative coating technique to merge visually with the copper colour of the roofing without significantly impacting on the efficiency of the solar cells. An intelligent energy management system maximizes the building's self-consumption of solar energy and at the same time its grid connectivity by optimizing solar yield, electricity demand and the charging or discharging of batteries for the building, its e-bikes as well as a thermal buffer storage tank.

To ensure comfortable indoor temperatures in the summer months, the demonstration unit built on the site features a passive cooling concept that employs a combination of effective shading and thermal mass (provided by earthen building materials) with night-time ventilation for cooling. The energy management system ensures optimal comfort by activating the shading system and opening skylight vents in the roof to control solar gain and provide natural ventilation as required. An interface within the unit allows the occupants to personally control and intervene in the automatic systems and at the same time provides hints, for example when opening windows may improve night-time ventilation cooling. To avoid the need for costly technical infrastructure and support the idea of sufficiency, the unit uses decentralized ventilation elements in the facades – obviating the need for a centralized system with ducts – as well as wireless light switches. Much like a bicycle dynamo, the action of pressing the switch generates sufficient electrical energy to transmit a radio signal to a remote light source to switch on or off. The entire lighting concept follows the same principle: by using flexible and portable wireless lamps, specific areas can be illuminated as desired, avoiding the need for superfluous or redundant light sources. The lighting illuminating the core services block is also adaptive, changing colour over the course of the day.

AN URBAN CARBON STORAGE

By designing and constructing future buildings as carbon sinks, architecture can serve as an instrument for reducing atmospheric CO_2. RoofKIT is therefore made predominantly of reclaimed organic materials and celebrates the idea of their reuse. Designed as a series of prefabricated timber modules, the RoofKIT unit was rapidly erected during the three-week event phase on site in Wuppertal, and also acts as an urban carbon sink due to the very high proportion of renewable materials in its construction.

The demonstration unit consists of three timber space modules, each made of two parts, and a terrace construction made of timber panels. All these elements were prefabricated over a period of several weeks by students working together with the carpentry Zimmerei und Tischlerei Kaufmann in their prefabrication workshop in Bregenzerwald, Austria. The module sections were prepared for transport to Wuppertal, where they were assembled and made habitable within a single day. The joining principle of the modules uses a system of paired beams that are bolted together on site, and all screws and bolts throughout the building are left visible so that the construction principle is legible for later disassembly.

The floor plan of the demonstration unit is optimized for communal and shared use of space. The individual, modular timber living units of the overall project are arranged around a public atrium that serves as a multifunctional space for communal activities and interaction. Smaller spaces afford greater privacy for personal use and are in turn placed around a central core unit that includes the kitchen, bathroom, technical infrastructure and storage space. This concentration of infrastructure also makes the prefabrication of the timber modules more effective: only one of the four modules erected as part of the demonstration unit therefore needed to contain core infrastructure elements, with the remaining modules connecting to it via plug-in connections. Prefabrication ensures a high degree of precision in the construction process and provides more social and safety benefits for those involved in it.

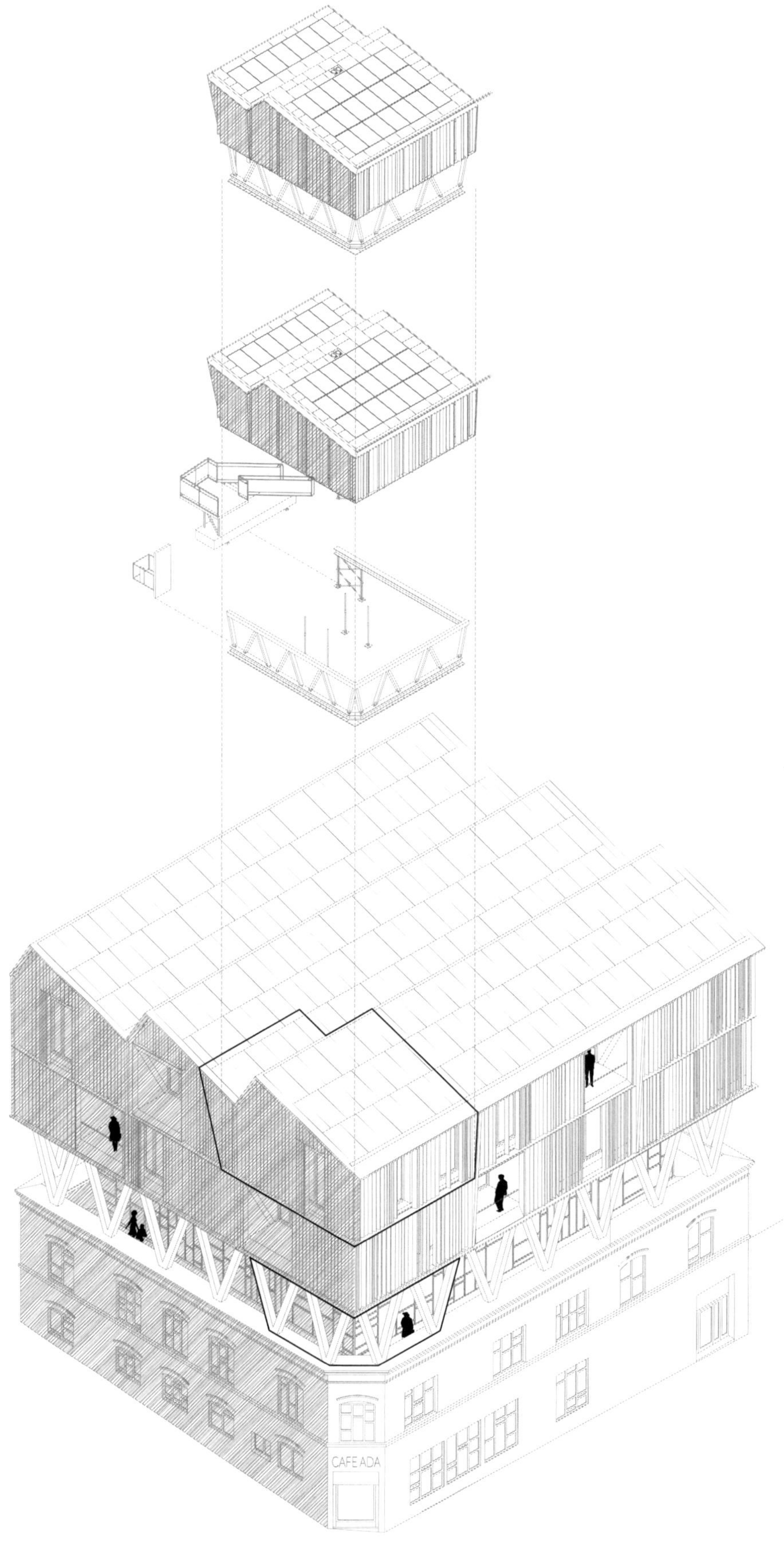

6

The demonstration unit in the context of the overall design.

7

The demonstration unit as built using prefabricated wooden modules at the Solar Campus in Wuppertal.

8 ↑↑

Reclaimed wood and found windows acted as design parameters for the facades.

9 ↑

A central installations core at the heart of the unit frees up the surrounding area for a variety of uses.

10 ↗

Curtains separate individual functions, in this case the bathroom and the sleeping area.

CIRCULARITY POTENTIAL, MONO-MATERIALS AND URBAN MINING

To ensure the circularity potential of the building and its materials, neither adhesives nor impregnations or paints nor foams or wet sealants have been used in the construction of the demonstration unit. Likewise, only mono-materials are used in its construction, i.e., no composites and no mixtures of materials. In addition to designing the building for the potential reuse of its parts in the future, RoofKIT also employs many components and materials that derive from existing urban mines and are thus given a second, and in some cases third or even fourth cycle of use. The demonstration unit uses wood from old barns in the Black Forest region, windows from a demolished building in Basel, an entrance door from a 19th-century building and bathroom and kitchen fittings from dismantled trade fair exhibition displays. While the reuse of parts is the most direct strategy for circular construction, RoofKIT also contains recycled materials that have been given a new form and function: the roof is made of 100% recycled copper, kitchen and bathroom surfaces of old yogurt pots, the entrance area is paved with reclaimed stone cobbles, and the toilet and shower are clad with panels of a ceramic material made of recycled glass bottles. The bathroom mirror is highly polished steel rather than the usual metal-glass laminates used in conventional mirrors.

In line with the principle of serving as a carbon sink, the structure is made of predominantly organic building materials. The internal wall surfaces are clay boards with a finish coat of clay plaster, which naturally regulate air humidity and air quality. The ceilings and core unit are clad with natural felt and all insulation is made of untreated,

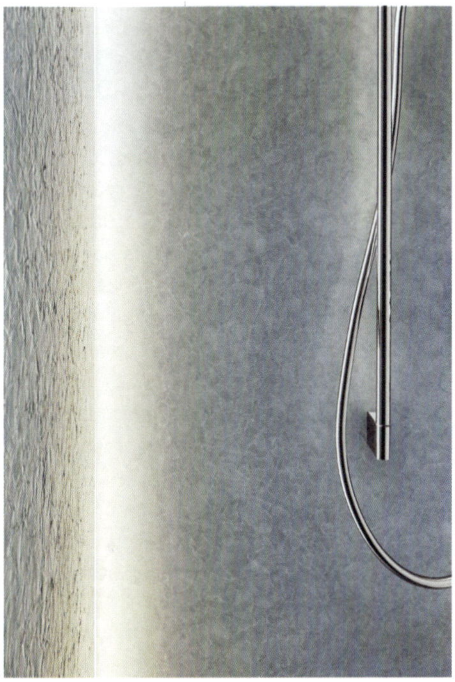

11 ↑↑↑

The floors are made of reclaimed and new timber, here both visible at the boundary between two modules.

12 ↑↑

Reused oak beams are combined with fresh wood.

13 ↑

Much of the reclaimed wood was sourced from the southern Black Forest region by Peter Rieger Historic Building Materials.

14 ↑

The wet areas of the shower and WC are lined with ceramic-glass panels, avoiding the need for wet seals.

15 ↑↑

The solar panels of the PVT system are coloured to match the recycled copper of the roof cladding, which is mounted on reclaimed wood underlay.

16 ↑

Air-dried earth blocks placed in the floor cavities increase the thermal mass of the wooden construction and are profiled to receive the coils of the underfloor heating.

17

The insulation consists of 100 % seaweed, a natural insulator that needs no synthetic additives to comply with fire safety regulations.

18

The substructure of the facade timbers is treated with living fungal cultures, which provide the wood with natural biological protection against the effects of the weather.

dried seaweed that is free of additives. Panel materials and lampshades are made of mycelium, the root system of fungi, with living fungal cultures used for natural biological weather protection for the underlying timber structure of the external facades. Construction wood is untreated and free of adhesives and no synthetic bonding agents have been used. Instead, reversible connections have been fabricated using digital milling systems so that they can be taken apart at a later point in time. To add thermal mass to the otherwise lightweight timber structure, air-dried earth bricks and boards were inserted into the floor cavities as an underlay for the underfloor heating. All these demonstrate how recyclability can be a determining aspect of the design solution without having to compromise on functionality.

DIGITAL DOCUMENTATION FOR CIRCULAR CONSTRUCTION

Using the digital Urban Mining Index tool,[2] the circularity potential of the demonstration unit was assessed and calculated at 98 % – the highest score of all Solar Decathlon participants, due largely to its consistent design strategy. Digital tools of this kind are hugely important in teaching and practice. They can be used both to roughly calculate initial design ideas and compare their circularity potential in the same way that carbon emissions are estimated in advance. In addition, these tools can be used to create a digital twin of a building that can, among other things, serve as a database of materials within a building, an invaluable tool for leveraging the potential of the built environment for future generations. Such digital representations also provide a basis for conducting accompanying simulations at the building and system level as well as for data exchange with other sectors.

CIRCULAR CONSTRUCTION AS AN ARCHITECTURAL PRINCIPLE AND POLITICAL POLICY

The RoofKIT project is in some ways a logical continuation of the Urban Mining and Recycling Unit (UMAR) presented in the first volume of *Building Better – Less – Different*.[3] Where UMAR was designed as part of a building-level research infrastructure, RoofKIT takes the urban environment and its existing structures as its field of research. Since the UMAR project started in 2016, undertaken together with Werner Sobek and his team, public and political awareness of circular construction has grown significantly. In response to the

2 See also: Anja Rosen, "The Economy of Urban Mining", in Felix Heisel, Dirk E. Hebel with Ken Webster, *Building Better – Less – Different: Circular Construction and Circular Economy*. Basel: Birkhäuser, 2022.

3 Felix Heisel and Dirk E. Hebel, "The Urban Mining and Recycling (UMAR) Unit", in Felix Heisel, Dirk E. Hebel with Ken Webster, *Building Better – Less – Different: Circular Construction and Circular Economy*. Basel: Birkhäuser, 2022.

19, 20

The terrace of the demonstration unit showing part of the communal area of the overall design. It is constructed primarily of reused elements including oak beams from the Black Forest, seating furniture made from former ceiling suspensions from Belgium and reclaimed windows from Switzerland.

various crises discussed in the introduction to this volume, the EU elevated circular construction to be a central theme of its Green Deal published in 2019. The consequences are manifold. In 2022, the German state of Baden-Württemberg, under the leadership of Minister President Winfried Kretschmann, initiated a strategic dialogue process called "Affordable Housing and Innovative Construction", a key pillar of which specifically addresses the topic of circular economy in construction. We are beginning to see architectural competitions that specifically address the aspect of reuse, for example the competition for the Walkeweg Nord quarter in Basel, where 150 new flats will be built on the site of a former multi-storey car park and must reuse concrete elements of its construction. Kerstin Müller, who also contributed to the first volume of this series,[4] acted as a consultant to the Canton of Basel with her office Zirkular.

The topic of reuse is also gaining ground in the USA. On 8 September 2022, San Antonio City Council adopted a deconstruction ordinance that requires certain projects seeking a demolition permit to be fully deconstructed as opposed to demolished. As a result, San Antonio became the largest city in the country to ensure that valuable materials are salvaged for reuse rather than crushed and landfilled. In its first phase, the ordinance applies to all small-scale residential structures built before 1920, with the year-built threshold rising in January 2025 to 1945 and even 1960 for properties that are designated as being historic.[5] Palo Alto in the state of California also recently passed a deconstruction ordinance that applies to all buildings in the city limits irrespective of their use or date of construction.[6]

RE-ERECTED FOR REUSE

As the competition winning entry to the international student competition Solar Decathlon Europe 21/22, RoofKIT shows that it is already possible to build sustainable architecture that conserves space and resources, produces energy while also formulating clear visions for how we can live together and transform the existing stock of buildings in today's cities. At the end of the event phase in Wuppertal in autumn 2022, the demonstration unit was disassembled cleanly and waste-free and then reassembled on KIT's South Campus in Karlsruhe where it will serve as a demonstrator of how construction and urban living can be made future-proof while conserving resources and minimizing impact on the climate. The building will be used as a temporary living unit for one to two people and thus continues to serve an active function as a living lab for research purposes.

4 Kerstin Müller, "New Buildings from Old", in Felix Heisel, Dirk E. Hebel with Ken Webster, *Building Better – Less – Different: Circular Construction and Circular Economy*. Basel: Birkhäuser, 2022.

5 San Antonio Reuse, Deconstruction Requirements, 2021, https://www.sareuse.com/deconstruction (accessed 18 May 2023).

6 City of Palo Alto, Zero Waste, Deconstruction and Construction Materials Management, https://www.cityofpaloalto.org/Departments/Public-Works/Zero-Waste/Zero-Waste-Requirements-Guidelines/Deconstruction-Construction-Materials-Management (accessed 18 May 2023).

Further Reading

▶ UMAR unit, "The Urban Mining and Recycling (UMAR) Unit", *Circular Construction and Circular Economy*, p. 142
▶ Circular construction, "Principles of Circular Construction", *Circular Construction and Circular Economy*, p. 22
▶ Clean energy transition, "The Clean Energy Transition in the Context of Sustainability", p. 20

21

The winning team of the Solar Decathlon Europe 21/22 in Wuppertal.

PROJECT CREDITS

Concept, Design and Construction Planning

Students of the KIT Faculty of Architecture, Project Management: Regina Gebauer (Architecture) and Nicolás Carbonare (Building Services), KIT

Building Services

Prof. Andreas Wagner, Nicolás Carbonare, Isabel Mino Rodriguez with Martin Kautzsch, KIT. Partners: Klaus Rohlffs, ip5 Karlsruhe; Prof. Jens Pfafferott, Offenburg University of Applied Sciences; Martin Wortmann-Vierthaler, Heinrich Meidinger Vocational Training School, Karlsruhe, David Wölfle, FZI Research Centre for Information Technology.

Circularity, Materials and Construction

Prof. Dirk E. Hebel, Regina Gebauer, Katharina Blümke, Elena Boerman, Hanna Hoss, Daniel Lenz, Manuel Rausch, with Michael Hosch, Benjamin Weber, Martin Kautzsch, Julian Raupp, KIT

Structural Design – Building

Prof. Karsten Schlesier, HCU Hamburg with Johannes Hasselmann and Jonas Benjamin Ernst, KIT

Structural Design – Foundations, Circulation Systems and Safety

Prof. Riccardo La Magna, David Andersson, KIT

Fabrication

Kaufmann Zimmerei und Tischlerei GmbH, Reuthe, Austria

Reused Components

Peter Rieger Historische Baustoffe, Concular, Rotor DC, Schweizer Bauteilbörse

Appendix

ACKNOWLEDGEMENTS

First of all, we would like to thank all the authors of this book: Martin Pehnt, Sebastian Herkel and Peter Schossig, Tianzhen Hong, Max Wei and Kaiyu Sun, Vincent Witt, Kathrin Dörfler, Oliver David Krieg, Kristin Slavin and Oliver Lang, Thomas Auer, Matthias Rudolph, Benjamin Weber, Jan Knippers and Achim Menges, Thomas Lützkendorf and Alexander Passer, Matthias Berning, M. Norbert Fisch, Mattheos Santamouris and Konstantina Vasilakopoulou, Martin Tamke and Mette Ramsgaard Thomsen, Daniel Fischer and Erik Zanetti, Hilke Manot and Julian Lienhard, Oliver Tessmann, Max Benjamin Eschenbach, Christoph Kuhn and Anne-Kristin Wagner, Gilles Retsin as well as Elena Boerman. Without their readiness to share their convictions, appeals, visions, activities, research and findings, this book and the discourse it has given rise to would not have been possible. Our thanks go also to both teams at KIT in Karlsruhe and Cornell University in Ithaca, and especially to Sebastian Kreiter and Luca Diefenbacher for their tireless work in drawing and improving the graphics. We would like to thank our universities, Karlsruhe Institute of Technology (KIT) and Cornell College of Architecture, Art, and Planning, and their departments of architecture for their continued motivation and support. And a special thank you to our editor Andreas Müller and Birkhäuser Verlag, our two translators Julian Reisenberger and Steffen Walter as well as the graphic designer of this book, Tom Unverzagt, for their trust, passion and outstanding creativity.

Felix Heisel, Dirk E. Hebel, Andreas Wagner and Moritz Dörstelmann

ABOUT THE AUTHORS

Felix Heisel is Assistant Professor of Architecture at Cornell University's College of Architecture, Art, and Planning, where he directs the Circular Construction Lab (CCL), a cross-disciplinary research hub working towards the systemic redesign of the built environment as a material depot in a continuous cycle of use and reconfiguration. Heisel is one of the founding partners of the Circularity, Reuse, and Zero Waste Development (CR0WD) network in New York State, as well as a founding partner of 2hs Architekten und Ingenieur PartGmbB Hebel Heisel Schlesier, Germany, an office specializing in the development of circular prototypologies. He has received various awards for his work and published numerous books and articles on the topic, including *Building Better – Less – Different: Circular Construction and Circular Economy* (Birkhäuser, 2022, with Dirk E. Hebel), *Cultivated Building Materials* (Birkhäuser, 2017, with Dirk E. Hebel) and *Building from Waste* (Birkhäuser, 2014, with Dirk E. Hebel and Marta H. Wisniewska). Felix Heisel graduated from Berlin University of the Arts and has taught and researched at universities around the world, including the Berlage Institute, the Ethiopian Institute of Architecture, Building Construction and City Development, the Future Cities Laboratory Singapore, ETH Zurich, Karlsruhe Institute of Technology (KIT) and Harvard GSD.

Dirk E. Hebel is Professor of Sustainable Construction and the Dean of the Faculty of Architecture at the Karlsruhe Institute of Technology (KIT), Germany. He is a founding partner of 2hs Architekten und Ingenieur PartGmbB Hebel Heisel Schlesier, practicing architecture with a focus on resource-respectful construction methods and materials. His work has been shown in numerous exhibitions worldwide, among them *Plastic: Remaking our world*, Vitra Design Museum Weil am Rhein, and *Environmental Hangover* by Pedro Wirz (both with Nazanin Saeidi, Alireza Javadian, Sandra Böhm and Elena Boerman), Kunsthalle Basel, both in 2022, as well as *Sorge um den Bestand*, BDA, Berlin and other venues, 2020–. Hebel published numerous books in the field of Sustainable Construction, most recently *Building Better – Less – Different: Circular Construction and Circular Economy* (Birkhäuser, 2022, with Felix Heisel) and *Urban Mining und kreislaufgerechtes Bauen* ("Urban Mining and Circular Construction") (Fraunhofer, 2021, with Felix Heisel). As Faculty Advisor together with Prof. Andreas Wagner, he won the first Solar Decathlon Competition 2022 held in Wuppertal, Germany, as part of the RoofKIT team (Regina Gebauer and Nicolás Carbonare).

Andreas Wagner is Professor of Building Science and Technology at the Faculty of Architecture at Karlsruhe Institute of Technology (KIT). After graduating in mechanical engineering from the University of Karlsruhe (TH), he worked for almost ten years in solar research at the Fraunhofer Institute for Solar Energy Systems (ISE) in Freiburg. In addition to teaching in Bachelor's and Master's programmes with a special focus on energy-optimized building, lighting design and simulation-based planning tools, his main research interests are concepts and performance analysis for energy-efficient buildings as well as comfort and user behaviour in office buildings. Andreas Wagner is (co-)author of more than 150 publications and six books and has reviewed more than 45 doctoral theses. He is a member of numerous scientific advisory boards for international journals and conferences. Since 2018, he has been Co-Operating Agent of the IEA EBC Annex 79 and, since February 2023, one of the two leaders of the working group "Energy Transition of the Built Environment" in the ESYS project of the German Academies of Sciences. He was Dean of the Faculty at KIT from 2000 to 2004 and from 2012 to 2015. In addition, he was a member of the steering committee and spokesperson for the area of "Efficient Energy Use" at the KIT Center for Energy for eleven years. Since 2021, he has been one of the spokespersons of the KIT Graduate School ENZo.

Moritz Dörstelmann is Tenure Track Professor of Digital Design and Fabrication (DDF) at the Faculty of Architecture at Karlsruhe Institute of Technology (KIT) and founding partner of the robotic construction company FibR GmbH. His academic work investigates digital circular construction concepts at the interdisciplinary interface of research and teaching through explorative prototyping of innovative material systems and construction technologies on 1:1 scale in application-oriented demonstrator projects. His construction company FibR realizes resource-efficient fibre composite lightweight structures as load-bearing structures, facades and interiors in architectural projects through computational design and robotic fabrication at industrial scale. At the intersection of application-oriented academic research and research-oriented industrial practice, Moritz Dörstelmann's work shows how digital design and manufacturing strategies can be used to explore a novel architectural design repertoire and enable socially relevant solutions to reduce resource consumption and enable circularity in construction.

Thomas Auer is Professor of Building Technology and Climate Responsive Design at the Technical University of Munich (TUM) and a partner at Transsolar. Based on a sound understanding of the architectural integration of energy and comfort strategies, he works with renowned architectural firms on numerous projects around the world. The resulting individual strategies are characterized by their holistic and innovative approach and have been awarded numerous prizes. Thomas Auer has taught at Yale University and many other universities and was appointed professor at TUM in 2014. His research focuses on the decarbonization of the building sector as well as climate adaptation and its impact on the quality of living. Its basis is always a robust optimization at the spatial, building and city levels. He is a member of the Akademie der Künste, Berlin, and the Convention of Baukultur at the Federal Foundation of Baukultur.

Matthias Berning is a senior scientist and project manager at ABB corporate research in Germany. He is part of the Sensor Solutions team, with a research focus on distributed sensing and information processing in different domains, including building automation. With more than ten years of experience in monitoring occupants and indoor environments, he is striving to exploit this information in building operation to optimize energy efficiency and comfort. During his studies in electrical engineering and information technology at the TU

Kaiserslautern, he started working on wireless sensor networks. He also used these in the field of pervasive computing during his doctorate at the TECO research group at Karlsruhe Institute of Technology (KIT).

Elena Boerman is a research associate in teaching, research and innovation at the Professorship of Sustainable Construction in the Faculty of Architecture at Karlsruhe Institute of Technology (KIT), where she studied architecture, obtaining her Master's degree in 2021. She received recognition from the Friedrich Weinbrenner Prize for her final thesis on urban planning and architectural strategies for dealing with existing building structures from the post-war modern era. Together with Sandra Böhm, she is responsible for setting up a novel material library at the Faculty of Architecture at Karlsruhe Institute of Technology (KIT) focusing on circular construction methods. She is a voluntarily member of the Karlsruhe chapter of Architects for Future, which she co-founded together with Alisa Schneider in 2020.

Kathrin Dörfler is an architect, researcher and educator in computational design and robotic fabrication. She has a Master's degree in architecture from the TU Wien and a PhD (Dr.-Ing.) in digital fabrication from ETH Zurich. Together with Romana Rust, she co-founded the architectural research studio dorfundrust. She undertook her doctoral thesis at Gramazio Kohler Research, ETH Zurich, as part of the National Centre of Competence in Research Digital Fabrication (NCCR DFAB). In 2019, Kathrin Dörfler joined the Technical University of Munich School of Engineering and Design (TUM SoED) as a tenure track professor to set up a research group for Digital Fabrication at the Department of Architecture. The research interests of her group lie at the interface between computational design and robotic fabrication, focusing on collaborative fabrication processes, on-site robotics and fabrication-aware design. In addition to research, Kathrin Dörfler has taught in Vienna, Zurich and Munich in architecture programmes as well as specialized postgraduate programmes in architecture and digital fabrication (MAS DFAB ETH Zurich).

Max Benjamin Eschenbach is a computational design researcher focused on the development of digital process chains as well as interactive and collaborative tools for digital design, planning and fabrication. He is currently a research associate and PhD candidate at the Digital Design Unit (DDU) of the Technical University of Darmstadt, working on computational tools for architectural design with reused components. He studied product design at the Kunsthochschule Kassel, where he also worked in research and teaching within the workshop for Digital Design & Fabrication (Digitale 3D-Technik) from 2019 to 2021.

M. Norbert Fisch is head of the Steinbeis Innovation Center energyplus (SIZ), Braunschweig and Stuttgart, CEO of EGS-plan Ingenieurgesellschaft, Stuttgart, and co-founder and shareholder of Green Hydrogen Esslingen. After completing his mechanical engineering studies with a focus on energy technology at the University of Stuttgart, he set up and managed the Department of Rational Use of Energy and Solar Technology at the university's Institute for Thermodynamics, and received his Doctorate of Engineering (Dr.-Ing.) in 1984. As head of department, he set future-oriented impulses and established numerous R&D projects for the technical use of solar energy. In 1996, he accepted an appointment as a professor at the Technische Universität Braunschweig and then headed the Institute for Building and Solar Technology (IGS) for 22 years. During this time he worked on well over 20 R&D projects in the fields of energy-efficient buildings, heat and cold storage, methods of optimizing the operation of non-residential buildings and the development and implementation of climate-neutral quarters. Since 2020 he has headed R&D projects at SIZ energyplus, an institute affiliated with the TU Braunschweig.

Daniel Fischer studied architecture in Karlsruhe, Tampere and Delft. After internships in Basel and Karlsruhe, he graduated cum laude with a degree in Digital Design & Architecture from TU Delft in 2018. After several years as a project architect, he joined the Professorship of Digital Design and Fabrication (DDF) at the Faculty of Architecture at Karlsruhe Institute of Technology (KIT) in 2021 with a particular research interest in digital wood construction and digital circular economy. He became a licensed and registered architect in 2022.

Sebastian Herkel heads the Energy Efficient Buildings department at the Fraunhofer Institute for Solar Energy Systems (ISE), where he works as a scientist in applied research in the fields of energy efficiency and renewable energy systems in buildings. His focus is on the transformation of the building stock, efficient heat supply systems and integral energy concepts for buildings as well as on scientific analyses of building performance and the digitalization of planning processes.

Tianzhen Hong is a senior scientist at the Building Technology and Urban Systems Division of Lawrence Berkeley National Laboratory in California. His research focuses on novel methods, data, computing, occupant behaviour and policy for the design and operation of low energy and resilient buildings and sustainable urban systems. Dr. Hong actively contributed to international collaborations such as IEA EBC Annex 53, 66, 79 and 81. He led the research projects that developed two building energy software systems, CBES and CityBES, which won the R&D 100 Awards in 2019 and 2022, respectively. He is an IBPSA Fellow and ASHRAE Fellow. He has published more than 180 journal articles and is a highly cited researcher.

Jan Knippers studied civil engineering at the TU Berlin, completing his doctorate (Dr.-Ing.) in 1992. He worked for several years in an engineering office before being appointed professor at the University of Stuttgart in 2000 as head of the Institute of Building Structures and Structural Design. In 2001 he founded Knippers Helbig Advanced Engineering and in 2018 Jan Knippers Ingenieure in Stuttgart. Jan Knippers focus is on teaching, research and practice with computational design and fabrication processes as well as fibre-based materials and bionics for resource-efficient load-bearing structures in architecture. He is Deputy Executive Director of the Cluster of Excellence "Integrative Computational Design and Construction for Architecture" (IntCDC) and Dean of the Faculty of Architecture and Urban Planning at the University of Stuttgart.

Christoph Kuhn is an architect and professor at the Technical University of Darmstadt, where he heads the Department of Design and Sustainable Building. His teaching and research revolve around the design, planning, construction and operation of sustainable buildings. After freelancing and working as a partner in various architecture firms, he has been co-founder and owner of Kuhn und Lehmann Architekten in Freiburg since 2015. From 2010 to 2013, he was a university professor at the Faculty of Architecture at the Karlsruhe Institute of Technology (KIT) after holding a two-year assistant professorship at the same institution. From 2007 to 2013 he was a lecturer at the Institut National des Sciences Appliquées de Strasbourg (INSA).

Oliver Lang + Oliver David Krieg + Kristin Slavin, Intelligent City. Oliver Lang is the CEO and Co-Founder of Intelligent City, Dr.-Ing. Oliver David Krieg is the Chief Technology Officer, and Kristin Slavin is the Director of Product. Intelligent City is a technology-enabled urban housing company. The firm has been working on deep technology and process integration for over a decade, to design and construct sustainable, net-zero multi-family urban buildings at lower costs for owners, operators and tenants. Its system incorporates mass timber, design engineering, Passive House performance, automated manufacturing and proprietary parametric software. The company calls this the Platforms for Life (P4L) model. It is a scalable and adaptable proprietary technology platform created to deliver highly desirable urban housing.

Julian Lienhard is a partner in str.ucture GmbH, a Stuttgart-based engineering firm for special structures, lightweight construction and digital building processes. After completing his award-winning doctorate (Dr.-Ing.) on bending-active structures at the ITKE of the University of Stuttgart in 2014, he taught at various universities in Germany and abroad. In 2016 and 2017, he was a visiting professor at the HafenCity University Hamburg (HCU). Since his appointment in 2019 as professor at the Institute for Structural Design at the University of Kassel, Julian Lienhard has conducted research on new hybrid constructions and establishing interdisciplinary work in digital value chains.

Thomas Lützkendorf has been Professor of Sustainable Management of Housing and Real Estate at the Faculty of Economics at Karlsruhe Institute of Technology (KIT) since 2000. His teaching and research focuses on topics concerning the implementation of principles of sustainable development in the construction and building sector. Thomas Lützkendorf studied at what is now the Bauhaus University in Weimar, where he completed his doctorate in 1985 and his habilitation in 2000. As a chairman at DIN and an expert in standardization at CEN and ISO, as well as in the development and testing of sustainability assessment systems, he is involved in the development and dissemination of fundamental principles and tools for capturing, assessing and influencing the ecological, economic and socio-cultural performance of buildings during the design process. He is a founding member of the International Initiative for a Sustainable Built Environment (iiSBE).

Hilke Manot has been undertaking her PhD at the Department of Structural Design, University of Kassel since 2022, where she worked as a student assistant during her architecture studies. She is interested in the design and construction of sustainable concepts and solutions with a focus on urban mining strategies and the reuse of existing building elements to advance circular construction. Her research focuses in particular on the reuse of structural steel in hybrid systems with natural materials.

Achim Menges graduated from the Architectural Association School of Architecture in London. He is an architect in Frankfurt and a professor at the University of Stuttgart. Since 2008, he has headed the newly founded Institute for Computer-based Design and Construction (ICD) and, since 2019, the Cluster of Excellence "Integrative Computational Design and Construction for Architecture" (IntCDC). He was previously a visiting professor at Harvard University for six years and at various other universities in the USA and Europe. In practice and research, Achim Menges investigates integrative approaches to computational design, fabrication and construction, as well as genuinely digital construction methods for sustainable architecture.

Alexander Passer is Professor of Sustainable Construction at TU Graz. Since 2011 he has headed the working group of the same name, which deals with topics of Life Cycle Sustainability Assessment (LCSA), its application in the design process and the optimization of the life cycle performance of buildings, taking into account systemic interactions. The focal areas of research for operationalizing sustainability in construction are Life Cycle Assessment (LCA), Life Cycle Cost Analysis (LCCA), Multicriteria Decision Models (MCDM) and Building Information Modelling (BIM). Alexander Passer is the Austrian delegate of the Committees of CEN/TC350 and CEN/TC 442 as well as other national and international technical committees. Since 2018, he has been chairman of the Sustainability Advisory Board of TU Graz. Also since 2018, he has been on the board of the Climate Change Centre Austria (CCCA). In 2014, he was a visiting professor at the Chair of Sustainable Construction at ETH Zurich. Since 2013, he has been subject editor of the *International Journal of Life Cycle Assessment* for the subjects of construction materials and buildings.

Martin Pehnt is Scientific Director and board member of ifeu – Institute for Energy and Environmental Research in Heidelberg. For over 25 years he has campaigned for a sustainable and just energy transition and societal transformation. Pehnt studied physics, energy technology and management in Tübingen, Boulder, Berlin and Stuttgart and previously conducted research at the National Renewable Energy Laboratory in the USA and the German Aerospace Center. In numerous projects, he has analysed energy policy instruments and strategies for renewable energies and energy conservation. He examines the impact of technology, life cycle assessments and the effect of energy policy, and accompanies pilot projects. His special focus area is implementing the heat transition towards sustainable buildings and climate-friendly heating systems. Pehnt is active in numerous advisory boards, cooperatives and committees for the energy transition, including Hamburg Climate Advisory Council and the Climate Expert Council Baden-Württemberg.

Mette Ramsgaard Thomsen examines the intersections between architecture and advanced computational design processes, investigating the profound changes that digital technologies instigate in the way architecture is conceived, designed and built. In 2005 she founded the Centre for Information Technology and Architecture (CITA) research group at the Royal Danish Academy of Fine Arts, Schools of Architecture, Design and Conservation where she has piloted a special research focus on the new digital-material relations that digital technologies bring forth. CITA has been central in forming an international research field examining the changes to material practice in architecture. This has been led by a series of research investigations developing concepts and technologies as well as strategic projects including the international Marie Curie InnoChain ETN network and the European Research Council (ERC) project "An Eco-Metabolistic Framework for Sustainable Architecture" that fosters interdisciplinary sharing and the dissemination of expertise, and supports new collaborations in the fields of architecture, engineering and fabrication. At the time of writing, Professor Ramsgaard Thomsen is General Reporter and Head of Science Track for the UIA2023CPH World Congress "Sustainable Futures – Leave No One Behind" examining how architecture can contribute to the Sustainable Development Goals of the United Nations (UN SDGs). In 2022 she was appointed Cret Visiting Professor at the University of Pennsylvania Weitzman School of Design.

Gilles Retsin is co-founder and CTO/Chief Architect of AUAR Ltd, a UK-based startup building a decentralized micro-factory network for regenerative timber housing, targeting 10,000 net-zero homes per year by 2032. He studied architecture in Belgium, Chile and the UK, where he graduated from the Architectural Association School of Architecture (PhD). His design work and critical discourse have been internationally recognized through awards, lectures and exhibitions at major cultural institutions such as the Museum of Arts and Design in New York, the Royal Academy in London and the Centre Pompidou in Paris. He has edited books on architecture, computational design and robotics and is also an associate professor at UCL, the Bartlett School of Architecture where he co-directs AUAR Labs, a research lab focused on innovating the full value chain of housing.

Matthias Rudolph is Professor of Building Technology and Climate-Responsive Design at the Architecture Faculty of Stuttgart State Academy of Art and Design. The focus of his academic work is on studying the interaction between ecology, site, space and form-finding as well as the microclimate adaptation of urban environments. He has more than 20 years of experience as a practicing Climate-Engineer. In interdisciplinary work with renowned architects within the company Transsolar, he creates strategies for climate-neutral buildings and urban developments in an international context. Matthias Rudolph is also a frequent lecturer at international conferences and industry events. Since 2017 he has been member of the executive board of the German Sustainable Building Council (DGNB).

Mattheos Santamouris is a Scientia Distinguished Professor of High Performance Architecture at the University of New South Wales (UNSW) and previously professor at the University of Athens. He was a visiting professor at the Cyprus Institute, Metropolitan University London, Tokyo Polytechnic University, Bolzano University, Brunel University London, Seoul University, National University of Singapore and UiTM Malaysia. He is Past President of the National Center of Renewable and Energy Savings of Greece. Mat Santamouris is author of 400 scientific articles, editor and author of 20 books and editor of numerous international journals. He is a reviewer of research projects in many countries including USA, UK, France, Germany, Canada and Sweden. He was ranked as the top world cited researcher in the field of Building and Construction by the Stanford University ranking system for 2019–2021, and figures prominently in many other academic rankings.

Peter Schossig has been working at the Fraunhofer Institute for Solar Energy Systems (ISE) in the field of thermal systems for over 25 years. Since 2017, he has been director of the Heat and Building division, which also includes research on the topic of heat pumps. After studying physics at the University of Freiburg, he completed his doctorate at the University of Karlsruhe (TH) on the topic of building-integrated heat storage. In recent years, he has significantly expanded the institute's work on heat pump development, especially with natural refrigerants, and extended the ISE's field of research to encompass grid-connected large-scale heat pumps and high-temperature heat pumps for industrial applications.

Kaiyu Sun is a principal scientific engineering associate at the Building Technology and Urban Systems Division of Lawrence Berkeley National Laboratory. Her research focuses on building energy modelling and development of simulation tools, the nexus between building energy efficiency and thermal resilience, automatic model calibration and occupant behaviour modelling. She is the lead developer of CBES: Commercial Building Energy Saver, which won the R&D 100 Award in 2019.

Martin Tamke is associate professor at the Centre for Information Technology and Architecture (CITA) in Copenhagen. He pursues design-led research on the interface and implications of computational design and its materialization. He joined the newly founded CITA in 2006 and shaped its design-based research practice, with a strong interdisciplinary focus in projects such as Durable Architectural Knowledge (DURAARK) or the international Marie Curie InnoChain ETN network. His latest research focuses on computational strategies and technologies for the transformation of the building industry towards sustainable and circular practices based on bio-materials. In 2019 Martin was appointed General Reporter for the scientific track of the UIA2023 Copenhagen World Congress of Architects and in 2022 guest professor at the University of Stuttgart at the "Integrative Computational Design and Construction for Architecture" (IntCDC) Cluster of Excellence. He is involved in the Danish-funded research project Predicting Response, the EU project Exskallerate, the ERC project "An Eco-Metabolistic Framework for Sustainable Architecture" and several industrial collaborations.

Oliver Tessmann is an architect and professor at the Technical University of Darmstadt where he heads the Digital Design Unit (DDU). His teaching and research revolves around computational design, digital manufacturing and robotics in architecture. From 2012 to 2015 he was assistant professor at the School of Architecture of the Royal Institute of Technology (KTH) in Stockholm. From 2008 to 2011 he was a guest professor at Staedelschule Architecture Class (SAC) and worked with the engineering office Bollinger+Grohmann in Frankfurt. In 2008 Oliver Tessmann received a doctoral degree (Dr.-Ing.) at the University of Kassel with research in the field of "Collaborative Design Procedures for Architects and Engineers". His work has been published and exhibited in Europe, Asia and the USA.

Konstantina Vasilakopoulou is a research-focused Lecturer at the School of the Built Environment of the University of New South Wales. She is the Acting Director of the Home Modification Information Clearinghouse and manages the school's Livability Lab. Her research interests focus on universal and inclusive design, light and lighting, energy efficiency in the built environment, urban climate mitigation techniques, etc. Her team undertakes research on the effects of the built environment on people's well-being, with a focus on the elderly and people with disability.

Anne-Kristin Wagner is an architect who researches and teaches in the field of sustainable building. Her current research focuses on reuse strategies and the life cycle assessment of materials and buildings. She has a strong interest in sustainability strategies in the building sector and at neighbourhood level to reduce the environmental footprint. She is a research associate and PhD student in the Department of Design and Sustainable Building at the Technical University of Darmstadt. Since graduating from TU Kaiserslautern, she has worked in energy consulting and sustainability certification for buildings at ee concept GmbH in Darmstadt.

Benjamin Weber studied architecture at Karlsruhe Institute of Technology (KIT), where he won the Solar Decathlon Europe as a member of the RoofKIT team. In his Master's thesis, which is a continuation of the competition, he dealt with the concept of building culture and historical rural building forms that serve as inspiration for circular, climate-adapted constructions made of locally available materials, and a climate-neutral low-tech concept in existing buildings. He was a fellowship student of the Norman Foster Foundation Energy Workshop and, since completing his studies, now works at haascookzemmrich Studio 2050 (one of the co-founders of the DGNB) on innovative, resource-saving projects around the world.

Max Wei is a staff scientist at the Sustainable Energy and Environmental Systems Department of Lawrence Berkeley National Laboratory (LBNL). His research focuses on developing greater resilience and equity in the built environment through urban-scale building modelling and policy development. He co-led the LBNL Resilience Task Force to develop greater resilience at the LBNL lab site and has led teams to develop modelling tools and quantification of the benefits of various passive and active measures for resilience to extreme heat. He has led the innovative integrated modelling of residential sector decarbonization scenarios across energy supply, buildings and transportation. Dr. Wei has over a decade of experience in the techno-economic modelling of emerging technologies and policy analysis of California decarbonization pathways. He co-led two past studies on pathways for California to meet its long-term climate goals for 2050; and has led studies quantifying the benefits of air conditioning with low global warming refrigerants and total cost of ownership of fuel cell-based cogeneration in commercial buildings.

Vincent Witt is a research associate at the Professorship of Digital Design and Fabrication (DDF) at the Faculty of Architecture at Karlsruhe Institute of Technology (KIT), graduating recently with a Master of Science degree in Architecture. As part of his studies, he completed an internship in Basel. His Master's thesis explored digital design and novel fabrication processes in relation to urban mining and their integration into the architectural design process.

Erik Zanetti is a research associate at the Professorship of Digital Design and Fabrication (DDF) at the Faculty of Architecture at Karlsruhe Institute of Technology (KIT). He holds a Master of Science degree with a specialization in computational design from Delft University of Technology, as well as a Bachelor of Science degree in Architecture from Politecnico di Milano. Prior to joining DDF, he worked as a computational designer and digital fabrication specialist at FibR GmbH in Stuttgart and as an external lecturer at the University of Innsbruck. His research focuses on circular building practices and materials, which he investigates through the use of digital design and digital fabrication techniques.

ILLUSTRATION CREDITS

Agentur Blumberg GmbH and Steinbeis Innovationszentrum (SIZ) energieplus 93: 4 (adaptations Sebastian Kreiter)
architectenbureau cepezed, Delft (adaptations Hilke Manot) 121: 5c
AUAR (Automated Architecture) 135: 2; 137: 3
Baumschlager Eberle Architekten 72: 2
Berning, Matthias 85: 1, 2 (adaptations Sebastian Kreiter); 86: 3
Braun, Zooey, Stuttgart 149: 7; 150: 8–10; 151: 11, 14; 153: 19, 20
Diefenbacher, Luca 13: 2
Dürr, René 72: 3, 4; 73: 5, 6
Element · A 66: 5 bottom
Eschenbach, Max Benjamin (Digital Design Unit DDU, TU Darmstadt) 126: 2; 127: 3; 128: 5
Gramazio Kohler Research, Department of Architecture, ETH Zurich 111: 1
Green Hydrogen Esslingen GmbH 94: 5, 6; 96: 10 (adaptations Sebastian Kreiter); 99: 12 (adaptations Sebastian Kreiter)
Green Hydrogen Esslingen GmbH and Maximilian Kamps, Agentur Blumberg GmbH 95: 7; 96: 9 (adaptations Sebastian Kreiter)
Hebel, Dirk E. 151: 13
Herkel, Sebastian (adaptations Sebastian Kreiter) 33: 1
Huber, Eduard, archphoto © Baumschlager Eberle Architekten 71: 1
Hufton + Crow 68: 7
Institute for Computational Design and Construction, University of Stuttgart 111: 2
Intelligent City Inc. 51: 1; 52: 2; 53: 3; 54: 4
Kaden + Lager, Berlin (adaptations Hilke Manot) 121: 5a
Khan, Ansar, Laura Carlosena, Samiran Khorat, Rupali Khatun, Quang-Van Doan, Jie Feng, Mattheos Santamouris (adaptations Sebastian Kreiter) 102: 2, 3
KIT Faculty of Architecture 144: 2; 145: 3; 146: 4, 5 (Sebastian Kreiter); 148: 6; 152: 12, 15–18
Kleinschmitt, Carla, Emilia Kühn (Digital Design Unit DDU, TU Darmstadt) 125: 1
Kreiter, Sebastian 15: 3; 17: 4; 18: 5
Liu, Yuxi 129: 7; 130: 8,9
Manot, Hilke, Julian Lienhard (adaptations Sebastian Kreiter) 117: 1, 2; 118: 3; 119: 4; 121: 6; 122: 7, 8
NAARO, photography & creative direction studio 133: 1; 138: 4
O'Brien, William, Andreas Wagner, Marcel Schweiker, Ardeshir Mahdavi, Julia Day, Mikkel Baun Kjærgaard, Salvatore Carlucci, Bing Dong, Farhang Tahmasebi, Da Yan, Tianzhen Hong, H. Burak Gunay, Zoltan Nagy, Clayton Miller, Christiane Berger (adaptations Sebastian Kreiter) 89: 4
Olsen Kundig, Seattle 67: 6; 69: 10
Professur Design of Structures dos, KIT Faculty of Architecture 114: 6
Professur Digital Design and Fabrication DDF, KIT Faculty of Architecture 113: 3–5; 115: 7–10
Santamouris, Mattheos, Jie Feng (adaptations Sebastian Kreiter) 101: 1; 105: 4
SDE Wuppertal 155: 21
Solar Decathlon Europe 22/23 143: 1
Steinbeis Innovationszentrum (SIZ) energieplus 91: 1, 2 (adaptations Sebastian Kreiter); 92: 3 (aerial photo Maximilian Kamps, Agentur Blumberg GmbH); 96: 8; 97: 11 (photo Maximilian Kamps, Agentur Blumberg GmbH); 99: 13 (adaptations Sebastian Kreiter)
Sun, Kaiyu, Wanni Zhang, Zhaoyun Zeng, Ronnen Levinson, Max Wei, Tianzhen Hong (adaptations Sebastian Kreiter) 37: 1; 40: 4, 5; 41: 6; 43: 7
Sun, Kaiyu, Wanni Zhang, Zhaoyun Zeng, Ronnen Levinson, Max Wei, Tianzhen Hong (based on: City of Fresno, Restore Fresno) 37: 2
Transsolar GmbH, Stuttgart 63: 1; 64: 2 (PK Odessa, Lanz und Schels); 65: 3, 4 (adaptations Sebastian Kreiter); 66: 5 top (PK Odessa, Lanz und Schels); 68: 8; 68: 9 (adaptations Sebastian Kreiter); 69: 11 (adaptations Sebastian Kreiter)
Unger, Malcolm 128: 4
Unverzagt, Tom 11: 1
Wagner, Anne-Kristin 129: 6
Waugh Tristleton Architects + Storey, London 121: 5b (adaptations Hilke Manot)
Witt, Vincent 19: 6 (N Scale People: Scottsmodelsremixes-andrescales, CC BY 4.0; Uline Sticky Note Pallet Scale Forklift: SamPerry, CC BY 4.0; Conveyor Belt: Cianon, CC BY 4.0; Le Corbusier's Maison Domino: Morgen, 3dwarehouse; Truck Turntable 10000mm Diameter: Australian Turntable Company, 3dwarehouse)

INDEX OF PERSONS

INDEX OF FIRMS, INSTITUTIONS AND INITIATIVES

INDEX OF PROJECTS, PRODUCTS AND PUBLICATIONS

COLOPHON

Layout, cover design and typesetting: Tom Unverzagt

Translation from German into English of the texts by Felix Heisel/Dirk E. Hebel, Andreas Wagner, Moritz Dörstelmann, Martin Pehnt, Sebastian Herkel/Peter Schossig, Moritz Dörstelmann/Vincent Witt, Kathrin Dörfler, Thomas Auer, Matthias Rudolph, Benjamin Weber/Andreas Wagner, Jan Knippers/Achim Menges, Thomas Lützkendorf/Alexander Passer, M. Norbert Fisch und Elena Boerman/Dirk E. Hebel/Felix Heisel/ Andreas Wagner: Julian Reisenberger

Editor for the publisher: Andreas Müller

Production: Anja Haering

Printing: Grafisches Centrum Cuno GmbH

Paper: 120 g/m² Amber Graphic

This publication is also available in a German language edition (Print ISBN 978-3-0356-2116-7, e-book PDF 978-3-0356-2718-3).

Library of Congress Control Number: 2023944976

Bibliographic information published by the German National Library

The German National Library lists this publication in the Deutsche Nationalbibliografie; detailed bibliographic data are available on the Internet at http://dnb.dnb.de.

ISBN 978-3-0356-2117-4

e-ISBN (PDF) 978-3-0356-2717-6

Im Westfeld 8, 4055 Basel, Switzerland

Part of Walter de Gruyter GmbH, Berlin/Boston

9 8 7 6 5 4 3 2 1
www.birkhauser.com